Communications in Computer and Information Science 302

Kam Cheong Li Fu Lee Wang Kin Sun Yuen
Simon K.S. Cheung Reggie Kwan (Eds.)

Engaging Learners Through Emerging Technologies

International Conference
on ICT in Teaching and Learning, ICT 2012
Hong Kong, China, July 4-6, 2012
Proceedings

Springer

Volume Editors

Kam Cheong Li
Open University of Hong Kong, China
E-mail: kcli@ouhk.edu.hk

Fu Lee Wang
Caritas Bianchi College of Careers, Hong Kong, China
E-mail: pwang@cihe.edu.hk

Kin Sun Yuen
The Open University of Hong Kong, China
E-mail: ksyuen@ouhk.edu.hk

Simon K.S. Cheung
The Open University of Hong Kong, China
E-mail: kscheung@ouhk.edu.hk

Reggie Kwan
Caritas Institute of Higher Education, Hong Kong, China
E-mail: rkwan@cihe.edu.hk

ISSN 1865-0929 e-ISSN 1865-0937
ISBN 978-3-642-31397-4 e-ISBN 978-3-642-31398-1
DOI 10.1007/978-3-642-31398-1
Springer Heidelberg Dordrecht London New York

Library of Congress Control Number: 2012940345

CR Subject Classification (1998): H.5, H.4, H.3, I.2, C.2, D.2, J.1

Typesetting: Camera-ready by author, data conversion by Scientific Publishing Services, Chennai, India

Printed on acid-free paper

Springer is part of Springer Science+Business Media (www.springer.com)

Preface

This edited volume consists of selected papers submitted to the 2012 International Conference on ICT in Teaching and Learning (ICT 2012). As the conference theme "Engaging Learners Through Emerging Technologies" highlights, the contents of the papers revolve around constructs, means and, especially, innovative ways for effective student engagement.

This volume begins with a conceptual paper on the construct of student engagement, outlining major perspectives of studying and researching this multidimensional notion.

The papers are presented in groups. The first group of papers is on emerging pedagogies supported by new technologies. This group focuses on the pedagogical impact and benefits of using technology in fostering educational innovations and enhancing student engagement. Through examination and analyses of students' attitudes toward online study experience, as well as their individual comments, perceptions and expectations in various educational settings, the papers shed light on ways to improve student engagement through ICT.

The second group focuses on the application of emerging technologies in teaching and learning. It explores the effectiveness of various ICT means, such as mobile tools and computer program, for enhancing teaching and learning. It also draws attention to the limitations of mobile devices in m-learning.

The third group presents research on and case studies of innovative applications of technologies in engaged learning. This covers a broad range of case studies, including a video-based learning system, a virtual experimental platform, online media tools and a blended learning approach for teaching enhancement.

Last but definitely not least, we have three papers on open textbooks, which address the current problems with conventional textbooks in Hong Kong. Textbooks being one major tool for learning, their various aspects (such as availability, format, design and cost) play a role in deciding students' engagement level.

Our many sincere thanks go to Eva Tsang and Linda Chow of the Education Technology and Publishing Unit of the Open University of Hong Kong (OUHK) for their effective administrative and editing support. We are obliged to the dedicated staff of the Centre for Research in Distance and Adult Learning of OUHK, especially Helen Lam, for their efficient assistance in the final stage of work with the papers. Grateful thanks also go to the ICT2012 Organizing

Committee for their unfailing support throughout the process of preparing this volume. We are indebted to members of the Program Committee. The high quality of this book could not have been maintained without their professional comments and advice in the paper-review process.

July 2012

K.C. Li
F.L. Wang
K.S. Yuen
Simon K.S. Cheung
Reggie Kwan

Organization

Organizing Committee

Chair

K.S. Yuen	The Open University of Hong Kong, Hong Kong

Vice-chair

Margaret Wong	St. Paul's Convent School, Hong Kong

Members

K.S. Cheung	The Open University of Hong Kong, Hong Kong
K.C. Li	The Open University of Hong Kong, Hong Kong
Eva Tsang	The Open University of Hong Kong, Hong Kong
Philips Wang	Association for Computing Machinery (HK Chapter), Hong Kong
Reggie Kwan	Caritas Institute of Higher Education, Hong Kong
Philip Tsang	Hong Kong Web Symposium Consortium, Hong Kong
F.T. Chan	The University of Hong Kong, Hong Kong
Bob Fox	The University of Hong Kong, Hong Kong
Andrew Lai	St. Paul's Convent School, Hong Kong
Titus Lo	Caritas Institute of Higher Education, Hong Kong
S.H. Tong	Hong Kong Baptist University, Hong Kong

Program Committee

Chair

K.C. Li	The Open University of Hong Kong, Hong Kong

Vice-chair

Philips Wang	Association for Computing Machinery (HK Chapter), Hong Kong

Members

Organizers

The Open University of Hong Kong

The Hong Kong Web Symposium Consortium

St. Paul's Convent School

Sponsors

Croucher Foundation

Sino-British Fellowship Trust

Wu Jieh Yee Charitable Foundation

Supporters

Fujitsu

Mobile Computer Land

Lenovo

Senco-Masslink Technology Limited

Education Bureau, HKSAR

REACH Global Services Limited

Pearson Education Asia Limited

Table of Contents

Research/Case Studies on ICT in Engaged Learning

Turning to a New Page of Open Textbooks

Student Engagement: Meanings, Approaches and Ideas for Educators Interested in ICT

K.C. Li[1] and Fu Lee Wang[2]

[1] The Open University of Hong Kong, Hong Kong SAR, China
kcli@ouhk.edu.hk
[2] Caritas Institute of Higher Education, Hong Kong SAR, China
pwang@cihe.edu.hk

Abstract. This paper attempts to offer a brief review of literature on the construct of student engagement. It summarizes key aspects of how student engagement has been interpreted and researched. It explains how the construct has been anatomised into components of academic, behavioural, emotional and cognitive engagement. By delineating the relationship between engagement and learning outcomes as well as environmental and student factors in play, it outlines the versatility and value of the construct. It also highlights the niche role of information and communication technology in facilitating and enhancing student engagement.

Keywords: student engagement, school engagement, learning behaviour, self-regulated learning.

1 Introduction

To gain any knowledge or skills, one must be engaged in learning. Substantial research suggests that student engagement is a key factor in effective learning and a predictor of learning development (Carini, Kuh, & Klein, 2006; Li, 2011; Mason, 2011; Wong & Li, 2011; Li, forthcoming). Effective educational delivery consists in getting learners engaged in learning activities or the learning process. While considerable efforts have been made and numerous research studies have been done on means to assist students' to learn effectively, all such efforts and research are futile, or at least substantially discounted, if students are disengaged.

Student engagement has been a key focus of educational research. A proper understanding of students' engagement levels and how they are related to the learner or curricular delivery will assist professors, teachers and instructional designers to engage students in effective learning. It has been well noted that student engagement is potentially important and a useful construct for educators and in educational research (Fredericks, Blumenfeld, & Paris, 2004; Appleton, Christenson, & Furlong, 2008).

However, the construct of 'engagement' has been conceptualized in myriad ways. This paper attempts to offer an overview of crucial ways the construct of student engagement has been understood and studied by reviewing relevant literature. It

K.C. Li et al. (Eds.): ICT 2012, CCIS 302, pp. 1–10, 2012.

summarizes how the construct has commonly been anatomized into components in literature and examines the factors influencing the components. Then, through the conceptualizations explained, this paper highlights a number of key aspects of information and communication technology (ICT) applications which may potentially benefit learning and teaching.

2 Perspectives

Literally, engagement means the act of being engaged and the engagement of students refers to how they participate, or are engaged, in what they are supposed to do – learn or study. For example, Kuh, Kinzie, Schuh, and Whitt (2005) refer to student engagement vis-à-vis the time and effort students put into their coursework and other educationally purposeful activities.

The interest in and study of engagement are to a large extent, etiological and outcomes oriented. Student engagement is considered or assumed to be conducive to learning achievement and is a predictor of performance (Appleton et al., 2008) Teachers and researchers are interested in engagement because they wish to enhance students' learning performance.

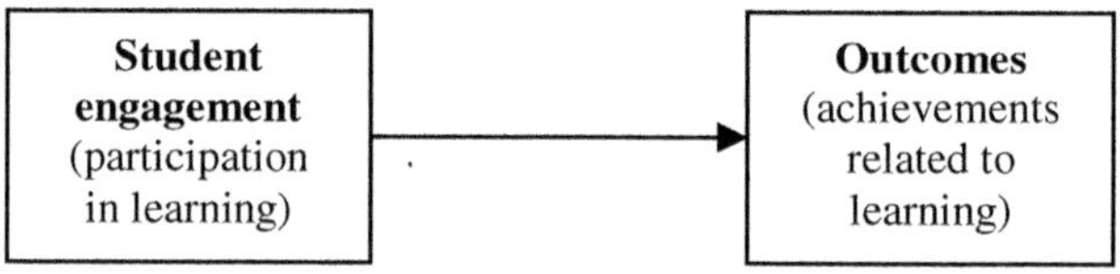

Fig. 1. Basic understanding of student engagement

Student engagement can be measured in terms of the amount of time they spend on relevant learning, the number of activities they complete, their willingness to work on the course or attend classes, etc. Learning outcomes may be considered in many ways, such as course grades, completion of a study programme or a period of study, or the ability to accomplish something.

With different emphases and diverse interests in their studies, researchers apply the term, engagement, in a broad range of ways, and the meanings of engagement have been construed in a plethora of ways. To clarify the concept and to facilitate in-depth studies, engagement has been anatomised into types. Studies adopting a two-dimensional or two-component model, usually earlier ones, typically include more observable 'behavioural engagement' and more implicit 'emotional (or affective/cognitive) engagement' (e.g. Finn, 1989; Marks, 2000). The behavioural one refers to explicit or external behaviour, and is measured in terms of participation, positive conduct or efforts such as time on tasks, completion of learning tasks and affective or emotional engagement as feeling and attitude or psychological commitment.

Seeing the multifaceted nature of the construct, a tripartite classification has become popular in the last decade. For example, Fredericks et al. (2004) highlight in their review three ways that engagement is defined, namely behavioural, emotional and cognitive engagement:

> "'Behavioural engagement' draws on the idea of participation; it includes involvement in academic and social or extracurricular activities and is considered crucial for achieving positive academic outcomes and preventing dropping out. 'Emotional engagement' encompasses positive and negative reactions to teachers, classmates, academics, and school and is presumed to create ties to an institution and influence willingness to do the work. Finally, 'cognitive engagement' draws on the idea of investment; it incorporates thoughtfulness and willingness to exert the effort necessary to comprehend complex ideas and master difficult skills."
>
> (Fredericks et al., 2004, p. 60)

In some studies (e.g. Reschly & Christenson, 2006a, 2006b), a four-type taxonomy is used, and in it, behavioural engagement in the above tripartite categorization is further subdivided into two dimensions: academic and behavioural. Academic engagements are concerned with involvement in the curriculum, using assignment completion, subjects passed or credits earned, and amount of time on task, as indicators. Behavioural engagement in the four-type model refers to physical participation, using class attendance, participation in class activities and extracurricular activities.

Engagement leads to learning outcomes. Like engagement, the construct of associated outcomes can be analyzed into components, which can broadly be classified as academic and psychological. Academic ones are results of learning achievements which are usually reflected in graduation, assessment scores and course grades. The psychological outcomes are basically emotional and social in nature and could be reflected in students' emotional control, sense of belonging and social skills, such as tactics to handle disagreements.

With such conceptualization and anatomy of the construct of engagement, Fig. 1 can be transformed as Fig. 2.

The relationship between engagement and outcomes is complex and this makes research on them interesting and attractive. Study results have shed light on and provided useful insights into many pedagogical issues. For example, as one consistent common result that Archambault, Janosz, Morizot, and Ragani (2009) note, students reporting low engagement from the beginning of high school presented higher risks of later dropout. All areas of engagement may have some bearing on each type of outcomes and the relationships rely on the context, say, the nature of the learning or the educational activity.

All relevant areas can be studied under the umbrella term engagement. Some studies focus on only one or two types of engagement (e.g. Downer, Rimm-kaufman, & Pianta, 2007; Rotgans & Schmidt, 2011). Some others concentrate on one educational context. Studies worked in general contexts and covered broad engagement areas. A common and well researched example is 'school engagement' (e.g. Jimerson, Campos, & Greif, 2003). This context can be remarkably reduced in

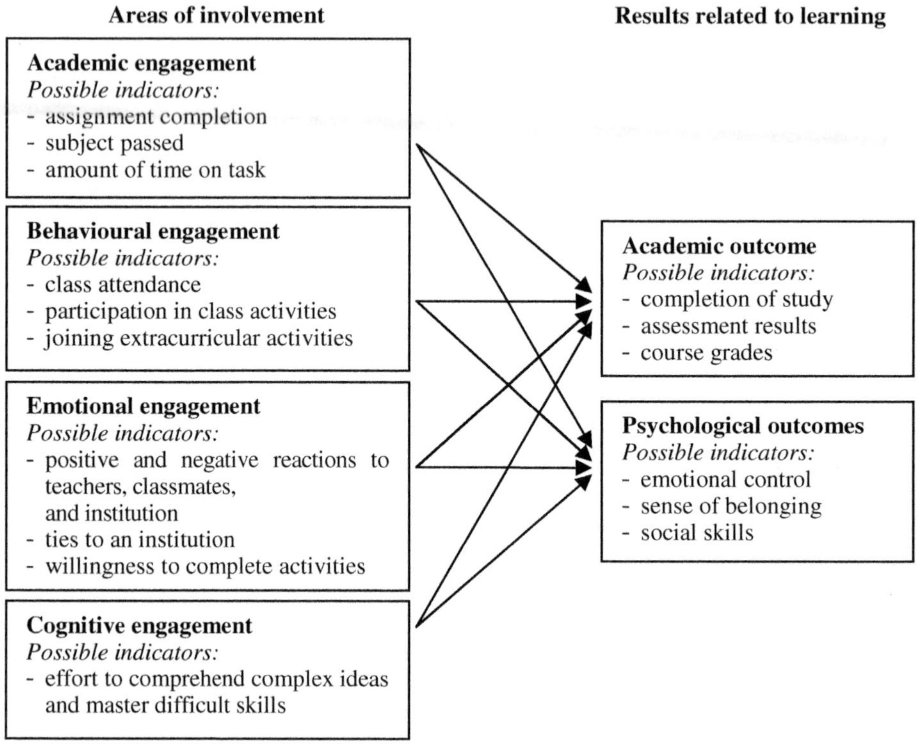

Fig. 2. Engagement and its results: components indicated

scope. A common example is 'classroom engagement' (e.g. Buhs, Ladd, & Herald, 2006; Blatchford, Bassett, & Brown, 2011) and the context to study can be even much smaller or highly specialised, such as 'engagement in out-of-school-time programmes' as reported in Bartko (2005).

All these imply that engagement is a versatile construct that has been utilized to cover a broad range of areas, and a huge number of studies employing this construct have made it expedient and popular. Embedded in the construct are assumptions that the students' attributes (such as learning attitudes and commitment to learning) and their learning are malleable. They can be changed or even revolutionized as a result of the student's interaction with the environment. The huge number of research studies reflects innumerable purposeful endeavours to seek ways to enhance learning. To maximize desirable outcomes from the course of learning, research studies are attempting to identify factors that exert influence on student engagement. Since engagement is multifaceted, factors exerting influence on engagement can be numerous (Lee & Shute, 2010).

3 Factors Affecting Student Engagement

The studies on factors affecting student engagement reveal a triangular cyclical cause-effect conceptual model as shown in Fig. 3. These elements, besides influencing student engagement, also shape what the educational outcome will be. The outcomes may reflect the factors directly or indirectly. For example, the aspect of provision of sufficient learning activities academically stimulating to the student facilitates academic engagement (such as time on tasks, and completion of the activities) of the student, which enhances achievement of academic outcomes (such as obtaining pass results). The outcomes may in turn exert influence on the components affecting engagement (indicated as dotted lines in Fig. 3, and similarly in Fig. 4), which appears an under-researched area as there is yet less literature on this.

The above mentioned factors affecting engagement are numerous and can be classified in diverse ways. They can be first divided into two broad groups, influences internal and external to the learner. Like engagement, internal or student factors, cover students' academic, behavioural, emotional and cognitive aspects. For example, academic factors include students' pre-course or pre-lesson knowledge of the subject matter, their learning capability and the extent to which they can self-regulate their academic participation in educational work. Connell (1990), Connell and Wellborn (1991), and Appleton et al. (2008) call these self-system processes.

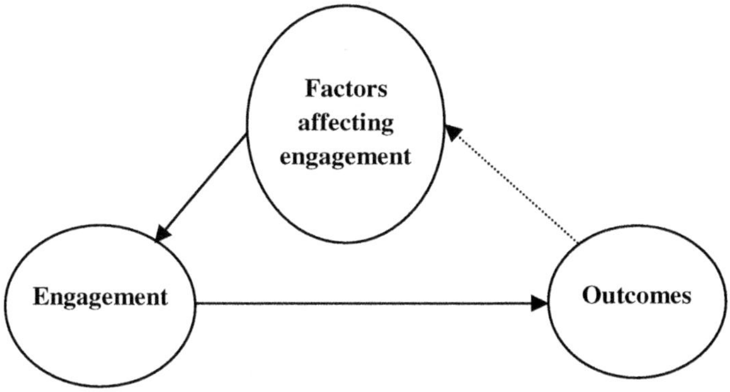

Fig. 3. Triangular relations among engagement, factors affecting it and its outcomes

The external influences can be referred to as environmental factors. They cover areas like the educational institution providing the course (such as school climate and learning activities), the physical environment of the study (such as lighting and ventilation) and the people supporting the students' learning [such as family (e.g. parental expectations and monitoring), peers (e.g. peers learning habits and beliefs, aspiration for learning) and teachers (such as praise and feedback). Graphically, the relationships of the factor, engagement and outcome are shown in Fig. 4.

Studies can cover broad areas such as things that encourage engagement in general (Russell & Slater, 2011), and may focus on a fine area such as the effect of class size on classroom engagement (Blatchford, Bassett, & Brown, 2010) and how classroom environment is linked to engagement and learning (Arbaugh, 2008).

It should be noted that while many researchers have found both environmental and student internal factors for the extent engagement reliable, some insist (Sinclair, Christenson, Lehr, & Reschly-Anderson, 2003, p. 31) that student internal causes be excluded. These scholars do not conceptualise engagement as an attribute of the student. They deem engagement as basically a state of being that is highly influenced by contextual factors. This stance (shown as semi-dotted lines in Fig. 4) highlights the responsibility of the institution and teacher to facilitate engagement and thus achieve learning outcomes.

Studies of factors have been found useful and the results offer a basis for predicting performance, and this provide insights for improvement measures and intervention as well as pedagogical enhancement. For example, empirical research by Frisch et al. (2005) has shown that life satisfaction predicts future higher levels of student engagement in school among college students, and thus a way to increase engagement is to enhance life satisfaction.

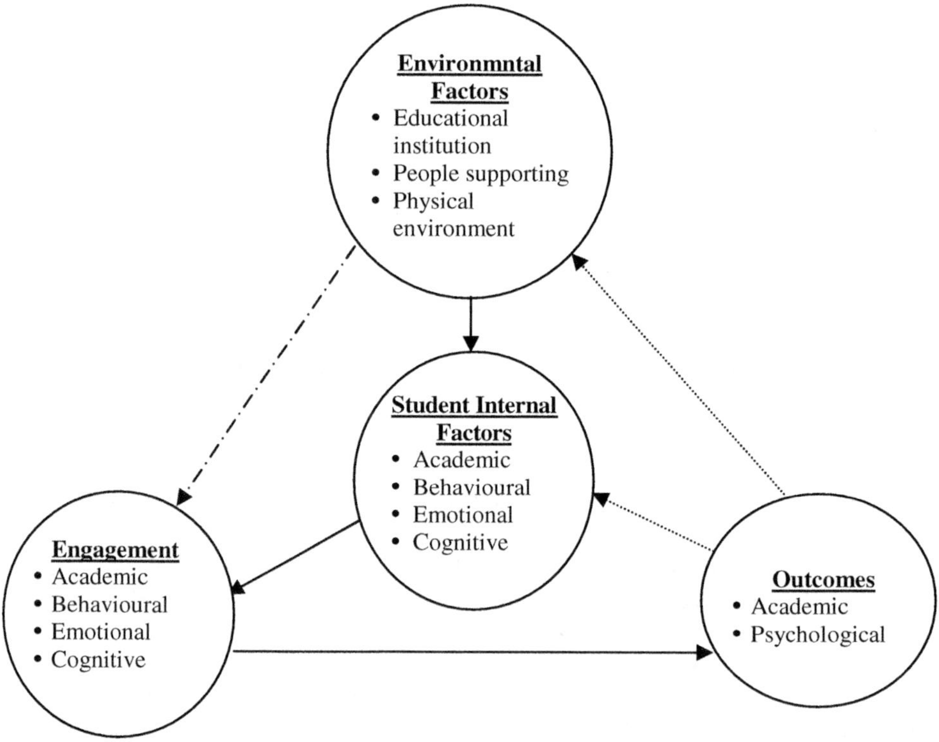

Fig. 4. Triangular relationships (factors in two groups, environmental and internal)

4 ICT as Key Tool to Provide Desirable Factors

As the conceptualizations and studies of student engagement suggest, the environment or context in which students are engaged in play key roles in deciding extents of engagement and thus extents of learning outcome achievement. This has created niches for ICT applications in learning and teaching and justifies investment of resources to the applications.

ICT has been considered one of the main tools that may provide desirable stimulus for high student engagement. However, it has been observed that students' levels of engagement in courses and their retention rates are relatively lower for online courses than for courses delivered in the conventional face-to-face mode (Nakazawa, 2009).

This calls for research to inform teachers and educators about pedagogical choices to make and what to consider when choosing from given options. Research on ICT in learning and teaching has been serving this need. For example, being interested in using games for teaching, Charles, Bustard and Black (2009) attempted to identify factors affecting engagement and elements of digital games that make them engaging, on the belief that, with careful design, e-learning systems may be able to achieve the levels of engagement expected of digital games. Nakazawa (2009) examined student engagement in online language learning, and noted that ICT provided students with more interaction opportunities using the target language and that students wished to have well-structured guidance, scaffolding and timely support from teachers.

Research warrants sound pedagogical reasoning to inform ICT use (John & Sutherland, 2005; Koehler & Mishra, 2008). The aforementioned work in this section, together with other research reported in other papers of this edited book, add to the efforts urgently needed for developing knowledge in this area and for the impartial reasoning.

Applications of ICT in learning and teaching involve integration of technology, pedagogy, subject matter domain and learning culture in education contexts (John & Sutherland, 2005). Mama and Hennessy's (2010) research suggests that the level of the teacher's integration of technology use with their pedagogical approach is dependent on the teacher's perception of technology's role in facilitating learning. ICT will only be effectively applied in education if educators develop in themselves proper knowledge of technology's role and how to integrate it with their teaching contexts.

5 Conclusion

This paper has attempted to summarize the meanings of student engagement from its myriad conceptualizations. It has been noted that the studies on this multidimensional construct is in general etiological, on the ground that engagement leads to educational outcomes, expecting that more effective pedagogical and curriculum design is built on a better understanding of the relationships between engagement and its outcomes as well as those between engagement and the factors facilitating it.

To a large extent, ICT applications in teaching and learning are for enhancing students' engagement in the learning process. It is to get them physically involved in useful learning activities, inspire them to be emotionally positive about learning and the involved processes and/or be cognitively productive in developing their knowledge and skills. Given the complexity of the construct and the diverse ways in which the term is used, to minimize confusion, we may need to foster the use of more specific terms such as school engagement, course engagement, learning process engagement, activity engagement.

Applications of ICT in teaching and learning often require a lot of resources, especially when new equipment and new skills are necessary for implementation. This calls for research to guide educators to proper decisions. Student engagement may offer useful conceptual and practical dimensions for gauging the usefulness of an application.

Yet as emphasized above, such research requires sound pedagogical reasoning. Axelson and Flick (2010) wisely raise this in their discussion of student engagement:

> "We know, or at least have reason to believe, that it is better for a student to be engaged—even behaviourally engaged...—than not to be. We know, or have reason to suspect, that many of the deeply embedded, rarely interrogated structures ... today may actually contribute to, rather than meliorate, the disengagement problem. Do we really consider the following a recipe for engagement: 15-week courses meeting for two hours twice a week with one professor, focused on a discrete but arbitrary subject upon which students are examined in a high-stakes final exam? Does our notion—and delivery—of general education follow such a recipe? Our majors?"
>
> (Axelson & Flick, 2010, p. 43)

When educators and researchers work diligently to integrate ICT applications in learning and teaching, they should accept the challenge posed by the questions raised. Unless they organize their study on sound pedagogical grounds, the deduced integration may not lead to engagement or learning productive engagement.

References

Appleton, J.J., Christenson, S.L., Furlong, M.J.: Student engagement with school: critical conceptual and methodological issues of the construct. Psychology in the Schools 45(5), 369–386 (2008)

Arbaugh, J.B.: Does the Community of Inquiry Framework Predict Outcomes in Online MBA Courses? The International Review of Research in Open and Distance Learning 9(2) (2008), http://www.google.com.hk/url?sa=t&rct=j&q=Arbaugh%2C+2000%2C+education&source=web&cd=3&ved=0CDgQFjAC&url=http%3A%2F%2Fwww.irrodl.org%2Findex.php%2Firrodl%2Frt%2FprinterFriendly%2F490%2F1045&ei=cVijT6u1GdSciQeasrzSDw&usg=AFQjCNFEwqwEeJksYTproaj6-LzZ8eThfA (retrieved March 15, 2012)

Archambault, I., Janosz, M., Morizot, J., Ragani, L.: Adolescent Behavioral, Affective, and Cognitive Engagement in School: Relationship to Dropout. Journal of School Health 79(9), 408–415 (2009)

Axelson, R.D., Flick, A.: Defining student engagement. Change: The Magazine of Higher Learning 43(1), 38–43 (2010)

Bartko, W.T.: The ABCs of engagement in out-of-school-time programs. New Directions for Youth Development 105, 109–120 (2005)

Blatchford, P., Bassett, P., Brown, P.: Examining the effect of class size on classroom engagement and teacher–pupil interaction: Differences in relation to pupil prior attainment and primary vs. secondary schools. Learning and Instruction 21, 715–730 (2010)

Blatchford, P., Bassett, P., Brown, P.: Examining the effect of class size on classroom engagement and teacher–pupil interaction: Differences in relation to pupil prior attainment and primary vs. secondary schools. Learning and Instruction 21(6), 715–730 (2011)

Buhs, E.S., Ladd, G.W., Herald, S.L.: Peer Exclusion and Victimization: Processes That Mediate the Relation between Peer Group Rejection and Children's Classroom Engagement and Achievement? Journal of Educational Psychology 98(1), 1–13 (2006)

Carini, R.M., Kuh, G.D., Klein, S.P.: Student engagement and student learning: testing the linkages. Research in Higher Education 47(1), 1–32 (2006)

Charles, M., Bustard, D., Black, M.: Game inspired tool support for e-learning processes. Electronic Journal of e-Learning 7(2), 101–110 (2009)

Connell, J.P.: Context, self, and action: A motivational analysis of self-system processes across the life span. In: Cicchetti, D., Beeghly, M. (eds.) The Self in Transition: Infancy to Childhood (The John D. and Catherine T. MacArthur foundation series on mental health and development), pp. 61–97. The University of Chicago Press, Chicago (1990)

Connell, J.P., Wellborn, J.G.: Competence, autonomy, and relatedness: A motivational analysis of self-system processes. In: Gunnar, M.R., Sroufe, L.A. (eds.) Self Processes and Development, vol. 23, pp. 43–77. Lawrence Erlbaum, Hillsdale (1991)

Downer, J.T., Rimm-kaufman, E.E., Pianta, R.C.: How do classroom conditions and children's risk for school problems contribute to children's behavioral engagement in learning? School Psychology Review 36(3), 413–432 (2007)

Finn, J.D.: Withdrawing from school. Review of Educational Research 59, 117–142 (1989)

Fredericks, J.A., Blumenfeld, P.C., Paris, A.H.: School engagement: Potential of the concept, state of the evidence. Review of Educational Research 74(1), 59–109 (2004)

Frisch, M.B., Clark, M.P., Rouse, S.V., Rudd, M.D., Paweleck, J.K., Greenstone, A., Kopplin, D.A.: Predictive and treatment validity of life satisfaction and the quality of life inventory. Assessment 12, 66–78 (2005)

Jimerson, S.R., Campos, E., Greif, J.: Toward an understanding of definitions and measures of school engagement and related terms. The California School Psychologist 8, 7–27 (2003)

John, P., Sutherland, R.: Affordance, opportunity and the pedagogical implications of ICT. Educational Review 57(4), 405–413 (2005)

Koehler, M., Mishra, P.: Introducing TPCK – Handbook of technological pedagogical content knowledge (TPCK) for educators. Routledge, New York (2008)

Kuh, G.D., Kinzie, J., Schuh, J.H., Whitt, E.J., Associates: Student Success in College: Creating Conditions That Matter. Jossey-Bass, San Francisco (2005)

Lee, J., Shute, V.J.: Personal and Social-Contextual Factors in K–12 Academic Performance: An Integrative Perspective on Student Learning. Educational Psychologist 45(3), 185–202 (2010)

Li, K.C.: Blended Learning Pilot Courses: A quest for effective instructional approaches. In: Tsang, P., Li, K.C., Wang, F.L., Chan, F.T., Tse, S. (eds.) Enhancing Learning Through Technology: Emerging research on ICT in Teaching and Learning, pp. 54–62. City University of Hong Kong Press, Hong Kong (2011)

Li, K.C.: Encountering pedagogical challenges: a case of three pilot blended learning courses. International Journal of Innovation and Learning (forthcoming)
Mama, M., Hennessy, S.: Level of technology integration by primary teachers in Cyprus and student engagement. Technology, Pedagogy and Education 19(2), 269–275 (2010)
Marks, H.M.: Student engagement in instructional activity: Patterns in the elementary, middle, and high school years. American Educational Research Journal 37, 153–184 (2000)
Mason, R.B.: Student engagement with, and participation in an e-forum. Educational Technology and Society 14(2), 258–268 (2011)
Nakazawa, K.: Student Engagement in Online Language Learning: A Case Study Examining the Online Delivery of Tertiary Language Courses. The International Journal of Learning 16(7), 405–414 (2009)
Reschly, A., Christenson, S.L.: Promoting successful school completion. In: Bear, G., Minke, K. (eds.) Children's Needs—III: Development, Prevention, and Intervention, pp. 103–113. National Association of School Psychologists, Bethesda (2006)
Reschly, A., Christenson, S.L.: Research leading to a predictive model of dropout and completion among students with mild disabilities and the role of student engagement. Remedial and Special Education 27, 276–292 (2006b)
Rotgans, J., Schmidt, H.G.: Cognitive Engagement in the Problem-Based Learning Classroom. Advances in Health Sciences Education 16(4), 465–479 (2011)
Russell, B., Slater, G.R.L.: Factors that Encourage Student Engagement: Insights from a Case Study of "First Time" Students in a New Zealand University. Journal of University Teaching and Learning Practice 8(1) (2011), http://ro.uow.edu.au/jutlp/vol8/iss1/7/ (retrieved March 11, 2012)
Sinclair, M.F., Christenson, S.L., Lehr, C.A., Reschly-Anderson, A.: Facilitating student engagement: Lessons learned from Check & Connect longitudinal studies. The California School Psychologist 8, 29–41 (2003)
Wong, S.N., Li, K.C.: Quality and Blended Learning: An Evaluative Exploration of Approaches to Learner Transformation. Paper presented at the 24th ICDE World Conference, Indonesia (October 2011)

Learning Management System: Japanese Student Perceptions and Expectations

Yoko Hirata and Yoshihiro Hirata

Hokkai-Gakuen University, Japan
{hira,hirata}@eli.hokkai-s-u.ac.jp

Abstract. Recently leaning management systems (LMS) have been widely used in Japanese tertiary institutions as tools to assist students to submit assignments and communicate with each other online. The system is also effective for the instructor in customizing materials, assessing student accomplishments, and recording their participation. Although the technical aspects and efficacy of LMS have been extensively discussed, little research has been conducted regarding how novice computer users perceive the use of this technology. This study examines Japanese undergraduate students' perceptions of using LMS in different educational settings. In addition, it looks at the benefits and drawbacks of LMS for their language studies. Based on a year-long empirical data study of the students' use of LMS in blended learning courses, their perceptions and expectations have been examined. The results suggest that the students' perceived benefits and drawbacks with LMS are different depending on individual students' ideas of and attitudes towards education.

Keywords: learning management system, language study, learner's perceptions.

1 Introduction

In the past decade there has been an increasing transition away from traditional, teacher-led face-to-face language learning towards language learning by using Learning Management Systems (LMSs) throughout the world (Abdulaziz, 2011; Nanaykkara, 2007). In spite of the fact that a large amount of money has been invested on installation and maintenance of LMSs, as Nanaykkara (2007) claims, this recent adoption has been made in order to offer more flexibility in teaching and to improve the quality of education in general. A study has indicated some potential benefits of LMSs for both the instructor and the students (Averious, Papasalouros, Retails, & Skordalakis, 2003). The benefits for the instructor include providing individual students with electronic materials, assessing students' grades systematically, and managing class activities efficiently (Alias & Zainuddin, 2005). In addition, an LMS provides students easy access to educational resources or materials and enables digital communication amongst students and with the instructor in an anytime from anywhere environment (Alias & Zainuddin, 2005). Because of these various benefits, adopting an LMS for large classes has been an emerging trend (Gew, Loughi, Cindio, & Ripamonti, 2004).

K.C. Li et al. (Eds.): ICT 2012, CCIS 302, pp. 11–24, 2012.

One of the challenges facing instructors and administrators when adopting LMS to courses provided by a tertiary institution is the effective and smooth conversion of traditional face-to-face learning environments to flexible, e-learning environments (Care & Scanlan, 2001). In addition, individual user perception is another important factor for the instructor to determine whether students can easily accept such an environments without encountering any problems (Nanaykkara, 2007). Studies have discussed that user acceptance of e-learning systems is influenced by sociocultural factors and functionalities of individual LMSs (Abdulaziz, 2011; Liaw, 2008; Nanaykkara, 2007). These studies have concluded that students react differently to different learning styles. In spite of the fact that a great deal of research has suggested that LMSs can be useful tools in the classroom (Abdulaziz, 2011; Deperlioglu, Sparpkaya, & Ergun, 2011; Hussein, 2011; Nanaykkara, 2007), there is still little research addressing how LMSs can be optimized so that students can facilitate their learning. Students possess "individual preferences, backgrounds, and priorities" when they are required to adapt to hybrid learning environments (Hinkelman, 2005). Instructors need to be aware of whether students are open to the use of LMSs and how these technologies should be used for different individual students in different educational settings.

2 Purpose of the Study

The purpose of this study is to examine Japanese undergraduate students' perceptions of the use of LMS in different educational contexts in order for them to pass English tests successfully. The focus was placed on the benefits of using LMS viewed by individual students in different educational situations.

2.1 Research Questions

1. How do students perceive LMS in different contexts: instructor directed and non-instructor directed?
2. What are the relationships between the students' views and sociocultural backgrounds, such as aims of study, and their perception of using LMS?

3 Methodology

3.1 The Setting and Student Profiles

The subjects of this study were 48 lower intermediate learners of English enrolled in a university English course. The study consisted of 26 male and 22 female full-time students, 18–22 years old. The study focused upon the faculties of Humanities, Economics, Law, and Engineering, the four faculties currently utilizing LMS in the course. The course was a two-semester blended learning course consisting of an instructor-directed, face-to-face learning environment and an online environment. The objective of this course is to help students develop their English listening, reading, as well as vocabulary skills. However, the majority of students taking this course for the purpose of gaining skills perceived it to be necessary to gain a high score on the Test of English for International Communication (TOEIC). In fact, almost 85% of students planned to take the test within a year of when this survey was conducted. This is due to Japanese university students taking English courses "for the specific purpose of taking the TOEIC" prevalent hiring factor for many businesses (Ockert, 2005). This course was offered weekly for ninety minutes in a computer assisted language learning (CALL) classroom. The students were required to use a textbook which was designed to improve and foster students' TOEIC scores. Although the students' computer skills were not high, they possessed sufficient knowledge of Web browsers and acquired computer literacy to be able to use LMS.

3.2 Procedures

The project described in this study was divided into two modules. In the first module, conducted during the first semester, students were required to attend a weekly class session and listen to the instructor's lecture on various skills required to foster improvement of TOEIC scores. Prior to beginning the course, students were required to take a placement test and only students who ranked in the top 50% were allowed to take this course. Half of the class involved direct, traditional teaching, using the textbook. The instructor provided keys and explanations of the exercises provided by the textbook. The remainder were taught using computer-based TOEIC exercises provided by an LMS named GOALS. The students were required to review the uploaded materials before attending class sessions. Exercises included cloze testing, multiple-choice, true-or-false, and listening & vocabulary activities.

In the second module, which was conducted in the second semester, students were given a choice between attending class on a regular basis and studying autonomously without attending class. Approximately 65% of the students decided not to attend the classes. Particularly for these students, the keys and explanations of the textbook were uploaded onto the server of GOALS.

At the end of the course when the test was administered, students were provided with a questionnaire which attempted to attain feedback on their perceptions of learning with LMS in the two different modules: guided use of LMS in the classroom and LMS outside of the classroom. The questions in the questionnaire were based on a study-suggested set of rules to consider when selecting survey questions (Stone, 2003). Eleven of the questions from the questionnaire referred directly to the students' views on using GOALS in the modules. These questions had a 10-point Likert scale, with "1" representing "strongly disagree" and "10" representing "strongly agree". The remaining questions offered option selection questions. The questionnaire also had an area in which students were asked to write down their opinions on any aspect of the course. This survey was administered in a paper version and the questionnaires were written in Japanese in order for students to fully understand the questions. The points were totaled and averaged, and a standard deviation was also attained. The data is presented in this paper as mean ±SD. In addition, the questionnaire was analyzed by using Spearman's correlation. Students' responses were also compared by *t*-test of the student ratings based on the questions mentioned above. In addition, the results of students' ratings were analyzed by using Spearman's correlation to determine correlations between responses and significant factors underlying their responses. Correlation is judged as significant at the .01 level (2-tailed).

3.3 The Learning Management System

In the present study, the Learning Management System, called GOALS, enables students to easily access assignments, tests, and exercises. It can also be designed to incorporate various media formats such as graphics and audio.

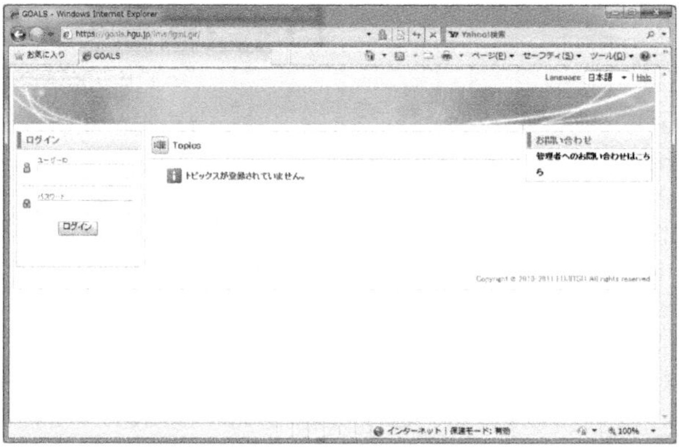

Fig. 1. Login screen

As shown in Fig. 1, the students are required to enter the system via this login page. Once logged in, their name appears at the top of the screen.

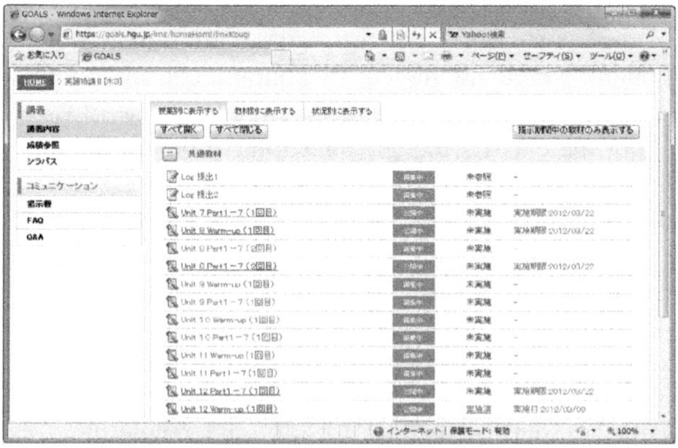

Fig. 2. Selection of tasks & exercises

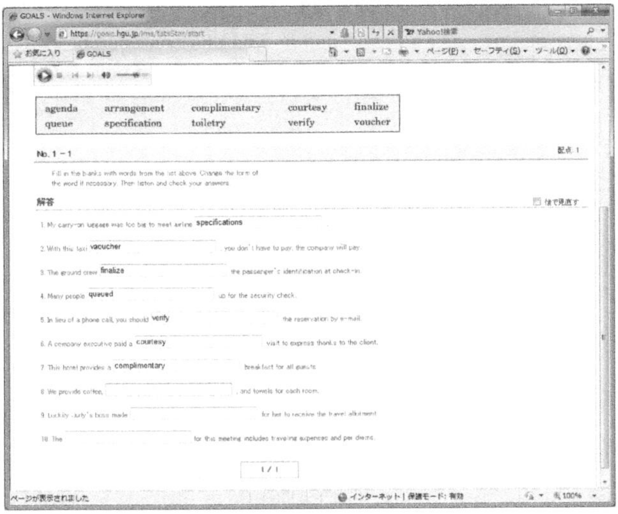

Fig. 3. Student exercises

After the login page, students are directed towards the 'Selection of tasks & exercises' page, as illustrated in Fig. 2. Here, students are presented with a list of titles of tasks and exercises they need to attempt. Columns of tasks, which were labeled according to the type of task, enable students to access an assigned task provided by the instructor. The system allows the instructor and administrators to create a content of materials, monitor students' assigned tasks, and grade them online. The materials and tasks are easily duplicated from one course to another. They can be made available for the use of other instructors as well. Students view the announcements about the courses and the task deadlines. Students are then guided to select tasks from amongst from listening, reading, grammar and vocabulary exercises. On the left side of the list is a discussion forum where students communicate with each other. This page also assists students in communicating to the instructor any issues they face while using this system. For example, if a student finds it difficult to improve his or her listening skills, the instructor may provide the student with suggestions and ideas for dealing with the problem.

When a task is selected from the list, the 'Exercise' page appears (Fig. 3). From here the students are required to complete listening exercises in a given amount of time. Students can download the materials, store it on their computer, and use it whenever they need to, depending on the tasks and exercises.

Upon completion, students are required to proceed to the 'Keys and explanations' page (Fig. 4). This page provides students with an opportunity to check the keys and explanations and review what they have done. The students' answers are automatically graded. No special computer skills are required in order to complete the entire process.

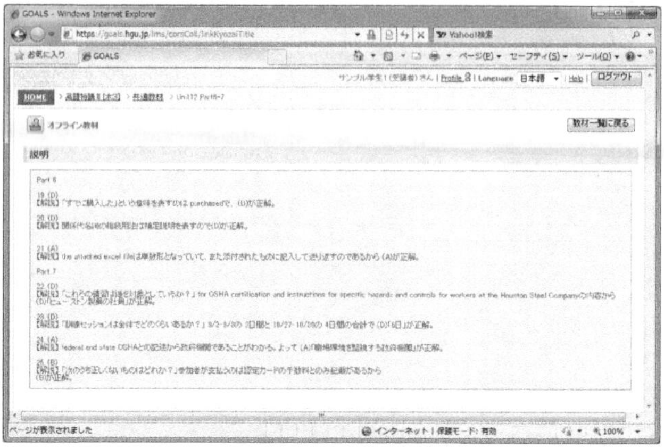

Fig. 4. Keys and explanations

4 Findings

The findings obtained by the survey are shown below. As shown in Fig. 5, with regard to the students' preferred learning style, almost half of them (23 students) thought the instruction provided only by the LMS was perceived to be better than teacher only instruction. Approximately 15% of students concurrently displayed preference for teacher instruction. However, approximately 40% of students thought that the instruction provided by both the teacher and LMS was better than the other options.

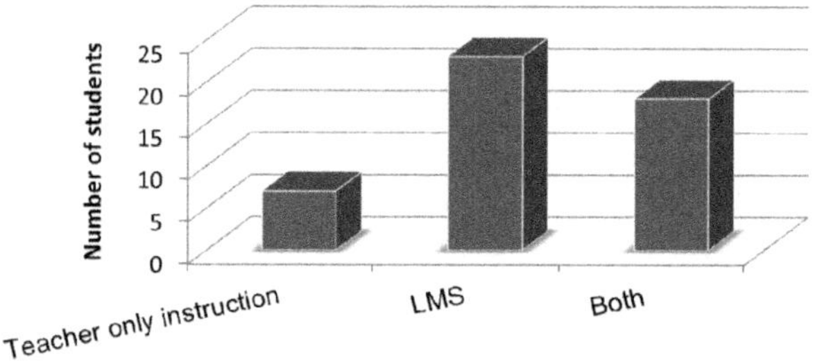

Fig. 5. Students' preferred learning style

With regard to the answer keys and explanations provided by the LMS, almost 96% of students stated that they definitely required them, as shown by Table 1 below. Table 2 expresses the preferences of approximately half of the students to complete exercises provided by the LMS outside of the classroom and the remainder preferring completion of exercises in the classroom.

Table 1. The keys and explanations provided by the LMS were necessary (%)

	Yes	No
Percentage of students	95.9	4.1

Table 2. Doing exercises provided by the LMS was important outside of the classroom (%)

	Yes	No
Percentage of students	45.9	54.1

As shown in Table 3, when asked about the purpose of taking the present course, almost 70% of the students stated their intention to gain high scores in the next TOEIC test. With regard to the keys and explanations provided by the LMS, approximately 85% of the students expressed a benefit towards study (Table 4).

Table 3. The purpose of taking this course is to gain high scores in the next TOEIC test (%)

	Yes	No
Percentage of students	68.8	31.2

Table 4. The keys and explanation provided by the LMS were beneficial to my study (%)

	Yes	No
Percentage of students	83.4	16.6

Table 5 shows the students' views upon the use of LMS. Many students thought that the exercises provided by the LMS were indispensable for their study. The Average (±SD) of this response was 6.25 (±2.26). They highly valued the convenience of working on exercises provided by the LMS. The instructor's enforcement of use is also influential. The average (±SD) of this response was 4.85 (±2.05). It is clear that not many students highly valued the instructor's explanations if the LMS was available. In addition, many students indicate that the use of LMS is worthwhile and therefore students stated that they used the LMS because of its efficacy. It is important to note that there were students who thought there was a big difference between the explanations provided by the LMS and those by the instructor. The average (±SD) of this response was 5.98 (±2.77). The students highly valued the instruction provided by the LMS without the instructor in the second module rather than the instructor's direct instruction in the first module. They thought that the LMS was important for them to study at their own pace. The average (±SD) of this response was 6.19 (±2.60).

Table 5. Students' views upon the use of the LMS

	Mean (SD)
1. The exercises provided by the LMS were indispensable for my study.	6.25 (2.26)
2. The exercises provided by the LMS were more convenient for me to study than those in the textbook.	6.02 (2.41)
3. I used the LMS because the instructor asked me to do so.	4.85 (2.05)
4. I didn't use the LMS because of the ineffective system.	3.90 (2.64)
5. I studied English more effectively in the second module than in the first module.	6.54 (2.65)
6. The LMS made my study worthwhile.	7.08 (2.64)
7. The instructor's explanations made my study worthwhile.	3.83 (3.51)
8. There was a big difference between the explanations provided by the LMS and those by the instructor.	5.98 (2.77)
9. The LMS helped me to study at my own pace.	6.19 (2.60)
10. I wish I could have used the discussion system of the LMS.	3.90 (2.10)
11. I'm satisfied with the overall functions of the LMS.	5.58 (2.50)

(N = 48)

The results of the *t*-test show a significant difference between the students who attended the classes throughout the course and those who didn't attend the course in the second semester. Compared with students who didn't attend the course in the second semester, the students who attended the classes throughout the course thought that the instructor's direct explanation was useful, and there was a big difference between the explanation provided by the LMS and that of the instructor (t = 10.99, t = 4.23 respectively; $p < .05$). In addition, there is a significant difference between the students who spent most of the time completing exercises outside of the classroom and those who spent most of the time inside the classroom. The students, who completed exercises outside of the classroom, thought the exercises provided by the LMS are more convenient than those in the textbook. Those, who did the exercises outside of the classroom, thought that they had studied more effectively in the second module than in the first module ($t = 3.39$, $t = 2.16$ respectively; $p < .05$). In addition, these students were satisfied with the overall functions of the LMS ($t = 3.03$; $p < .05$).

In addition, the results of the *t*-test show a significant difference between the students who thought the keys and explanations provided by the LMS were beneficial to their study and those who didn't think the keys and explanations were beneficial. Compared with the students who didn't see the keys and explanations as beneficial, the students, who highly valued the keys and explanations provided by the LMS, thought the materials provided by the LMS were more convenient than those in the textbook. Students who highly valued the keys and explanations provided by the LMS also preferred the second module to the first module ($t = 3.63$, $t = 3.46$ respectively; $p < .05$). In addition, these students thought that the LMS made their study worthwhile and therefore they were satisfied with the overall functions of the LMS ($t = 2.58$, $t = 4.04$ respectively; $p < .05$). These students used the LMS due to the instructor's enforcement ($t = 2.56$; $p < .05$). There is a significant difference between the students who took the course in order to gain high TOEIC scores and students who took the course in order to acquire a credit for the course. Compared with students who took the course in order to gain high scores, those who took the course in order to acquire a credit for the course were satisfied with the overall the functions of the LMS ($t = -2.88$; $p < .05$).

Table 6. Correlation between factors regarding the exercises by the LMS and the instructor

	Exercises provided by the LMS were indispensable.	Exercises provided by the LMS were more convenient than those in the textbook.	I used the LMS because the instructor asked to do so.
Exercises provided by the LMS were indispensable.	1.00	-----	-----
Exercises provided by the LMS were more convenient than those in the textbook.	.687**	1.00	-----
I used the LMS because the instructor asked to do so.	.325**	.380**	1.00

*Notes: Correlation Matrix (N = 48), **p < .01.*

Table 6 shows that there was a moderate correlation (r < .6) between those who thought that exercises provided by the LMS are indispensable and those who thought that exercises provided by the LMS are more convenient than those in the textbook (r = .687, $p < .01$). There was a weak correlation (r < .4) between those who thought exercises provided by the LMS are indispensable and those who used the LMS because the instructor asked them to do so (r = .325, $p < .01$). In addition, there was a weak correlation (r < .4) between those who thought that exercises provided by the LMS are more convenient than those in the textbook and those who used the LMS because the instructor asked them to do so (r = .380, $p < .01$).

As shown in Table 7, there was a moderate correlation (r < .6) between those who thought exercises provided by the LMS were more convenient than those in the textbook and those who valued the second module rather than the first one (r = .465, $p < .01$). There was a weak correlation (r < .4) between those who thought that exercises provided by the LMS are more convenient than those in the textbook and those who thought that the LMS made their study worthwhile (r = .361, $p < .01$). The correlation of .714 was also significant between those who valued the second module rather than the first one and those who thought that the LMS made their study worthwhile.

Table 7. Correlation between factors regarding the use of LMS and its effects

	Exercises provided by the LMS were more convenient than those in the textbook.	I studied more effectively in the second module than in the first module.	The LMS made my study worthwhile.
Exercises provided by the LMS were more convenient than those in the textbook.	1.00	-----	-----
I studied more effectively in the second module than in the first module.	.465**	1.00	-----
The LMS made my study worthwhile.	.361**	.714**	1.00

*Notes: Correlation Matrix (N = 48), **p* < .01.

Table 8 shows that there was a moderate correlation (r < .6) between those who thought the instructor's explanations made their study worthwhile and those who saw a big difference between the explanations provided by the LMS and those by the instructor (r = .550, $p < .01$). There was a negative weak correlation (r < –.4) between those who thought the instructor's explnations made their study worthwhile and those who thought that the LMS helped them to study at their own pace (r = –.459, $p < .01$). The correlation of -.405 was also significant between those who saw a big difference between the explnation provided by the LMS and those by the instructor and those who thought that the LMS helped them to study at their own pace.

Table 8. Correlation between factors regarding the role of instructor and learning style

	The instructor's explanations made my study worthwhile.	A big difference between the explanations provided by the LMS and those by the instructor.	The LMS helped me to study at my own pace.
The instructor's explanations made my study worthwhile.	1.00	-----	-----
A big difference between the explanations provided by the LMS and those by the instructor.	.550**	1.00	-----
The LMS helped me to study at my own pace.	–.459**	–.405**	1.00

*Notes: Correlation Matrix (N = 48), **p* < .01.

The students expressed distinct but different opinions about the LMS. Some students commented favourably about the LMS as follows.

> *"The benefits of using the LMS included listening and doing excises repeatedly at anytime, anywhere even at home."*

> *"The LMS was an easy and convenient tool for me to study for TOEIC tests."*

> *"The explanations of the keys provided by the LMS were helpful for my study because, in the regular classroom, I always miss some important parts of the instructor's explanations. I usually just grin and bear it."*

> *"Using the LMS is a useful tool for students who don't want to come to school and who want to do something else during the class time."*

On the other hand, there were students who made negative comments about the LMS as follows.

> *"I didn't use the LMS at all because I didn't have my own computer. It is easier for me to listen and take notes than working with a computer. However, I admit that submitting an electronic file to the instructor is more convenient than submitting a paper-based file."*

> *"The instructor's explanations were more valuable for me than the explanations provided by the LMS. This is the reason why I've attended all the classes throughout the course, even though attending them was not mandatory."*

"I know that working with a computer is easy and educational to some extent, but I'm sure that working with a textbook will help me achieve high TOEIC scores."

"I understand that checking the keys and the explanations provided by the LMS makes my study for TOEIC a bit easier. But I don't want the instructor to increase the amount of time I have to work with the LMS at all."

5 Discussion of Findings

Although the course in the present study was carried out in an experimental set up, a careful examination of the findings clearly revealed distinctive student views on the use of the LMS. One of the major findings from the survey indicates that there were two groups of students who viewed the use of the LMS differently. The survey indicates that there are many students, with positive attitudes towards the LMS, who were satisfied with the "open, flexible delivery mode" of this learning type (Hinkelman, 2005). In addition to the fact that these students easily accepted LMS implementation, they found so many advantages in the use of the LMS. They highly valued the out-of-class engagement in learning at their own pace. They preferred studying with the LMS without the instructor. They preferred the second module in which class attendance was non-mandatory. It is interesting to note that, however, as the results of the *t*-test have shown, these students' self-motivation to study independently with the aid of the LMS was not high. Even though they fully acknowledged the efficacy of the LMS, they are inclined to use it only with the instructor's strict enforcement. It is obvious that focus should be placed on how to maximize this technology for those who are capable of but non-receptive to using LMSs. A more detailed study is needed for this issue.

On the contrary, the findings also indicate that there were students who had negative attitudes towards the use of LMS. They showed reticence towards new ideas of learning with the LMS. These students were not willing to do exercises online but were more willing to read the printed versions (Avgerious et al., 2003). The comments collected from the students suggest that they resorted to taking notes by hand even when they used online materials. Another important comment implies that repetitive on-screen exercises were seen as merely mechanical processes based on individual students' intentions (Pacneco, 2005). The results of the *t*-test, Spearman's correlation, as well as students' comments have shown that, compared with the students who didn't attend the course, the students who attended all the classes throughout the course were more willing to listen to the instructor's explanations, rather than the explanations provided by the LMS. They depended more upon traditional, in-class instruction rather than the self-directed, independent, on-screen learning process. It is also demonstrable that the present study hasn't identified the students' educational goal as a potentially important facilitator of e-learning acceptance (Abdulaziz, 2011). Compared with those who took the course for the purpose of gaining high TOEIC scores, those who took the course because of acquiring a credit for the course were positive towards the functions of the LMS.

The findings of the present study suggest that the instructor and administrators should determine the LMS's pedagogical impact upon students. They should not consider LMS only from a technical perspective and should not regard LMS simply as a tool to provide educational content and management of student learning processes (Phan, 2010). Although the findings revealed several positive aspects of using the LMS, it would seem odd to claim that the users fully appreciated the efficacy for their own study. There is a strong possibility that these students highly valued simply the easy accessibility and the clear presentation of exercises. As Avgerious and colleagues (2003) claim, it is important for the instructor to acknowledge the LMS's inability to supervise the students' engagement because of a lack of a physical interaction with the students. In order for the instructor to encourage students to make the maximum use of LMSs, the focus of attention should be on shifting from traditional teacher-centered classrooms to learner-oriented environments (Pacneco, 2005). It is also important to develop approaches which give more control to students based on their own individual learning preferences and needs. This will help students become more involved in their own activities and facilitate own language learning.

6 Conclusions

This study examines how Japanese university students perceive the use of LMS in instructor-directed and non-instructor-directed educational contexts. It also attempts to look at the benefits and drawbacks of using LMS for their English language studies in a blended learning environment. The results reveal that the LMS in the present study may not serve as an alternative instructor and therefore new methodologies for diverse users of LMS should be developed. In spite of the fact that there is now a great deal of research which supports the use of LMS, there is not much from the perspective of students' use of such systems. Although this study was exploratory and only conducted upon forty-eight students, it has created an opportunity for those who are involved with e-learning, to ensure how to instruct students with LMS. As LMS has been widely adopted by many tertiary institutions, it would be advisable to conduct further in-depth studies to acquire a more comprehensive understanding of the long-term relationship between the use of LMS and socio-educational effects upon students.

References

Abdulaziz, I.F.: EFL students' readiness for e-learning: factors influencing e-learners' acceptance of the Blackboard in a Saudi university. The JALT CALL Journal 7(1), 19–42 (2011)

Alias, N.A., Zainuddin, A.M.: Innovation for Better Teaching and Learning: Adopting the Learning Management System. Malaysian Online Journal of Instructional Technology 2(2), 27–40 (2005)

Avgerious, P., Papasalouros, A., Retails, S., Skordalakis, M.: Towards a Pattern Language for Learning Management Systems. Educational Technology & Society 6(2), 11–24 (2003)

Care, W.D., Scanlan, J.M.: Planning and Managing the Development of Courses for Distance Delivery: Results from a Qualitative Study. Online Journal of Distance Learning Administration 4(2) (2001), http://distance.westga.edu/~distance/ojdla/summer42/care42.html (retrieved)

Deperlioglu, O., Sarpkaya, Y., Ergun, E.: Development of a relational database for learning management systems. Turkish Online Journal of Educational Technology 10(4), 107–120 (2011)

Gew, P., Loughi, I., Cindio, F.D., Ripamonti, L.A.: Applying an LMS to Large Language Classes. In: Proceeding of the IASTED International Conference on Web-based Education, Innsbruck, Austria (February 2004), http://jli.retecivica.milano.it/papers/wbe04.pdf (retrieved)

Hinkelman, D.: Blended Learning: Issues Driving an End to Laboratory-based CALL. JALT Hokkaido Journal 9, 17–31 (2005)

Hussein, H.B.: Attitudes of Saudi Universities Faculty Members Towards Using Learning Management System. Turkish Online Journal of Educational Technology 10(2), 43–53 (2011)

Liaw, S.: Investigating students' perceived satisfaction, behavioural intention, and effectiveness of e-learning: A case study of the Blackboard system. Computer & Education 51(1), 864–873 (2008)

Nanaykkara, C.: A model of user acceptance of learning management systems: a study within tertiary institutions in New Zealand. The International Journal of Learning 13(2), 223–232 (2005)

Ockert, D.: Substantive Scale Verification: A Likert Scale Analysis and Critique of University Student Pedagogical Activity Preferences. JALT Hokkaido Journal 9, 48–64 (2005)

Phan, M.: Evaluation of E-Learning in Vietnam. Lap Lambert Academic Publishing, Saarbrucken (2010)

Pacneco, A.Q.: Web-based Learning: A Challenge for Foreign Language Teachers. Revista Electronica Actualidades in vestigativas en Education 5(2), 1–25 (2005), http://revista.inie.ucr.ac.cr/uploads/tx_magazine/web.pdf (retrieved)

Stone, M.: Substantive scale construction. Journal of Applied Measurement 4, 282–297 (2003)

e-Assessment: A Case of Student-Centred Learning

Madeleine Tsoi and Reggie Kwan

Caritas Institute of Higher Education, Hong Kong SAR, China
mtsoi@cihe.edu.hk

Abstract. There is a growing trend worldwide to adopt a student-centred learning approach as the central pedagogy at both school and university levels. Over the years, many such epithets as *self-directed learning, learner-focused learning, autonomous learning, independent learning, collaborative learning, experiential learning, etc.* have been used to define the approach and its process. This paper reports on a case of student-centred learning using an online self-regulating and diagnostic assessment system to facilitate students in a sub-degree institute in the HKSAR to undertake self-directed and self-controlled learning in English academic writing skills. It has taken the project team two years to install the system, conduct pilot study and test stringently as well as repeatedly. The system is now in full operation and feedback from the institute's student population drawn from diverse backgrounds has indicated that the system has indeed fulfilled its mission of providing a practical and convenient means of enabling students to conduct autonomous learning wherever and whenever they wish.

Keywords: e-Assessment, e-learning, computerized adaptive testing, item response theory.

1 Introduction

A tertiary institute in the HKSAR which offers sub-degree Associate Degree and Higher Diploma programmes has established an online e-Assessment platform. The system has self-regulating and diagnostic features which facilitates users to engage in self-directed, self-controlled and self-paced learning in English academic writing. The system mainly features a data bank which contains 400 multiple choice questions on almost all aspects of English academic writing skills. Users of the system initially receive random questions but the level of difficulty of subsequent questions depends on responses. If the user supplies a correct answer, the immediate question that follows increases in difficulty and conversely, if the user supplies an incorrect answer, the subsequent question decreases in difficulty. More importantly, the system provides feedback on users' overall performance, result analysis and suggestions for further improvement.

2 Literature Review

A student-centred learning approach as the central pedagogy has been a catch-cry at both school and university levels for years. Epithets developed over the years include

K.C. Li et al. (Eds.): ICT 2012, CCIS 302, pp. 25–30, 2012.

but not limited to *self-directed learning, learner-focused learning, autonomous learning, independent learning, collaborative learning, experiential learning and child-centred education.* Gibbs (1995) argues that this type of learning should focus on learners' being active rather than passive. Learners would have to decide what is to be learned, how and when it is to be learned, with what outcome, criteria and standards. Similarly, Donnelly and Fitzmaurice (2005) describe the approach as a shift in power from the expert teacher to the student learner. It puts more responsibility on the learners to decide what to learn and how to learn it. Students will learn by doing, rather than just by listening passively and by engaging in meaningless tasks, like theory memorization. Simon (1999) links student-centred learning with the process of development or 'readiness', a student will learn when s/he is ready. Burnard (1999) identifies student-centredness as 'students might not only choose *what* to study, but *how* and *why* that topic might be an interesting one to study'. In other words, a student-centred learning approach should emphasize the concept of students having "choices" in their learning. Many researchers and educators maintain that the student-centred approach to education is far more superior to the traditional teaching environment where students resort to becoming passive, apathetic and bored. According to Simon (1999), a student-centred learning approach is related to an emphasis on learning process and competence, instead of content. In fact, research has indicated that constant feedback and reinforcement during the learning process lead to improvement and increased level of competence. Candy, Crebert and O'Leary (1994) also identifies adult learning as a continuous process by which adults manifest attributes of personal autonomy in self-managing learning efforts. In essence, many researchers identify student-centred learning as the process by which learners control both their learning objectives and pace of learning.

3 e-Assessment Project

The e-Assessment Project is a government funded project and the project period straddled two years as it took time to acquire and install the hardware and software, design the four hundred questions in the data bank and conduct numerous tests before its full implementation.

As the underlying concepts for the development of this e-Assessment System were based on "Computerized Adaptive Testing" and "Item Response Theory" which were more commonly used in mathematical and scientific applications, the Project Team had to conduct frequent and regular meetings to discuss ways of adapting this system for present use. An in-depth survey study of online learning and assessment websites on English Academic Writing was also conducted. Survey findings indicated that websites of this kind were generally text-heavy, grammatically oriented and non-level specific. The lexical density of some websites was so high that they literally put users off. A focus group of ten students was also formed to attempt twenty multiple-choice questions initially designed in paper and pencil format to provide some indication of the scope of the future data bank.

The main aim of the Project was to develop a self-directed online e-Assessment system that would promote the concept of "learning through assessment" and to harness the diverse learning needs of students with varied abilities, particularly sub-degree students. The system should be a self-regulating, diagnostic system which would promote student-centred, self-controlled and self-paced learning. To this end, the multiple choice questions would be categorized under the curriculum domain, which would denote the "breadth" of the system, whilst questions in each category would further be designed under the skills domain, which would denote the "depth" of the system. Two hundred questions were designed initially and students of the institute were invited to try those questions. Feedback questionnaires were distributed and responses were scrutinized by the Project Team for further improvement and refinement. Internal and external subject specialists were also consulted on a needs basis.

Coupled with the refining process, additional questions were added which brought the total number of questions to 400. Levels of difficulty were more clearly defined to identify participants' skills and knowledge attainment. The questions were categorized into: S1 – Format, Structure and Process; S2 – Style and Tone; S3 – Reading, Summarizing and Paragraphing; S4 – Language, Grammar and Proofreading; and S5 – Research and Referencing. The questions in each category were subdivided further into three levels of difficulty. Since the categories differed in their nature and complexity, the number of questions contained in each category also differed.

Student users were able to log into the system using their student identity numbers to attempt the e-Assessment questions. Analytical reports on the users' strengths and weaknesses were available after each test. They were followed by explanatory notes, relevant reading lists and recommendations for further improvement. Unlimited access was available to users and they could engage in a cyclical process as follows: e-Assessment – Weak areas diagnosed – Improvement – Reassessment. Since the system randomly generated questions based on a user's performance each time, the user would only be able to improve his/her subsequent performance through "genuine competence", not memorization of test answers.

Several rounds of testing on the validity of questions were conducted and participants were encouraged to use the diagnostic function of the system to analyze their own mistakes in English academic writing. Remedies and solutions offered by the system gave directions and pointers for further improvement. Computer generated results indicated that participants fared better in questions under the Category of "Style and Tone" in Academic writing. Regardless of the Levels, participants seemed to show more familiarity with the kind of language style and tone they should use for academic writing. Accuracy of responses also depended on how the questions were phrased. Based on the testing results, the Project Team sought to modify the questions. As such, ambiguous terminology and ways of questioning were eliminated.

A series of training workshops for lecturers were organized in May and early July of 2011. Language instructors and academic representatives from different departments of the Institute, as well as teachers and lecturers from other local tertiary institutions and secondary schools participated in these workshops. Participants in these workshops were impressed by the diagnostic and tracking functions of the system. Their feedback and opinions were taken into consideration by the Project Team when dealing with system modification and improvement. Training sessions for students and other staff members continued for the remainder of the project period.

After directing conscientious effort towards perfecting the questions in the data bank and addressing some minor technical problems, the e-Assessment system has now been implemented in full scale. Checks and evaluations will be administered continually throughout the lifetime of the system. Evidence demonstrating the Diagnostic Function of the system is shown below.

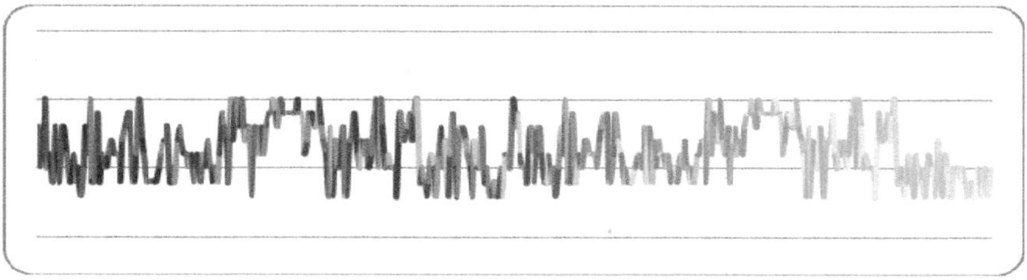

Fig. 1. Accuracy rate of users

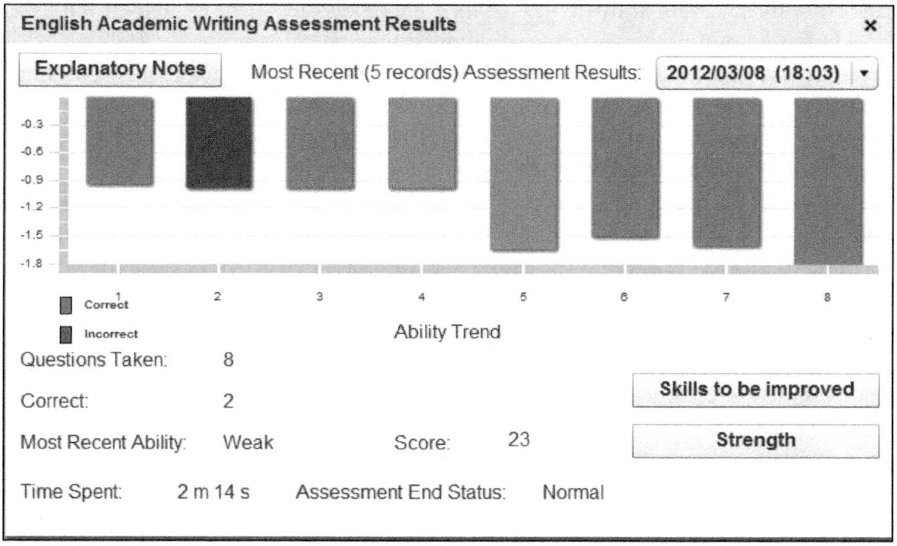

Fig. 2. Assessment results and analysis

3.1 Feedback and Major Findings

The testing sessions have proven the effectiveness of the system in tracking down participants' strengths and weaknesses. This feature of the system will be useful for

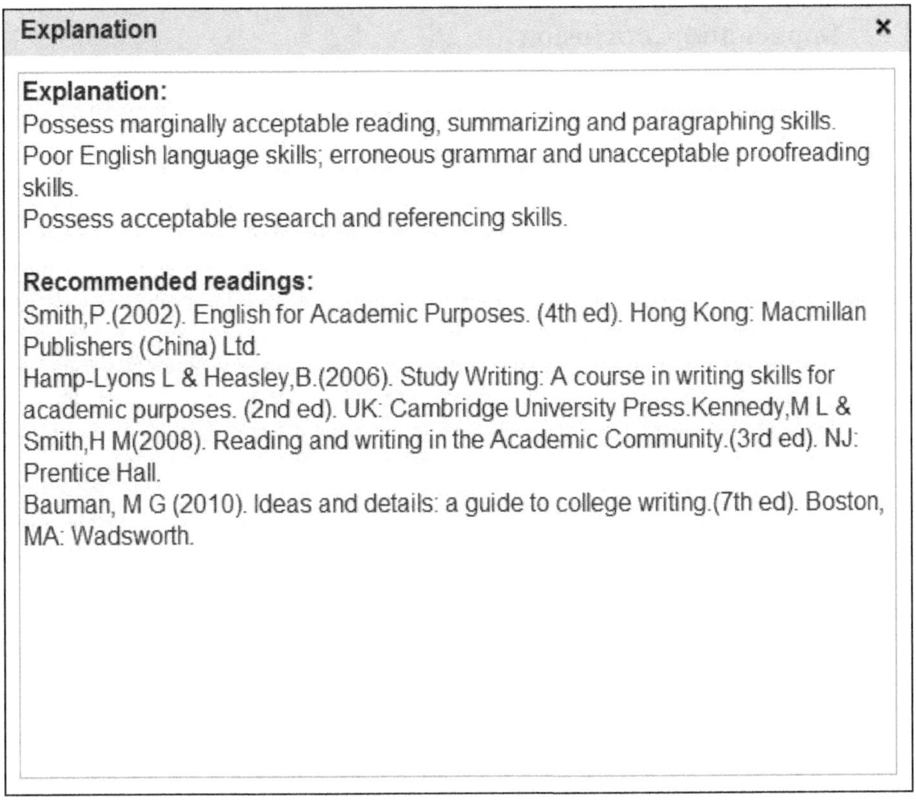

Fig. 3. Explanation and recommendation

educators and language instructors to actively relate curriculum planning to the abilities of the students they teach, i.e. to customize curriculum content to address learners' weak areas, in this case educators may put greater emphasis on the training of research, summarizing and referencing skills in English academic writing.

Student feedback also underscores the importance of how a question should be phrased in an assessment task. Long, ambiguous language and phraseology should be replaced by direct and succinct phraseology. This is worth reflecting on as many teachers tend to put the blame of poor examination results solely on students. As no time limit is set on completing the e-Assessment test, students involved in the testing sessions experience no stress as their counterparts in many formal assessment situations. Indeed the aim of using assessment as a means to facilitate learning has been achieved. To a certain degree, this also helps to change the mind set of many students who view assessment as a laborious, nerve-wrecking and painful experience. Contrary to popular beliefs, many students are not quite ignorant about the structure and language style of academic essays but instead they are less in tune with how, when and why they have to acknowledge other writers' literary works.

4 Impact and Conclusion

Various analyses conducted by the Project Team indicate that the effectiveness of the e-Assessment System outweighs its costs as the System is highly adaptable and can be extended to incorporate other courses. Our test results have established the rationale behind this project: assessment can indeed be modified to become a stress-free tool that is conducive to learning, and more significantly, a self-directed and self-controlled type of learning that coincides with contemporary education theories which emphasize "learner autonomy", or "student-centred" and "learner-oriented" learning. During our training sessions, teacher participants from other tertiary institutions and secondary schools approved of such a system as it could be combined with the traditional assessment system to provide more assessment alternatives. Student participants in the training sessions also welcomed the system and regarded this form of assessment more relaxing and satisfying as they could see their progression from easy to harder questions.

In conclusion, the e-Assessment System for English academic writing allows educators to effectively track the progression of individuals and groups of students in their self-learning process. It both empowers learners to be aware of their own strengths and weaknesses, thus aiding in their personal growth within the subject, and educators in tailoring the curriculum to meet the needs of their students. The platform embodies what many teachers and professional educators have been lacking for years: a tool that effortlessly and effectively facilitates assessment for the sake of learning and development, but not for intimidating and stifling learners.

Acknowledgement. This project has been funded by the Education Bureau of HKSAR Government under the Quality Enhancement Grant Scheme.

References

Burnard, P.: Carl Rogers and postmodernisation: Challenged in nursing and health sciences. Nursing and Health Sciences 1, 241–247 (1999)

Candy, P.C., Crebert, G., O'Leary, J.: Developing Lifelong Learning through Undergraduate Education. (NBEET Commissioned Report No. 28). Australian Government Publishing Service, Canberra (1994)

Donnelly, R., Fitzmaurice, M.: Designing Modules for Learning. In: Moore, S., O'Neill, G., McMullin, B. (eds.) Emerging Issues in the Practice of University Learning and Teaching. AISHE, Dublin (2005)

Gibbs, G.: Assessing Student Centred Courses. Oxford Centre for Staff Learning and Development, Oxford (1995)

Simon, B.: Why no pedagogy in England? In: Leach, J., Moon, B. (eds.) Learners and Pedagogy. Paul Chapman Publishing, London (1999)

A Report on the Online Learning Experience of Students in Accounting Course

J. Lam, R. Chan, and K. Yan

Centre for Cyber Learning, HKU SPACE, Hong Kong SAR, China
jeanne.lam@hkuspace.hku.hk

Abstract. Blended learning, the incorporation of different learning environments, is widely adopted in higher education institutions. The term usually refers to the combination of traditional face-to-face classroom methods with more modern computer-mediated activities. Through a blended learning approach, online learning plays an important role in the learning process which allows learning to happen at anytime, anywhere. In this paper, we review the use of online learning in an accounting course in our institution. The online courseware is launched in our new e-learning platform, SOUL 2.0. A survey is conducted to investigate the online learning experience of students and their perception of various online course materials. The results show that most of the students were satisfied with the provision of online course materials which made their study more flexible and accessible.

Keywords: blended learning, online learning, e-learning, accounting course.

1 Introduction

Blended learning can be defined as an appropriate mix of e-learning and traditional classroom learning that improves the learning experience of students (Lam, Hung, Chan, Zhang, Yan, & Woo, 2011; Lam, Hung, Chan, Yan, & Woo, 2011). It is one of the latest education trends emerging in open and distance learning institutes as well as conventional universities, continuing education institutions and corporate training (Yau, Lam, & Cheung, 2009), with its evident advantages of flexibility, richness, resource-sharing, and cost-effectiveness (Zhang, 2011). Shankar and Malthouse (2006) point out that the rapid changes in media is affecting one's perception, such that a two-way communication with capability of personalization and information control (Vlašić & Kesić, 2007), which allows real-time interaction without time and geographical constraints, turns out to be the most appropriate online learning means in this trend.

In the 21st century, online learning is regarded as one of the main media to deliver training and education resources, with the benefits in terms of cost-effectiveness, accessibility and up-to-date information (Anderson, 2011). A study from US by Allen and Seaman (2007) reveal online learning has been growing continuously with an increase in student access and demand for online learning. Online platform acts as the mean for providing learning in the virtual environment. Researchers advocate

K.C. Li et al. (Eds.): ICT 2012, CCIS 302, pp. 31–44, 2012.

pedagogy-driven approach in blended learning development and emphasize the importance of online learning contents. Zhang (2011) states that an e-learning platform and its functions are the basic tools only. He believes specifically designed and developed e-courses are the most important elements in blended learning.

To act in concert with the e-learning advancement, the School of Professional and Continuing Education of the University of Hong Kong (HKU SPACE) launched a new learning management system in 2011, namely SOUL 2.0. The SOUL 2.0 system, a comprehensive e-learning solution for managing and delivering instructional resources (Clark & Mayer, 2011), serves as a one-stop portal allowing the School community to access online courses and e-learning resources, and supports interactions and collaborative learning between teachers and students, and between students and students. With the provision of a feature-rich learning environment (Lam, Lau, Yau, & Cheung, 2009), students can access a set of easy-to-use SOUL 2.0 functions in their learning.

To provide higher flexibility in learning, HKU SPACE fully supports the design and development of e-learning courses. As a pilot study, the Centre for Cyber Learning worked with the Accounting programme team to offer an online course website containing a variety of online learning components developed based on modern pedagogical theories and instructional design concepts. Four courses of Advanced Diploma in Accounting programme were selected for e-learning implementation. The online components of the first course "Basic Accounting" were offered to students from January 2011 and would be given to students in subsequent intakes. The online components included chapter reviews, MC quizzes and long questions that could be accessed via SOUL 2.0. Each student was provided with a set of login information to access SOUL 2.0, and a copy of login procedure was sent to them by post.

This paper aims to evaluate the effectiveness of the use of online learning in an accounting course in our institution. A survey was conducted at the end of the semester on the course "Basic Accounting" to gather students' feedback towards their online learning experience and views on the impact of online learning in their studies. The results helped to review the design of online learning and identify ways to improve the provision of online learning, hence improving the effectiveness of teaching and learning.

2 Blended Learning Implementation

HKU SPACE developed its first e-learning platform, namely SOUL (SPACE Online Universal Learning) system, in 1999. In light of technological advancement, a revamped e-learning platform, SOUL 2.0, was designed and developed based on the solid theoretical foundation of blended learning (Huang & Zheng, 2011). The functions of SOUL 2.0 could be classified into six categories, including course content functions, communication and collaboration functions, assignment and assessment functions, administration and management functions, learning functions, and evaluation functions.

In this study, the course "Basic Accounting" of the Advanced Diploma in Accounting programme is being investigated. The programme is offered to part-time students for acquiring a solid foundation in accounting. To extend the student learning continuum and provide a flexible self-learning environment, blended learning is implemented such that the course is designed and developed based on the six-step process of instructional design (Shim, Lam, Lau, Hung, Yuen, & Tsang, 2011). The online components are built with various e-learning tools and offered as supplementary activities in SOUL 2.0.

To engage students in the learning process, students are provided with course materials, streaming courseware, interactive learning courseware, and link to supplementary materials. For instance, the Chapter Summary covers the key topics in each chapter, of which the presentation makes use of visual slides and audio narration.

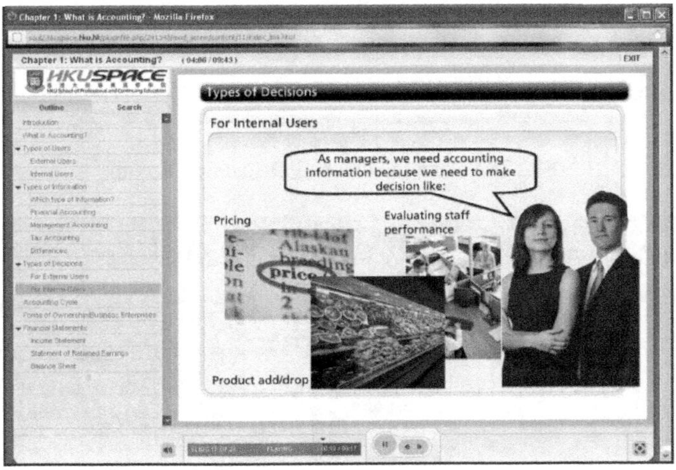

Fig. 1. A Sample Screen of Chapter Summary

To encourage communication and collaborative learning, the Discussion Forum and Q&A Corner allow students to share views and understanding regarding to the course. Coates and Humphreys (2001) state that participating in relevant discussion forum result in a positive impact towards students' learning.

Alexander (2001) states that students' experience in learning and the context are the key elements in determining a successful e-learning project. To examine students' knowledge and comprehension in each chapter, Chapter Quiz and Self-test Question are provided for students to make use of their accounting knowledge for problem solving.

Other built-in functions in SOUL 2.0, e.g., Announcement, Calendar, Grading, and User Activity Report, etc., are also applied in the course setting. The self-help tools including 1-minute demos, FAQs and user guides are offered via the SOUL 2.0 Support Centre. This reassures the user support for e-learning services and facilitates the learning process.

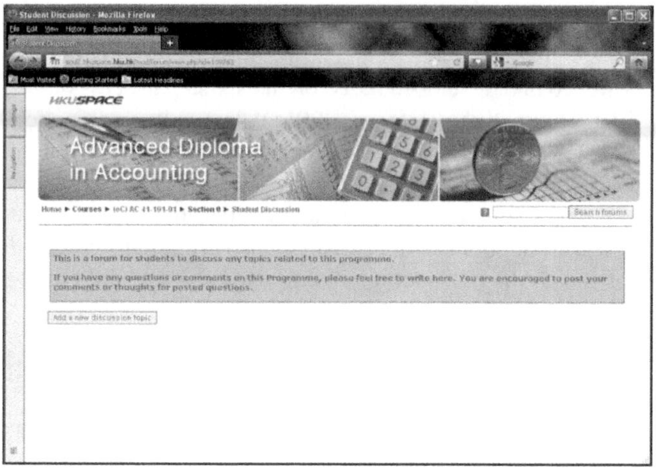

Fig. 2. A Sample Screen of Discussion Forum

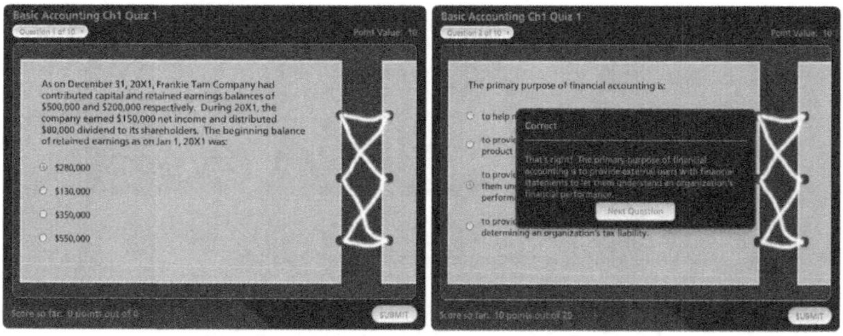

Fig. 3. Sample Screens of Chapter Quiz

Fig. 4. A Sample Screen of Course Announcement

3 Survey Results and Findings

This survey was conducted on the "Basic Accounting" course that the intake of part-time students in May 2011 was invited to the survey at the end of the semester in August 2011. A total of 128 responses were received, constituting a response rate of 82.1%.

3.1 SOUL 2.0 Access Information

For an in-depth exploration of system usage and learning habit of part-time students, the access information of the "Basic Accounting" course in the SOUL 2.0 system from 8 May to 21 August 2011 is retrieved for further analysis. The following figures show the information of access rate to the course and course resources.

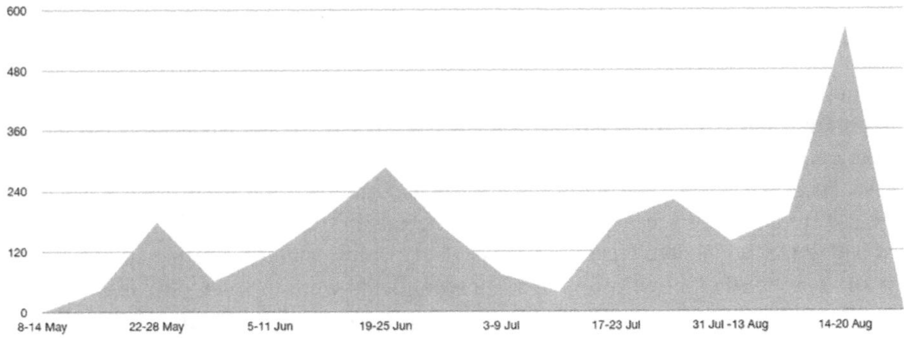

Fig. 5. Total number of access from May to August 2011

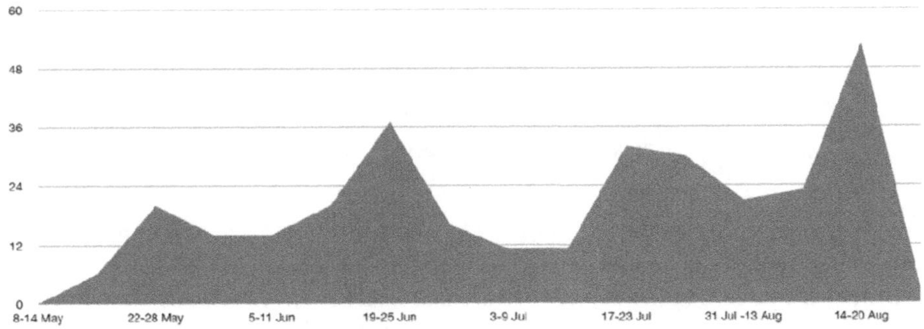

Fig. 6. Number of unique users from May to August 2011

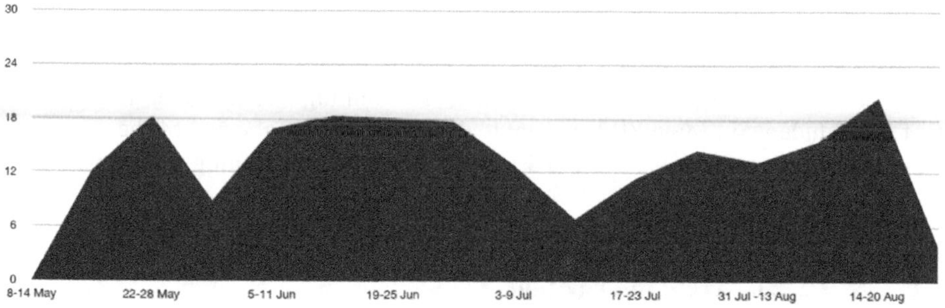

Fig. 7. Average access per user from May to August 2011

The findings show that a total of 95 out of 156 enrolled students accessed the course in SOUL 2.0 during the said period, i.e., an access rate of 60.9%.

3.2 Summary of Survey Results

This survey consisted of three parts with 18 questions in total. These questions were categorized under Online Course Design, Online Course Materials and Overall Comments.

At the beginning, a screening question was conducted. A total of 100 out of 124 enrolled students had accessed the online materials of the course in SOUL 2.0 while the rest had not. Students who had not accessed any online materials reflected that they did not know about the online resources. These students were instructed to answer the last question regarding the types of online learning means which facilitated their learning process.

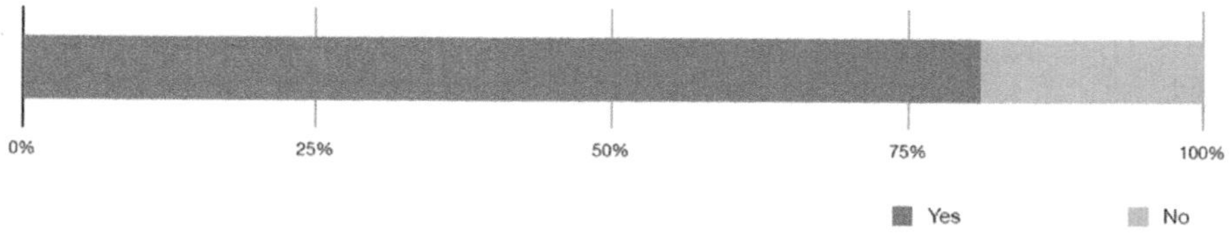

Fig. 8. Percentage of students accessed online course materials

Part I: Online Course Design. In the first part of the survey, the students were asked about the design of the course setting. Among the four questions, 59% and 50% of the respondents agreed that the course website and instructions in each activity were very clear or clear. 50% agreed that the ease of navigation was very easy or easy. Meanwhile, a moderate percentage of the respondents (53%) considered that the overall graphic design of the course website had room for enhancement. Their responses to the questions are illustrated below.

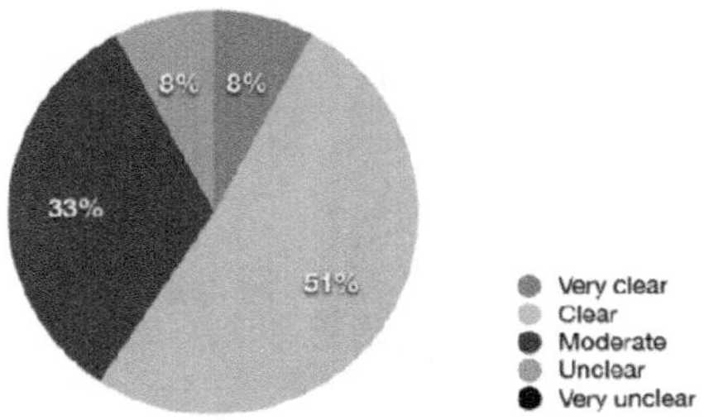

Fig. 9. Was the course website clear to meet your expectation at the start of the course?

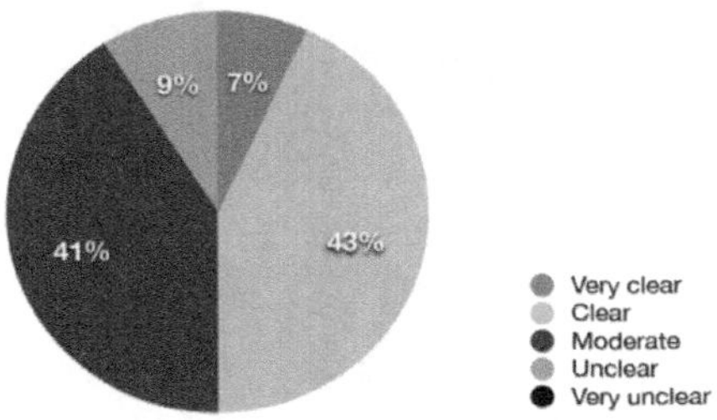

Fig. 10. Was the instruction clear to guide you in each activity?

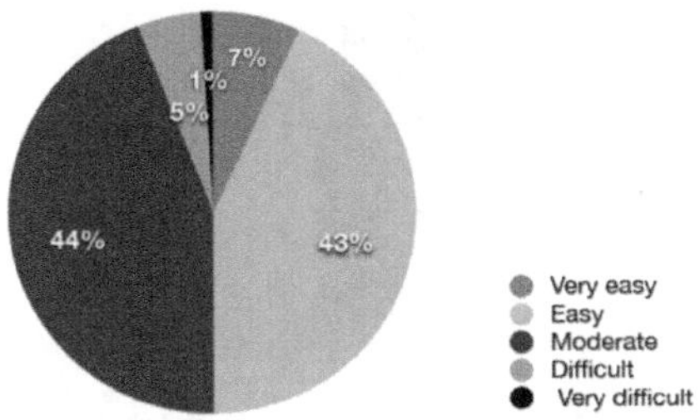

Fig. 11. Were the online course materials easy to navigate?

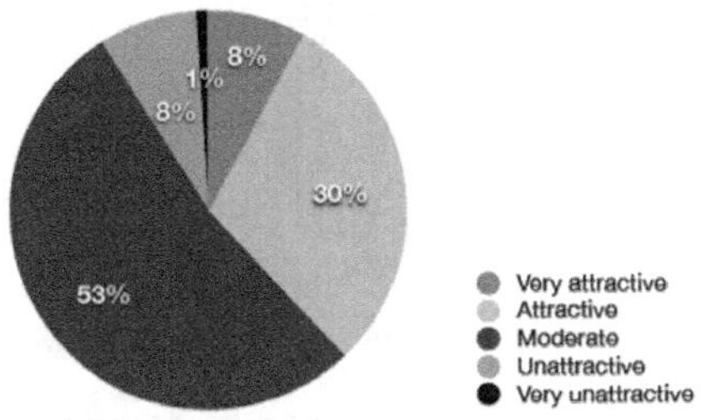

Fig. 12. Was the overall graphic design of the course website attractive?

Part II: Online Course Materials. In the second part of the survey, the students were asked about the online course materials. Five questions are set up to explore students' perception on the online course materials and whether these materials were beneficial to the learning process.

For Chapter Summary, four statements are prepared for the rating. In general, 49% of the respondents strongly agreed or agreed that Chapter Summary helped to consolidate and deepen their knowledge, whereas 48%, 53% and 51% of the respondents strongly agreed or agreed that the narration, contents, and charts and graphics were clear and appropriate.

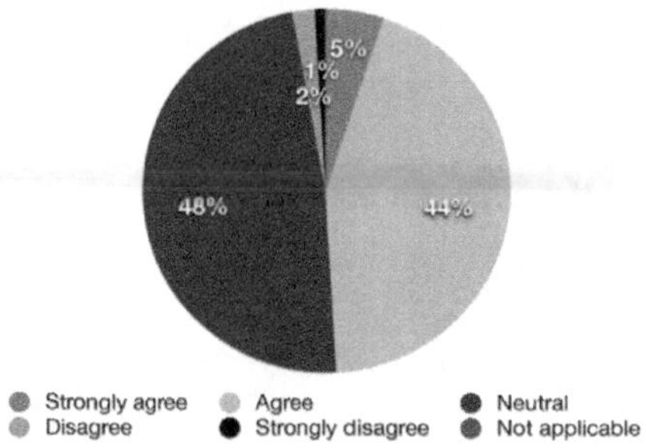

Fig. 13. The Chapter Summaries helped to consolidate and deepen my knowledge

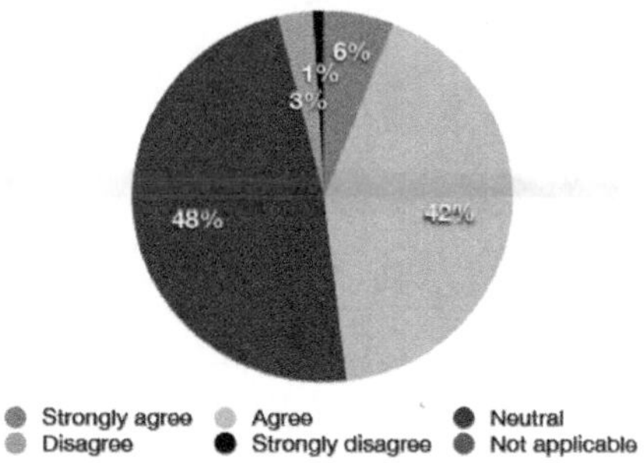

Fig. 14. The narration was clear and easy to follow

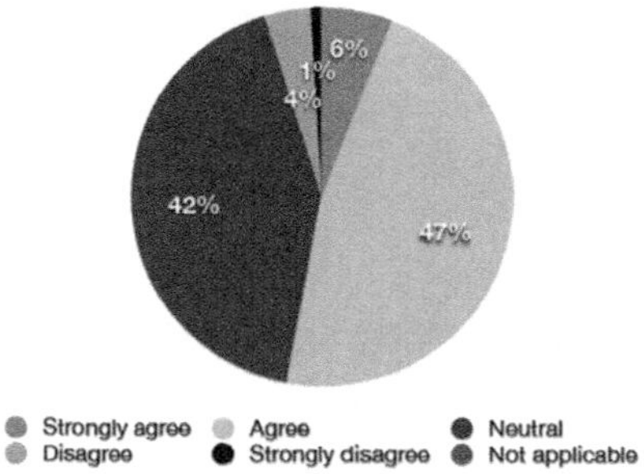

Fig. 15. The contents, i.e., fonts, contrast and alignment, etc., were clear and easy to read

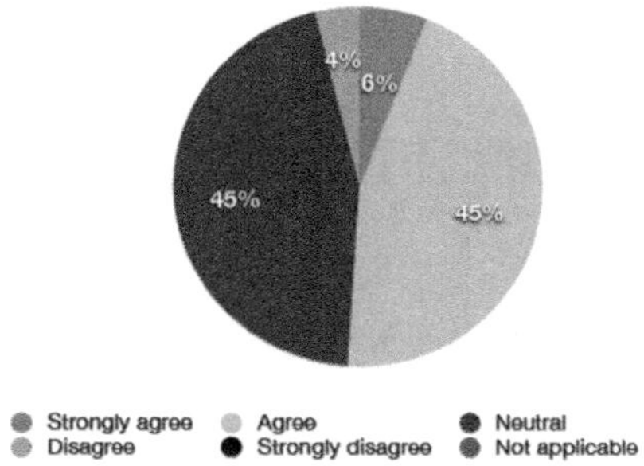

Fig. 16. The charts and graphics were appropriate and helped my understanding

For Chapter Quiz, 48% of the respondents strongly agreed or agreed that the function enhanced their practice and a half deemed that the questions were useful and allowed them to test their knowledge. For Chapter Exercise, 45% of the respondents strongly agreed or agreed that the exercises were practical and interactive. Overall, 39% of the respondents reflected the workload for the online course materials was appropriate, whereas 44% of the respondents perceived the online course materials helped them in reviewing the course contents after class.

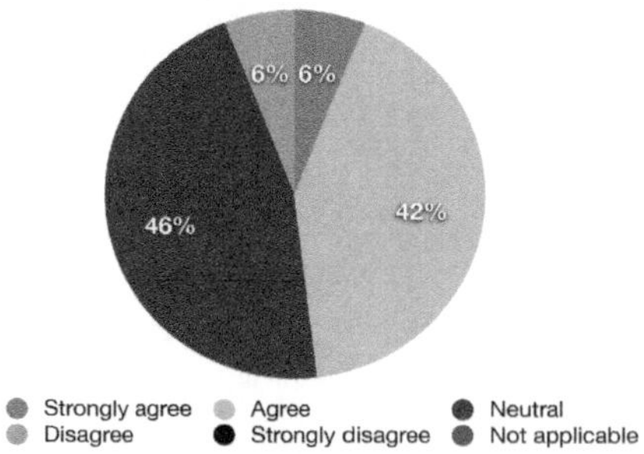

Fig. 17. The Chapter Quizzes enabled me to enhance my practice

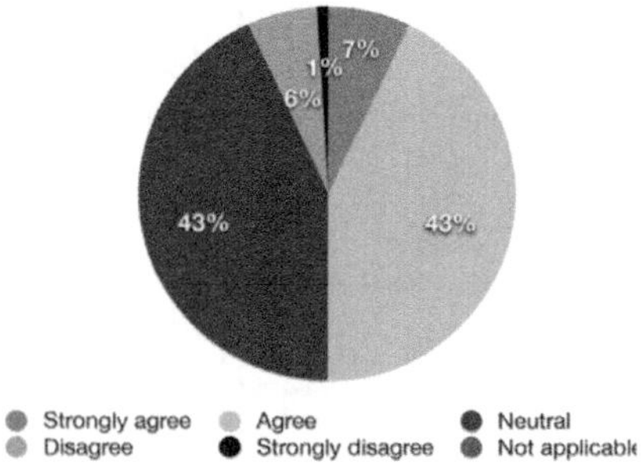

Fig. 18. The questions were useful and allowed me to test my knowledge and skills

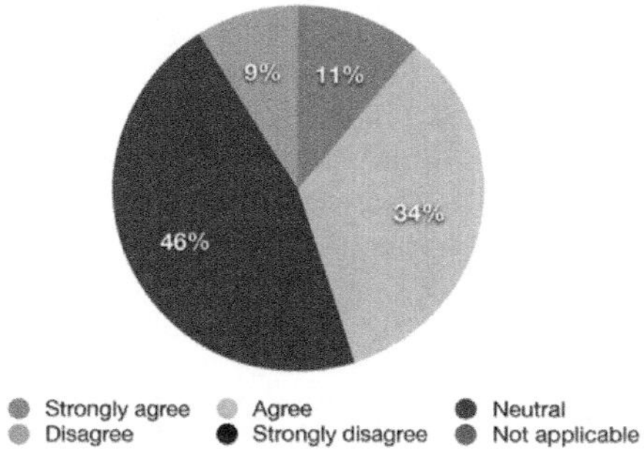

Fig. 19. The Chapter Exercises were practical and interactive

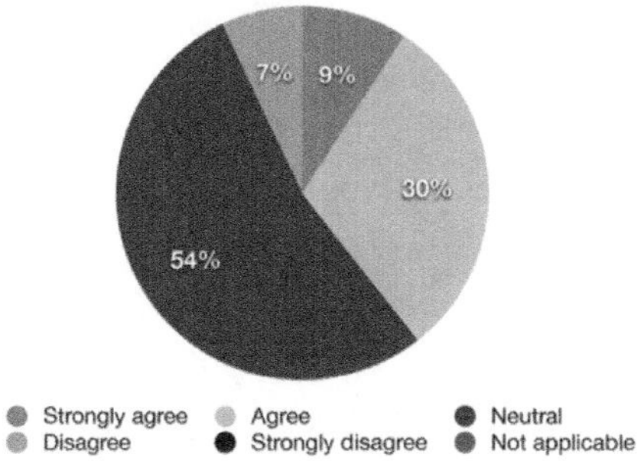

Fig. 20. My workload for the online course materials was appropriate

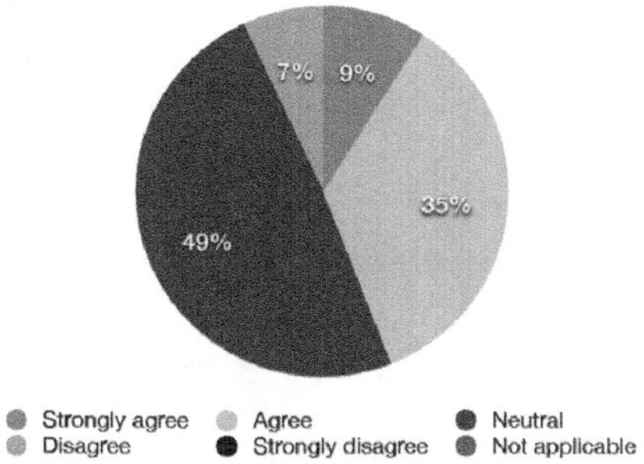

Fig. 21. Overall, the online course materials helped me in reviewing the course contents after class

Part III: Overall Comments. Finally, the students were asked about the overall learning experience in this project. Among the first six questions, 49% and 41% of the respondents showed the online course materials received an impact of higher flexibility and accessibility, as well as more interesting and engaging in the learning process. Nearly half of the respondents indicated the online course materials enhanced their understandings of the topics covered and enriched their learning experience. In reviewing the whole project, 97% of the respondents were satisfied with the quality of the online course materials, whereas 94% of the respondents thought their instructor was helpful in facilitating online learning to achieve the learning goals.

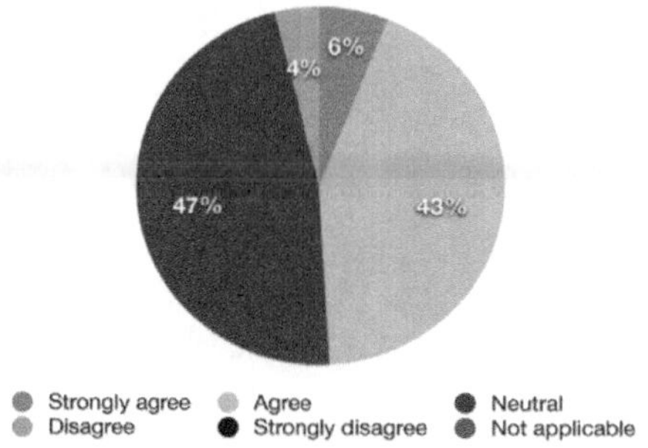

Fig. 22. The online course materials made my learning more flexible and accessible

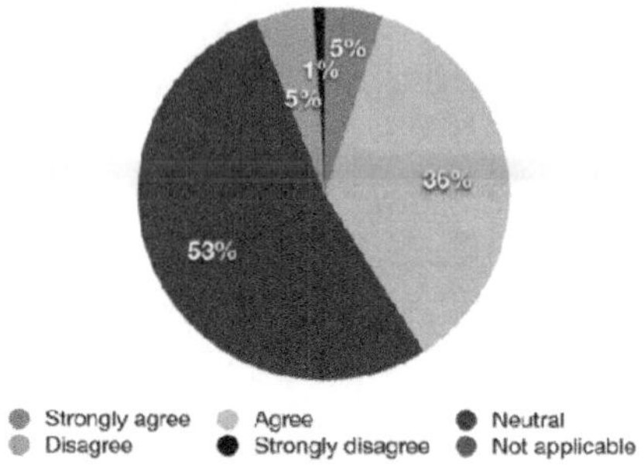

Fig. 23. The online course materials made my learning more interesting and engaging

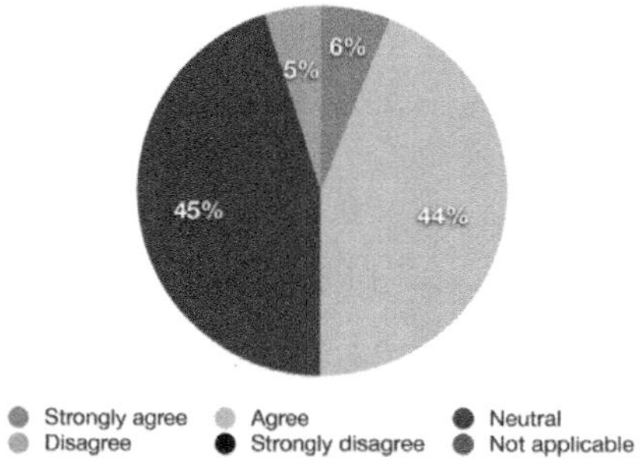

Fig. 24. The online course materials enhanced my understanding of the topics covered

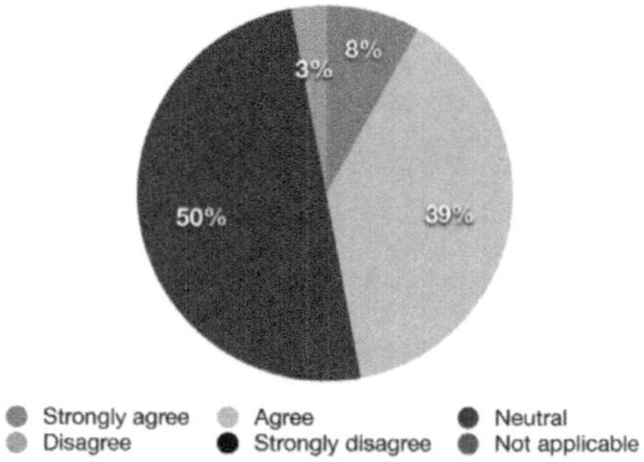

Fig. 25. The online course materials enriched my learning experience

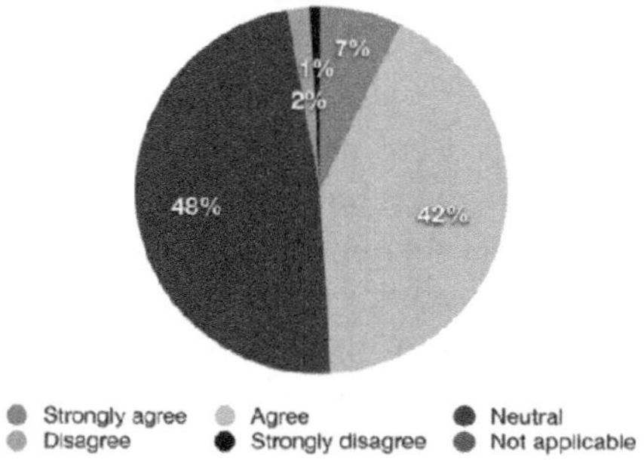

Fig. 26. Overall, I was satisfied with the quality of the online course materials

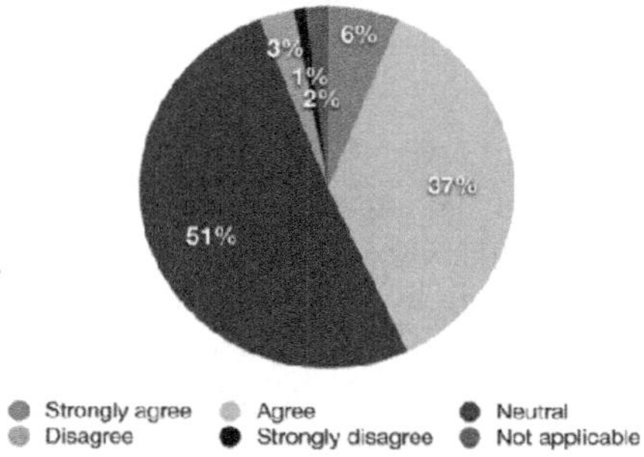

Fig. 27. Overall, the facilitation by the instructor for online learning in SOUL 2.0 was helpful in achieving my learning goals

As SOUL 2.0 is an entirely new system, one-fourth of the respondents had encountered problems in using the platform. It was reported that some students had difficulties in navigating between pages and therefore the user interface should be enhanced and the user support should be strengthened. In general, no students reported

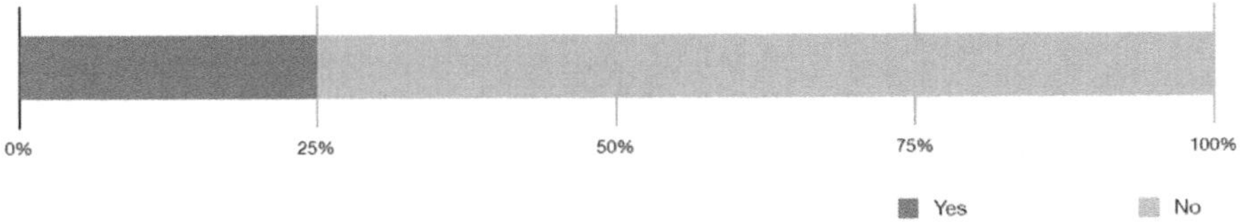

Fig. 28. I have encountered problems in using SOUL 2.0

any problem concerning the online course materials and access to the course website. It is considered that the system is running smoothly in supporting the delivery of online learning.

To investigate which courseware weighed in terms of usefulness and effectiveness in the learning process, the students were asked to rate the selected course materials in order of preference. 39% and 36% of the respondents opted for Chapter Summary and Chapter Exercise respectively while the rest chose Chapter Quiz. A sub-question was prepared to acquire more personal perception on the issue and a total of 9 feedbacks were received. For Chapter Summary, the respondents reflected that it did help in enhancing understanding of the course and act as a supplement to cover the insufficiency of other online materials. For Chapter Quiz, the respondents stated that it was a good test which helped to get familiarize with the MC questions in the textbook. Last but not least, the Chapter Exercise played the role to reflect learning mistakes and enabled students to drill answering technique in the exercise.

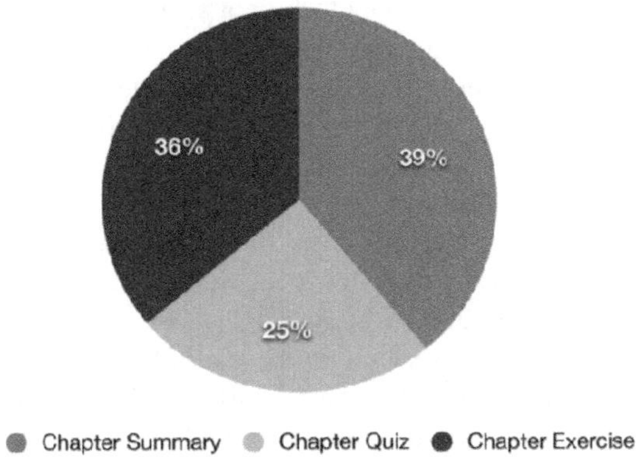

Fig. 29. Which of the following can be regarded as the most useful material in your online learning process? Chapter Summary, Chapter Quiz or Chapter Exercise

All respondents were invited to answer the last question regarding their preference of types of online learning tools. This question is aimed at exploring the development trend of online learning tools for part-time students. For this question, more than one-third of the respondents recommended Video Podcast as an impressive learning

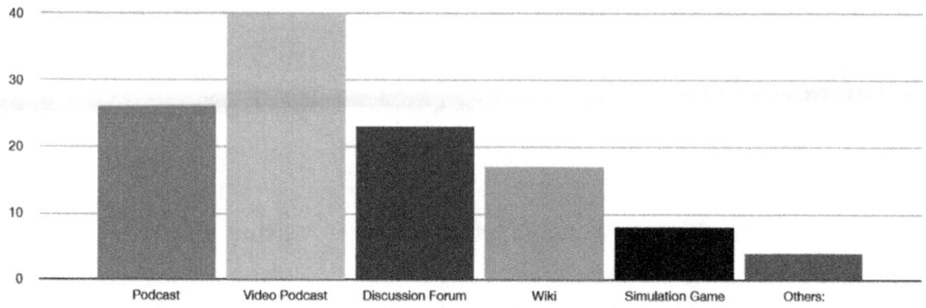

Fig. 30. This type of online learning material helps in enhancing learning in my experience

tool. Podcast (Audio) and Discussion Forum were the second and third alternatives respectively. Some respondents perceived Wiki and Stimulation Game as the splendid materials in online learning.

3.3 Discussion of Survey Results

In the study, the course "Basic Accounting" of Advanced Diploma in Accounting programme was selected for e-learning implementation. The students were provided with a set of login information to access the online course materials in SOUL 2.0. However, one-fifth of the enrolled students did not know about the online resources and had not accessed any online materials. In order to maximize the effectiveness of blended learning, the instructors should raise their students' awareness of the online materials and encourage their students to participate in online activities. The instructors may also incorporate online activities as part of the course assessment.

In terms of the design and delivery of the online course, the course setting was clear and the navigation between pages could be done with ease. In order to assist those students who had encountered problems in using the platform, the instructors may introduce the course setting at the beginning of the semester. Students are also encouraged to attend the training session on the use of SOUL 2.0 or seek assistance via the user support channel. In general, nearly half of the respondents agreed that the online course materials enhanced the flexibility and accessibility of their learning, as well as strengthened their understanding and enriched their learning experience. To increase the access rate to the course and course resources, the instructors should act as a facilitator in online learning. The instructors can also work with the instructional designer and e-learning professionals to deliver a series of content-rich course activities for their students.

To investigate the popularity of various types of online learning tools, the students were invited to indicate their preference. The results serve as a reference for e-learning development in the future. The instructional designer can help to design online activities in different formats in order to meet the needs of the students, hence integrating online activities into classroom teaching through the proper alignment of teaching and learning experiences with the learning goals and objectives.

4 Conclusion

This paper has reviewed the provision of online course materials for an accounting course in HKU SPACE. A summary of the survey results is provided to give a clear picture of the system usage with learning outcomes. In general, the responses are very positive and encouraging for our colleagues to continue developing quality e-courses in other academic areas.

However, the design of the blended learning course still has room for improvement. Current design limits the use of online content in different devices. The design of the website and online materials are not suitable for smart phones with small display screens. With the popularization of portable devices such as media players (iPod), smart phones (iPhone), tablet computers (iPad) and personal digital assistants (PDA), as well as the availabilities of high-bandwidth network connection and the advance in wireless technologies such as Wifi, Bluetooth and Cloud Computering technology, information access and communication becomes more interactive and shareable (Lam, Yau, & Cheung, 2010). It is expected the provision of learning contents in mobile supported formats can enrich students' learning experience. Extended development and research in this area can be performed.

With the latest technology and modern pedagogical theories for the e-learning era as well as the stability of Internet service and Internet device penetration in the society, the increasing use of online learning in the lifelong learning sector is foreseeable.

References

Alexander, S.: E-learning developments and experiences. Education + Training 43(4), 240–248 (2001)

Allen, I.E., Seaman, J.: Online Nation: Five Years of Growth in Online Learning. The Sloan Consortium, Massachusetts (2007)

Anderson, T. (ed.): The Theory and Practice of Online Learning, 2nd edn. Athabasca University Press, Athabasca (2011)

Clark, C.R., Mayer, E.R.: E-learning and the Science of Instruction: Proven Guidelines for Consumers and Designers of Multimedia Learning, 3rd edn. Pfeiffer, San Francisco (2011)

Coates, D., Humphreys, R.: Evaluation of Computer-Assisted Instruction in Principles of Economics. Educational Technology & Society 4(2), 133–144 (2001)

Huang, R.H., Zheng, L.Q.: Can Using Hand-held Devices Improve the Instructional Quality in Blended Learning Context? A Case Study of the "Introduction to Educational Technology" Course. In: Workshop Proceedings of ICHL 2011: Blended Learning – Maximization of Teaching and Learning Effectiveness, pp. 41–51 (2011)

Lam, J., Hung, A., Chan, F.T., Yan, K., Woo, G.: Project Management Model for Blended Learning Course Development. International Journal of Continuing Education and Lifelong Learning 4(1), 107–122 (2011)

Lam, J., Hung, A., Chan, F.T., Zhang, W.Y., Yan, K., Woo, G.: Blended Learning Course Development Model. In: Workshop Proceedings of ICHL 2011: Blended Learning – Maximization of Teaching and Learning Effectiveness, pp. 52–64 (2011)

Lam, J., Lau, N., Yau, J., Cheung, K.S.: A Survey on the Readiness in Adopting e-Learning among Teachers and Students. In: Local Proceedings of ICHL 2009: Hybrid Learning: The New Frontier, pp. 143–158 (2009)

Lam, J., Yau, J., Cheung, K.S.: A Review of the Use of Mobile Learning in Education. Paper Presented at International Conference on ICT in Teaching and Learning 2010, Singapore (June 2010)

Shankar, V., Malthouse, E.: Moving Interactive Marketing Forward. Journal of Interactive Marketing 20(1), 2–4 (2006)

Shim, C., Lam, J., Lau, N., Hung, A., Yuen, K., Tsang, D.: The Role of Instructional Design in Blended Accounting Courses. In: Workshop Proceedings of ICHL 2011: Blended Learning – Maximization of Teaching and Learning Effectiveness, pp. 65–74 (2011)

Vlašić, G., Kesić, T.: Consumers' attitudes toward interactive marketing communication and relationship personalization – contemporary developments in marketing communications. Journal of Marketing Communications 11(2), 9–27 (2007)

Yau, J., Lam, J., Cheung, K.S.: A Review of e-Learning Platforms in the Age of e-Learning 2.0. In: Wang, F.L., Fong, J., Zhang, L., Lee, V.S.K. (eds.) ICHL 2009. LNCS, vol. 5685, pp. 208–217. Springer, Heidelberg (2009)

Zhang, W.Y.: Entering the 3rd Generation of e-Learning: Characteristics and Strategies. In: Workshop Proceedings of ICHL 2011: Blended Learning – Maximization of Teaching and Learning Effectiveness, pp. 1–9 (2011)

An Enhanced e-Assessment System for the Acquisition of Putonghua

Carole Chen, Kenneth Wong, Kat Leung, and Reggie Kwan

Caritas Bianchi College of Careers, Hong Kong SAR, China
{ychen,kwong,kleung,rkwan}@cihe.edu.hk

Abstract. This paper presents the design and development of a Putonghua e-Assessment System for the sub-degree students at Caritas Institute of Higher Education and Caritas Bianchi College of Careers. A software prototype of Computerized Adaptive Testing (CAT) has been developed to promote assessment for learning and enhance students' Putonghua self-learning capacity. It is to help individual students identify the various approaches available to learn "how to learn" through self-directed, self-controlled and, to some extent, customized "assessment" opportunities. An adaptive algorithm based on the one-Parameter Logistics Model from Item Response Theory (IRT) is utilized in this software prototype, which could select questions for each user based upon their ability as measured during the test. Further learning support is obtainable within the system, including immediate feedback such as detailed study guides with full explanations and illustrative examples, and follow-up exercises for self-improvement. A full usability test and evaluation will be conducted in the coming academic year. In the first part of this paper, the background of developing the system will be discussed, followed by a brief introduction of improvements and new features of the new version. Then, further development of the system will be presented with conclusions.

Keywords: computerized adaptive testing (CAT), Putonghua assessment, assessment for learning, item response theory (IRT).

1 Introduction

The paper reports the design and development of a Putonghua e-Assessment System for the sub-degree students in Caritas Institute of Higher Education and Caritas Bianchi College of Careers, with the purpose to enhance students' Putonghua self-learning ability. Putonghua e-Assessment System (Version One) was developed in the summer of 2011, which consists of 800 sets of multiple-choice questions on the tones of Putonghua. It was a Computerized Adaptive Testing (CAT) system based on the one-Parameter Logistics Model from Item Response Theory (IRT). During the testing process, questions are presented to users depending on their language capacity as measured by the system. The updated version, i.e. Version Two, retains the IRT concept but more features are added, such as extended curriculum and varied question formats.

K.C. Li et al. (Eds.): ICT 2012, CCIS 302, pp. 45–58, 2012.

In the first part of the paper, the background of developing the system will be discussed, followed by a brief introduction of improvements and new features of the updated version. Then, further development will be presented with conclusion.

2 Literature Review

CAT has been flourishing in higher education for several decades. It is considered a promising approach to enhance the efficiency of teaching, learning, and assessment (Linacre, 2000; Wong, 2002, 2008). CAT system could, based on users' response to previous questions, select questions of appropriate difficulty level from a pre-set data pool. For example, from users' perspective, if a user answers a question correctly, he/she will then be presented a more difficult item. Or, if a user gets a question incorrectly, he/she will be presented an easier item. The user's ability is evaluated throughout the testing process (Rudner, 1998). To implement of question selection function, an item selection algorithm is needed. Previous researches suggested that IRT was a reassuring theory for CAT (Lord, 1980; Rudner, 1998).

IRT models could provide a framework for evaluating how well assessments work, and how well individual questions on assessments work. It calculates user's responses and predicts the ability of the user (Lord, 1980). It mathematically describes the relationship between a person's trait level and performance on an item (Stocking, 1997). The prerequisite of item response function is a data pool with items calibrated with a psychometric model. After the question items are dichotomously scored, the item response function estimates the probability of user's ability to provide a correct response. There are three commonly used IRT models: one-parameter, two-parameter and three-parameter IRT models. The Rasch model based on objective measurement (Keeves & Alagumalai, 1999) is known as one-parameter IRT model. Rasch model could correlate the ability of the user and difficulty of the question items. The mathematical formula of Rasch Model is as follows:

$$P(\theta) = \frac{e^{(\theta - b)}}{1 + e^{(\theta - b)}} \tag{1}$$

Where

P: probability of a correct response.

θ: user parameter – user's ability

The Rasch Model Test Characteristic Curve (Wright, 1996) (Fig. 1) demonstrates the relationship among the probability of a correct response (P), the user's language ability (θ), and the difficulty level of an item (*b*).

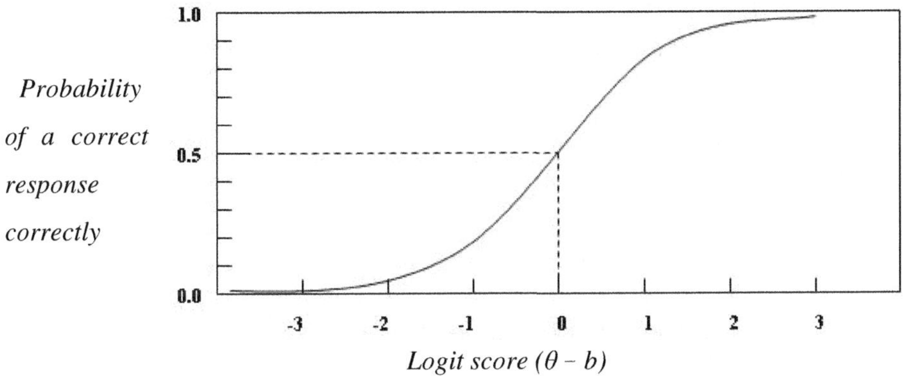

Fig. 1. The Rasch Model Test Characteristic Curve (Wright, 1996)

In the Putonghua test, item parameters pertain to the difficulty level of the item, while user parameters pertain to the Putonghua ability of the user. The higer a user's ablity relative to the difficulty level of an item, the higher the probability to answer the quetsion correctly, according to the Rasch model. For example, when a user's parameter *(θ)* equals to an item parameter *(b)*, the user would have a chance of 50% to provide a correct response. When a user's parameter is higher than an item parameter, the user would have a chance of more than 50% to get the answer correctly, and vice versa. The benefit of this item selection algorithm is that the difficulty level of an administered item is close to the ability level of a particular user.

As it was described by Rudner (1998) and Wong (2002), the advantages of CAT include:

- Immediate Scoring and Feedback. The most significant benefit of computerized test is being able to obtain results immediately.
- Increased Efficiency (i.e. quicker and shorter tests). Computerized tests have been proven efficient, and CAT is considered even better.
- Easier Test Revision. Users could make revisions easily with CAT.
- Self-Pacing. CAT allows users to work at their own pace.
- Challenging. Users are tested with question items of appropriate level.

3 Background

Because of the fasting growing interaction between Hong Kong and Mainland China, the recognition of Putonghua in Hong Kong is rising splendidly. Putonghua has become a *lingua franca* in academic and business contexts. More local secondary schools and post-secondary institutes have used Putonghua as medium of instruction for Chinese related courses. After a series of interviews of sub-degree students, it was found that students do need a Putonghua self-learning system which could enhance their Putonghua competency effectively.

In lieu of this, an online assessment system (e-assessment system) was developed in 2011. The question bank consists of a considerable amount of listening exercises regarding tones in the form of multiple choice questions, based on the idea of

Computerized Adaptive Testing and Item Response Theory (Siu, 2011). During the trial period of the e-Assessment system (Version One), Putonghua lecturers, together with students from several Associate Degree programmes and Business and Technology Education Council (BTEC) programmes, have been invited to participate in tests and to comment on the system. The users' suggestions mainly fall on the following two aspects.

- **General Structure of the System.** Most of the users, especially lecturers, complimented the CAT concept and the item response function. It was regarded as an effective approach for students to acquire Putonghua capacity through self-directed, self-pace and customized "assessment" opportunities. In addition, the assessment report at the end of each test could help users better understand their strengths and weaknesses, and further improve their Putonghua capacities.
- **Assessment Report.** Some students found the assessment report in pie chart not clear enough to display their Putonghua strengths and weaknesses. They considered it not easy to understand the difficulty level of each question and why they have made a mistake.

4 New Features of the System

With the feedback from users during trial period of the project, the system has been enhanced in several significant ways to give users a better test experience and understanding of their Putonghua capacities.

New features of the system will be discussed on three aspects: extended curriculum, questions formats, and assessment reports.

4.1 Extended Curriculum

The previous curriculum of the Putonghua e-Assessment System covered three major topics of Putonghua Phonetics. These topics are Tones (聲調), Initials (聲母), and Finals (韻母). Because of time constraint, the majority of the questions were to assess students' capability to distinguish among the four tones.

However, as a tonal language, Putonghua is far more complicated than merely four tones. Apart from the first tone (high-level tone), second tone (rising tone), third tone (dipping tone) and fourth tone (high-falling tone), there is a neutral tone (輕聲), which is also named fifth tone or zeroth tone. In addition, the rules of tone sandhi and the rules for placing the tone marks are also significant in mastering the speaking skill. Therefore, the current curriculum (Fig. 2) is extended to better reflect the knowledge users need in daily and professional contexts.

Aside from phonetics, Chinese grammar, especially the distinction between standard Chinese and Cantonese, is also crucial to the mastery of Putonghua. As a result, it is included in the current curriculum (Fig. 3). It is to test users' competence to distinguish a Putonghua term or sentence from several Cantonese terms or sentences.

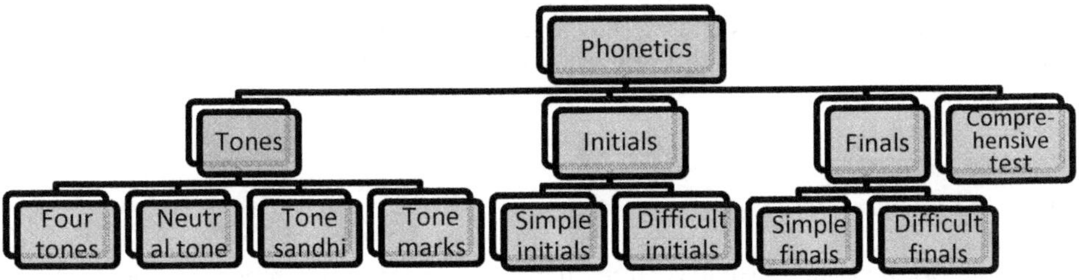

Fig. 2. The extended phonetics curriculum

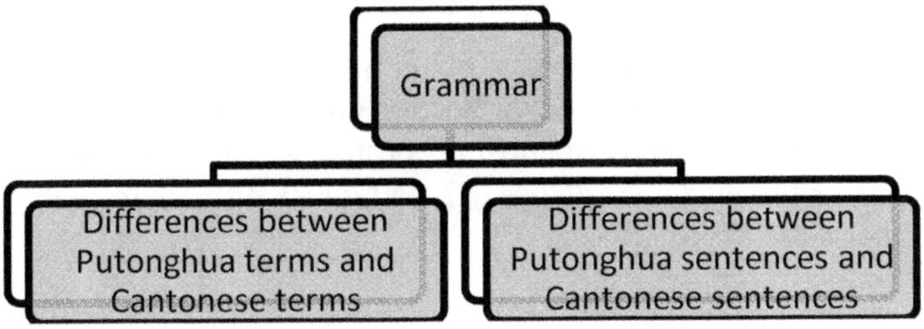

Fig. 3. The grammar curriculum

With the new curriculum, the current system is made up of two parts: Part 1 phonetics and Part 2 grammar. Part 1 consists of four sections, which are Section 1 Tones, Section 2 Initials, Section 3 Finals, and Section 4 Comprehensive Test; while Part 2 consists of two sections, Section 5 Term distinction and Section 6 Sentence distinction.

4.2 System Rationale of the New Curriculum

Similar to the previous version, CAT and IRT are again adopted. However, it is an updated version. Users could choose to enter one section at a time at their own preference. At the start of each section, a question of medium difficulty is to be generated from the data bank as a reference point of the user's Putonghua skill. As the user answers one question, the system scores the answer and uses it to determine which question to present next. Correct responses would prompt questions of increased difficulty; while incorrect responses result in questions of lesser difficulty. The process would continue until the standard error of successive answers calculated is less than a defined value (e.g. 0.01), and the system would notify the user that the assessment of a particular section has been finished at this time. The scores of the previous sections will not affect the question difficulty of the next section.

Although a timer is presented on the lower right corner of the interface, there is no time limit for each section. Users could take their time and pace to work with the questions. They could even exit the test before completing all the questions generated in each section. When they come back to the assessment system, they could choose to continue with the previous test or start a new one. If they decide to continue with the previous test, the system would present questions based on the assessment records of the specific user.

4.3 Question Formats

Both the original and current versions make use of multiple-choice questions. As for the original version, one Chinese phrase (either two-word or three-word ones) is presented in the question stem, and the four tone marks as four choices are provided. Users could listen to the sound bites of the stem words by clicking the sound icon against of the questions.

In the current version, new types of question are used to improve assessment experience and increase difficulty. For Section One - Tones, there are three more types of multiple-choice questions: choosing proper Chinese word/phrase (Type A), choosing proper pronunciation (Type B), and choosing a word with a different tone from the other three (Type C).

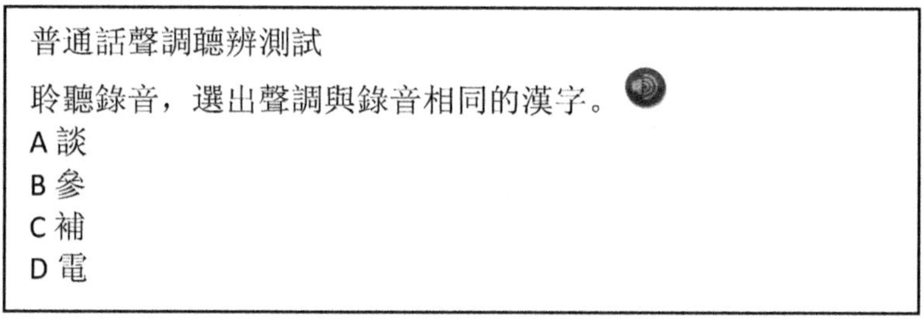

Fig. 4. Choosing proper Chinese word
(When users click the sound icon, they will hear "考"the third tone. C is the correct choice.)

When users come up with a question Type A, they could listen to the phrase by clicking the sound icon, and then choose one suitable Chinese phrase from the four choices (Fig. 4). As for question Type B, one Chinese phrase is provided in the question stem, and students could listen to the four choices and select a proper pronunciation (Fig. 5). Regarding question Type C, the tone of one choice would be different from the other three. (Fig. 6)

As for Sections Two, Three and Four, the above three mentioned question types are applicable, but question Type C should be revised to fit with the contents of the questions (Fig. 7). For example, in Section Two, users might be required to choose a two-word phrase which is with different initials from the other three choices.

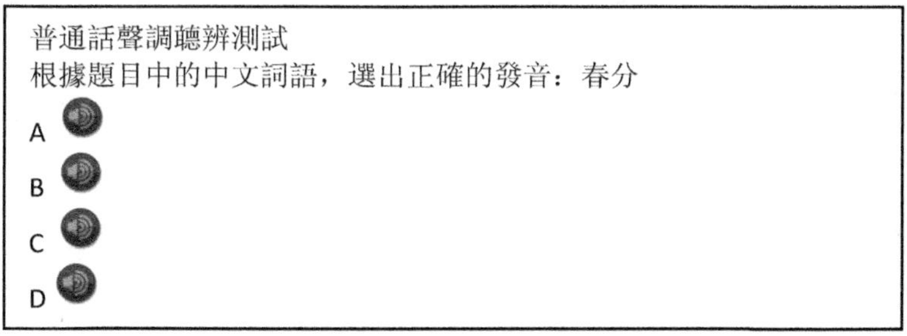

Fig. 5. Choosing proper pronunciation
(Only the choice which pronounces "chūnfēn" is correct.)

普通話聲調聽辨測試
從以下四個漢字中，選出聲調與其它三個漢字不同的選項。
A 小
B 楚
C 脂
D 導

Fig. 6. Choosing a word with a different tone from the other three
(C is correct, because 脂 is the first tone and the other three words are the third tone.)

普通話聲母聽辨測試
從以下四個詞語中，選出聲母與其它三個詞語不同的選項。
A 城鎮
B 成長
C 沉重
D 曾經

Fig. 7. Question Type C should be revised to fit with the contents of the questions
(D is correct, because the initials of the two words are "c" and "j" respectively, and the initials of the other three phrases are "ch" and "zh".)

Questions in Part 2 are a bit different from those in Part 1. In Sections Five and Six, users might either be requested to choose a standard Chinese term or sentence from the four choices (Type D) (Fig. 8 and 9), or to choose a suitable term or sentence to fix into the context (Type E) (Fig. 10 and 11).

普通話語法測試
從以下四個詞語中，選出適當的普通話詞語。
A 腰脊
B 脊梁
C 背脊骨
D 腰骨

Fig. 8. Choosing a standard Chinese term
(B is correct, because only B is commonly used in Putonghua.)

普通話語法測試
從以下四個句子中，選出符合普通話語法的表達。
A 高過頭沒用的。
B 這麼着急就先走吧。
C 吃多點吧。
D 打電話給他。

Fig. 9. Choosing a standard Chinese sentence
(B is correct, because only B is grammatically correct in Putonghua.)

普通話語法測試
從以下四個詞語中，選出適當的普通話詞語，使句子意思完整。
剛才一場爭吵，讓小明非常___。
A 光火
B 激氣
C 火滾
D 惱火

Fig. 10. Choosing a suitable Putonghua term
(D is correct, because only D is commonly used in Putonghua.)

普通話語法測試
從以下四個句子中，選出符合普通話語法的表達，使以下對話/文章的意思完整。
甲：我清楚記得你曾經這麼說過。
乙：________。
甲：你撒謊！
A 沒有，我不是這樣說的。
B 不，我不是這樣說的。
C 是啊，我是這樣說的。
D 是嗎？你還記得。

Fig. 11. Choosing a suitable sentence (B is correct.)

5 Assessment Report

When users have completed the questions in one section, they are to be directed to the result page. The detailed assessment report on this page explains in a clear, graphical format the users' Putonghua strengths, weaknesses, and improvement suggestions.

Compared with the previous version, the current assessment report:

- Displays the difficulty and result of each question in a bar chart (Fig. 12). The X-axis of the chart indicates question ID, and the Y-axis tells the level of difficulty and result of the question. When users move the cursor to a specific bar, for example, question No. 8, a popup box would appear telling the difficulty and result of the question. If the user gets a question correctly, the bar would be in blue, while if it is incorrect, the bar would be in pink. Instead, the original version displayed these details with only one color in a pie chart.

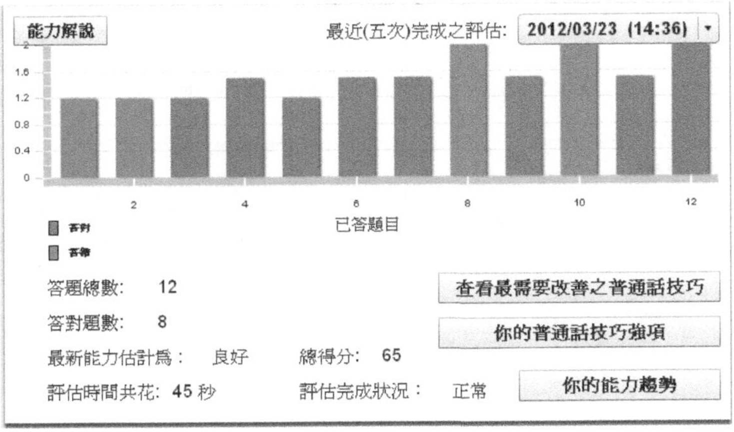

Fig. 12. Assessment report

- Provides detailed explanation for each question. When users click the bar of a particular question, a pop-up box would be available telling why such an answer is correct or incorrect (Fig. 13).
- Contains a summary of users' competency on a particular section. The summary would be available by clicking the "Explanatory Note" icon. Based on the data collected during the assessment, the system would generate a report which could demonstrate the users' strengths and weaknesses with improvement suggestions. For example, if one user gets most of the questions concerning "zh, ch, z, c" correctly, but he/she could not distinguish "n" and "l" in Section Two Initials, the system would generate a report indicating this user is good at alveolar affricates and retroflex affricates, but more work is needed to improve his/her ability to tell the differences between alveolar nasal and alveolar liquid. To make it more user friendly, these technical terms would be associated with examples so that users could understand easily. Moreover, recommended readings and useful links are also provided in the summary (Fig.14).

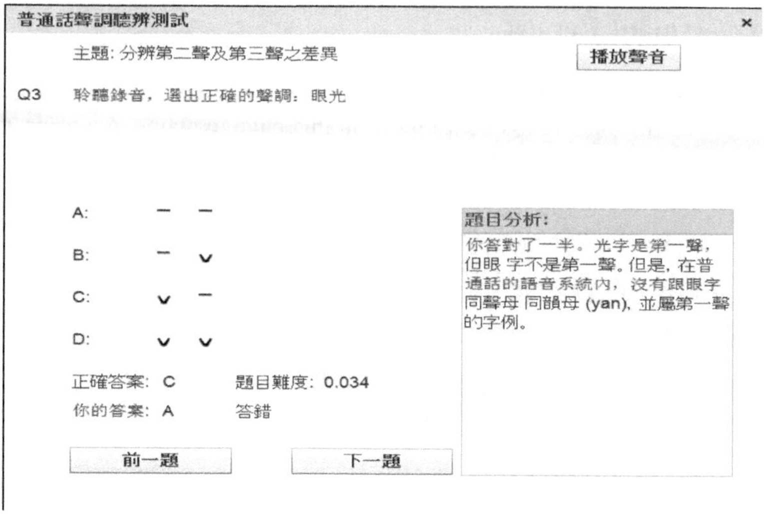

Fig. 13. Detailed explanation for each question

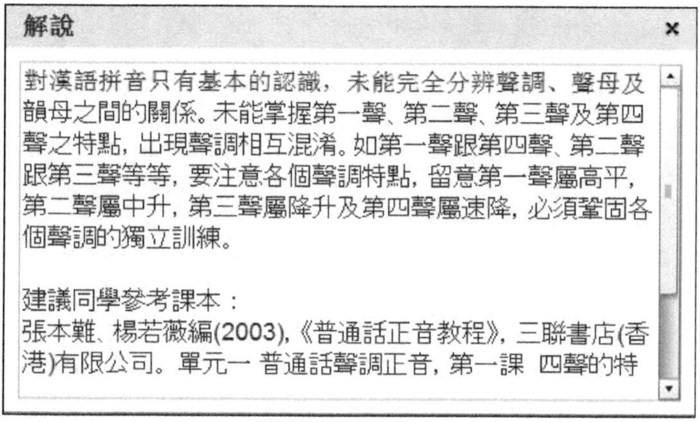

Fig. 14. A summary of users' competency on a particular section

— Offers thorough explanation on users' weaknesses and strengths. When users tend to obtain more information on how good/weak they master a specified skill within a section, they could click the "Skills to be improved" or the "Strength" icon. A column chart would pop-up when a user clicks the "Strength" icon. The Y-axis indicates all the skill items in a section, and the X-axis tells the extent to which the user good/bad at an individual skill item (Fig. 15).

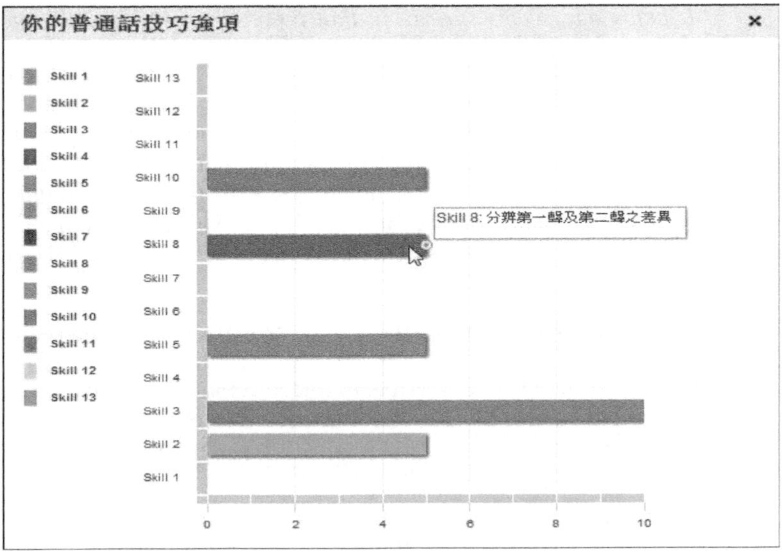

Fig. 15. Column chart display the data of "Strength Skills" of individual student

6 Evaluation of the Prototype

Six voluntary students were invited to participate into the usability test. Before conducting the usability test, the student participants had completed a traditional paper-and-pencil test (PAPT). The traditional PAPT contained 20 multiple-choice questions, and all items were selected randomly from the item bank. Each participant were requested to complete all the 20 questions in 20 minutes without leaving the testing venue. The usability test was videotaped and observed by one of the researchers.

The actual executed time of each participant to complete the e-test was recorded automatically by the system. The average executed time of the participants was 2 minutes 58 seconds. The average time spent by student participants in the traditional PAPT test was about 6 minutes. To compare the executed time of the current version with that of the previous version, the average executed time spent by student participants in the previous prototype was 5 minutes 4 seconds. Therefore, the current e-Assessment system was more efficient than the previous version.

To collect quantitative data, all participants had completed a questionnaire with 28 questions of 5-point Likert scale format and 6 open-ended questions. Based on the data collected, all participants agreed that the e-Assessment system was user-friendly. The majority of the participants enjoyed using the e-Assessment system and felt confident to try it again. All participants agreed that the e-Assessment could be a useful revision aid. Furthermore, the majority of the participants agreed that the questions and reports within the e-Assessment system were clear and easy to be understood. Half of the participants gave the following comments:

> *"It helps and seems surprising that there is a system could analyse my weakness and provide some advices when I finish the questions"*

Among the feedback of the previous prototype, participants commented that the assessment report was not easy to be understood and quite complicated. However, the findings from the current usability test show the improvement of the assessment report. Interestingly, the majority of the participants agreed that they would use the e-Assessment system in mobile devices, such as iPhone. This comment is inspiring to the research team and more work will be on this issue.

7 Potential Use of the Enhanced e-Assessment System

The current system is an updated version of the original Putonghua e-assessment system. It is expected to be able to serve the following purposes:

- It could better reflect users' overall Putonghua capacity.

  The new curriculum covers tones, initials, finals, and grammar differences between Putonghua and Cantonese. Skills on all these aspects are crucial to the accuracy and fluency of spoken Putonghua. Users could drill up their skills on these items by participating on the tests regularly. It would be effective and efficient if they could pay close attention to their weak points.

- It could better reflect users' overall Putonghua capacity.

  Various types of questions could make the test more challenging. Questions of diverse formats could be of different level of difficulty, even if they are with the same content.

  For example, one set of testing material is to be converted into question Type A (choosing proper Chinese phrase) (Fig. 16) and question Type B (choosing proper pronunciation) (Fig. 17). The difficulty level of the two questions differs. With question Type A, users could read the four options in advance, and then decide which option is appropriate after listening to the sound bite; while, with question Type B, users have to listen to the four options carefully and even take some notes before selecting a suitable option to match up with the phrase in question stem. Therefore, question Type B is more difficult than question Type A in this situation.

普通話聲調聽辨測試

聆聽錄音，選出聲調與錄音相同的漢字。

A 昌盛

B 蒼生

C 槍聲

D 長生

Fig. 16. Choosing proper Chinese phrase

(When users click the sound icon, they will hear "槍聲". C is the correct choice.)

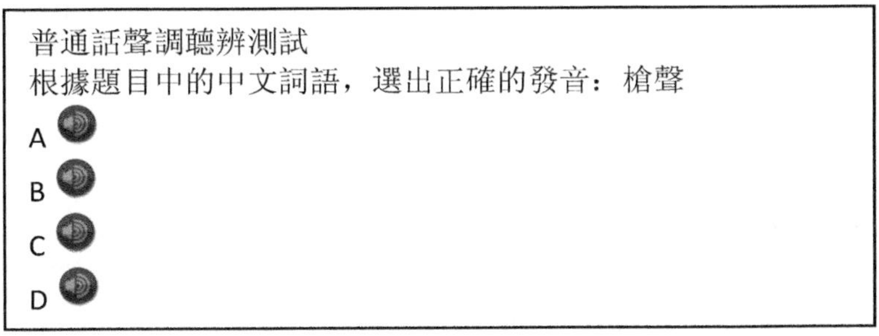

Fig. 17. Choosing proper pronunciation
(Users would hear昌盛，蒼生，槍聲 and 長生 when they click the sound icon against A, B, C and D respectively. They need to determine which pronunciation is correct.)

- It could help users better understand their strengths and weaknesses.

  The detailed assessment report indicates not only the users' strengths and weaknesses in each section, but also in the sub-branches under each section. For example, a user might be good at tones in general, but he/she might not master the rules of tone sandhi. The thorough assessment report could tell the user of such information.

- It could serve as a reference for classroom teaching and learning.

  Since the e-assessment system could help to identify the strengths and weaknesses of students from different progarammes and at different years, Putonghua lecturers could adjust the difficulty of the teaching materials based on their results of online tests. For example, if the system indicates that most of the students in a class could not tell the differences between alveolar affricate (z, c) and alveolopalatal affricate (j, q), this item could be re-visited in subsequent face-to-face classes accordingly.

8 Conclusion

The current version of the Putonghua e-Assessment System is an updated version of the one constructed in 2011 (Wong, 2010; Siu, 2011). It is expected to provide a better test experience and to better reflect students' Putonghua competency. Further research will focus on how this system could improve students' Putonghua competency. After the usability test, the participants provide a lot of useful suggestions to the research team. In general, the e-Assessment system is user-friendly and participants feel confident to use the e-Assessment system as a useful revision aids.

Furthermore, with the popularity of portable devices, the research team is now working on a mobile app for the Putonghua e-Assessment System. Students would be able to access the system and conduct tests anytime, anywhere in the near future. However, it is not yet proven that computer based assessment in higher education could reduce lecturers' workload. More research would also be carried out on this aspect.

Acknowledgement. This project is funded by the Education Bureau of Hong Kong SAR Government under the Quality Enhancement Grant Scheme.

References

Keeves, J.P., Alagumalai, S.: New Approaches to Measurement. In: Masters, G.N., Keeves, J.P. (eds.) Advances in Measurement in Educational Research and Assessment, pp. 23–48. Pergamon Press, New York (1999)

Linacre, J. M.: Computer-Adaptive Testing: A Methodology Whose Time Has Come (Research Memoranda No.69) (2000) Institute for Objective Measurement website, Inc., http://rasch.org/memo69.pdf (retrieved)

Lord, F.M.: Applications of item Response Theory to Practical Testing Problems. Lawrence Erlbaum Associates, Hillsdale (1980)

Rudner, L.M.: An On-line, Interactive, Computer Adaptive Testing Mini-Tutorial. ERIC Clearinghouse on Assessment and Evaluation (1998)

Siu, K., Woo, Y.T., Leung, K., Wong, K., Kwan, R., Tsang, P.: e-Assessment System as a Positive Tool in the Mastery of Putonghua. In: Kwan, R., et al. (eds.) ICT 2011. CCIS, vol. 177, pp. 351–365. Springer, Heidelberg (2011)

Stocking: Item Response Theory. In: Keeves, J.P. (ed.) Educational Research, Methodology, and Measurement, p. 836. Elsevier Science Ltd., U.S. (1997)

Wong, K., Kwan, R.: Building a Web-based Computerized Adaptive Testing System. Paper Presented at International Conference on Information and Communication Technologies in Education, Badajoz, Spain (2002)

Wong, K., Leung, K., Kwan, R., Tsang, P.: Developing a simple Web-based Intelligent Tutoring System in e-Learning using Cognitive Diagnostic Assessment and Adaptive Testing Technology. Paper Presented at the International Conference on Hybrid Learning 2010, Beijing, China, August 16-18 (2010)

Kwan, R., Wong, K., Yu, C.-W., Tsang, P., Leung, K.: Building an Assessment Learning System on the Web. In: Fong, J., Kwan, R., Wang, F.L. (eds.) ICHL 2008. LNCS, vol. 5169, pp. 91–102. Springer, Heidelberg (2008)

Wright, B.D.: Reliability and Separation. Rasch Measurement Transactions 9(4), 472 (1996)

Using a Facebook Closed-Group as Part of an Online Course

Daniyar Sapargaliyev

Eurasian National University, Kazakhstan
dsapargalieff@gmail.com

Abstract. This paper presents the results of a survey among international students after using a Facebook closed-group as part of an online course. We posted educational materials of one session from the online course: "Developing teachers' critical thinking through educational designing" on Facebook and integrated it with the educational platform Moodle. The students studied the course materials in six sessions during the semester. We specifically created a Facebook closed-group to offer students the option to use not only PCs, but also mobile devices to access the online course. After completing of the course, we asked the students (n = 10) to evaluate the use of Facebook in learning. The findings showed that students indicate imperfections in the organization of course materials on Facebook. Nevertheless, the majority of students noted the positive role of Facebook in the development of relationships between each other.

Keywords: Facebook, online course, Moodle, mobile device, student survey, closed-group.

1 Introduction

Facebook, launched in 2004, is now the most popular social networking service and has more than 845 million active users worldwide. The influence of social networks in our daily lives grows day by day. The spread and penetration of Internet social services inevitably changes our society, but at the same time, the emergence of Facebook impacts on education. The increasing use of Facebook in the higher education system is obvious. Many universities have their own web pages on social network sites. More and more teachers and students use Facebook for learning and improving interpersonal communication. We try to consider how Facebook has recently been used for educational purposes in different universities.

Many researchers are trying to find the influence of Facebook on the educational activities of students. For example, Vivian (2009) reports the findings from one online discussion group with 15 students from the University of South Australia. The author found that students accessed and used Facebook for informal learning via the use of status updates, private messaging, instant chat, tagging and 'groups'. Some students reported that they increased their use of Facebook during assessment periods and a number of students used 'SNS self-control' practices that inhibited or reduced their use of Facebook.

Grosseck, Bran and Tiru (2011) investigate how students are engaged in Facebook academic activities. The authors found that the majority of first year students spend a significant amount of time on Facebook more for social uses and less for academic

K.C. Li et al. (Eds.): ICT 2012, CCIS 302, pp. 59–68, 2012.

purposes, even if they take part in discussions about their assignments, lectures, study notes or share information about research resources.

Meanwhile, Selwyn (2009) presents an in-depth qualitative analysis of the Facebook 'wall' activity of 909 undergraduate students in a UK university. The author concludes that rather than necessarily enhancing or eroding students' 'frontstage' engagement with their formal studies, Facebook use must be seen as being situated within the 'identity politics' of being a student. Survey data showed that Facebook provides a ready space where the 'role conflict' that students often experience in their relationships with university work, teaching staff, academic conventions and expectations can be worked through in a relatively closed 'backstage' area.

Sometimes using Facebook for educational purposes is perceived negatively. For example, Roblyer and colleagues (2010) argue that faculty members have a track record of prohibiting classroom uses of technologies that are frequently used by students. The authors conducted a survey to determine how likely higher education faculty are to use Facebook for either personal or educational purposes. A comparison of faculty (n = 62) and student (n = 120) responses indicate that students are much more likely than faculty to use Facebook and are significantly more open to the possibility of using Facebook and similar technologies to support classroom work. Meanwhile faculty members are more likely to use more traditional technologies such as email.

Junco (2012) presents a large sample (n = 1,839) of college students to examine the relationship among multiple measures of frequency of Facebook use, participation in Facebook activities, and time spent preparing for class and actual overall GPA. The author points out that time spent on Facebook was strongly and significantly negatively related to overall GPA, while only weakly related to time spent preparing for class. However, using Facebook for collecting and sharing information was positively predictive of the outcome variables while using Facebook for socializing was negatively predictive.

Moreover, Odell, Nevin and Roberts (2008) describe a research project on the potential value of Facebook as a social networking tool within higher education. The authors clarify the positive and negative factors associated with the use of Facebook for educational purposes. There were educational gains to be made through the use of social networking sites — with the usual caveat that the tool should be a good fit in the educational context. At the same time, there are many examples where the use of social networks to help improve the educational environment at universities. For example, Shambare and Mvula (2011) argue that Facebook's usage in classrooms is still low despite the many opportunities for facilitating teaching and learning in universities. Authors studied students' Facebook usage habits and investigated the perceived usefulness of Facebook in education. Data was collected from a sample of 194 undergraduate students (Business Management course) using self-administered questionnaires. Findings confirmed Facebook's popularity and utility in education.

Of course one important aspect in Facebook usage is the development of cooperation in the classroom. For example, Lampe and colleagues (2011) examine how undergraduate students use Facebook to engage in classroom-related collaborative activities. Surveys data showed (n = 302, n = 214) that predictors of Facebook use for class organizing behaviors include self-efficacy and perceived motivation to communicate with others using the site. Facebook intensity did not predict either positive or negative collaboration, suggesting that how students used the site, rather than how often they used the tool or how important they felt it was, affected their propensity to collaborate.

Nevertheless, new technologies and social networks do not always help in the educational process. For example, Wood and colleagues (2012) examine the impact of multi-tasking with digital technologies while attempting to learn from real-time classroom lectures in a university setting. The authors point out that four digitally-based multi-tasking activities (texting using a cell-phone, emailing, MSN messaging and Facebook) were compared to three control groups (paper-and-pencil note-taking, word-processing note-taking and a natural use of technology condition) over three consecutive lectures. This study indicated that participants who did not use any technologies in the lectures outperformed students who used some form of technology. Interestingly, some researchers consider Facebook as an alternative platform for online learning. For example, Bunus (2010) presents experience in using social networking applications and video content distribution as a complement of traditional classroom education. The author's solution has been based on effective adaptation, extension and integration of Facebook, Twitter, Blogger, YouTube and iTunes services for delivering educational material to students on mobile platforms like iPods and third generation mobile phones.

Reid (2011) explores what happens to interpersonal and power dynamics when tutors use closed-group Facebook pages as a social networking tool in their tutorial groups with first and second year Bachelor of Education students. The author argues that this literacy practice creates an alternative pedagogical space that enables critical practices in relation to writing. The research analyses how this space changes issues of power, access, diversity and design by creating new relationships and new forms of interaction, language and texts.

Shiu, Fong and Lam (2010) consider using Facebook for conducting courses as a replacement of expensive traditional electronic learning platforms. Authors determine how people use Facebook for teaching and learning and argue that Facebook came to existence as a social networking website that supports many features. The framework of Facebook actually provides free of charge software that was provided by traditional electronic learning.

All these examples of using social networks in higher education have prompted us to study Facebook's possibilities in the classroom and online learning. In this article we will try to describe our experience of using Facebook in teaching of international students. We focused on the use of a closed Facebook group for the development of communication between students and published educational materials. That is, we used Facebook as an additional platform for online learning.

2 Creating a Facebook Closed-Group

In 2011, the Faculty of Educational Studies of Adam Mickiewicz University in Poznan offered an online course: "Developing teachers' critical thinking through educational designing" that consisted of six sessions. This course was available for international students of Educational Studies in winter and spring semesters. The

30-hour online course is based on lectures followed by discussions and students' tasks supported by the e-learning platform Moodle.

The author of this course, Professor Dylak, described module as: 'the course is focused on the designing process for education. The basic categories of educational designing are: aims and objectives, teaching material, learning styles, teaching strategies, assessment, evaluation and teacher's competences. The main task of this course is to introduce the culture of educational designing and planning with reference to theories of knowledge. As a main result of the course, participants should create a scenario of lesson or other educational form. Students are expected to prepare a portfolio that may include written tasks, production of classroom based resources, and personal comments' (Dylak, 2011). Participants of the "Developing teachers' critical thinking through educational designing" course were obliged to complete all sessions and fill in the designing chart that sums up the whole module. The designing chart can be perceived as a helpful tool in preparing participants' own curriculum. Each session consists of four main blocks of tasks: Introduction, Revisiting, Developing and Implementing. the course started in November of 2011 and ended in January of 2012. Students had registered for the course at the beginning of the semester.

It is important to note that the primary online platform for the students was Moodle. Only one from six sessions of the course: "Building a structure of the teaching-learning content" was placed on Facebook. We have created the closed Facebook group "Educational Design" for this purpose. This group had 13 members consisting of 11 students, a technical helper and professor. We have placed a direct Web link to the group on the Moodle platform.

Students first learned the academic material on Moodle, and when it came time to study them with a session on the Moodle website a link was passed to the private group which already had pre-placed posts. Generally 21 posts with learning materials and tasks of the session were available on Facebook. Also, we posted short videos of lecture episodes, photos and text documents on the Facebook closed-group for sharing learning information. It was not possible to place other types of files. For example, in our session we also had MP3 files and PDF files with tables and texts. We decided not to change the file formats and in order to place these types of files we used the program Dropbox. There were posted public links of additional files on the Facebook closed-group.

We tried to allow students to have access to the course not only with laptops or desktops, but also from mobile devices because it was important using both desktop and mobile technologies for sharing learning information. More than 2,500 mobile phone models support Facebook applications. Among them, smartphones and landline phones with access to the Internet. It allows students to write and read comments and also see photos, videos and audio files of course materials. This technical aspect was particularly important for our study. Not all platforms for online learning were supported by mobile devices. If a student has access from several types of devices (PCs, tablets, and mobile phones) to learning content, it will greatly contribute to deliver educational materials and support. The main problem with using Facebook for organization and posting learning content was the movement of these posts while students had added comments. The platform for e-learning (such as Moodle) has the possibility of fixed location of learning materials, but on Facebook the learning materials initially were replaced after each update and posting of comments. When students were commenting on the posts then these 21 posts subsequently mixed. This condition somewhat disoriented students.

3 Student Survey

After successfully completing our course, we asked students to evaluate the use of our Facebook group for learning. It should be noted that the students firstly used social network for educational aims. The main purpose of our survey was to determine the effectiveness of Facebook for learning and the development of relationships among students. We prepared a paper-based questionnaire. The questionnaire includes two closed-ended questions and six open-ended questions. The student survey was conducted in an anonymous form.

3.1 Participants

The participants of the survey were 10 students (100% female) of Adam Mickiewicz University in Poznan. The students were from two age groups (under 21 (40%) and from 22 to 31 (60%)). The international students were from two countries (Italy and Spain). The survey was conducted in January 2011.

3.2 Results of the Student Survey

(Q1) How long have you been using Facebook? We decided to find out how long students have been using Facebook. Half of the students said they have used social network for more than two years. Two of the ten students answered that they have used Facebook for less than two years. At the same time 20 per cent of respondents indicated that they have used the social network site for less than 12 months. Only one of the ten students said that she had used Facebook for less than half a year. It is important to note that all students participating in the survey have had experience of using Facebook (Fig. 1).

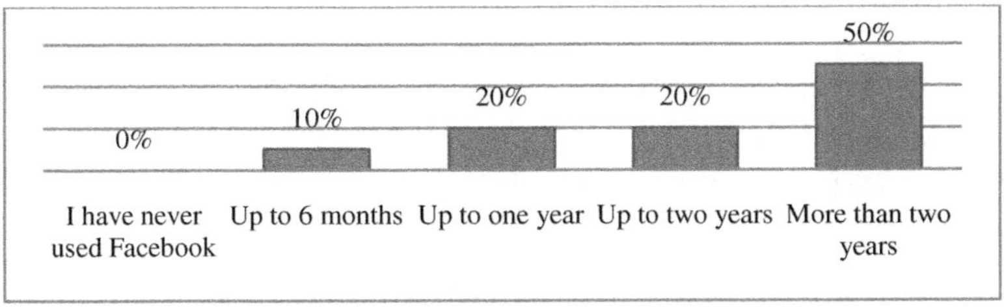

Fig. 1. Periods of using Facebook by students

(Q2)How often do you use Facebook? In our study, we attempted to determine how often students use Facebook. Six in ten respondents use Facebook every day. Four in ten use the social networking site multiple times throughout the day. Two in ten students check Facebook at least once a day. However, 40 per cent of respondents said they use it just a few times a week. It should be noted that students use Facebook frequently (Fig. 2).

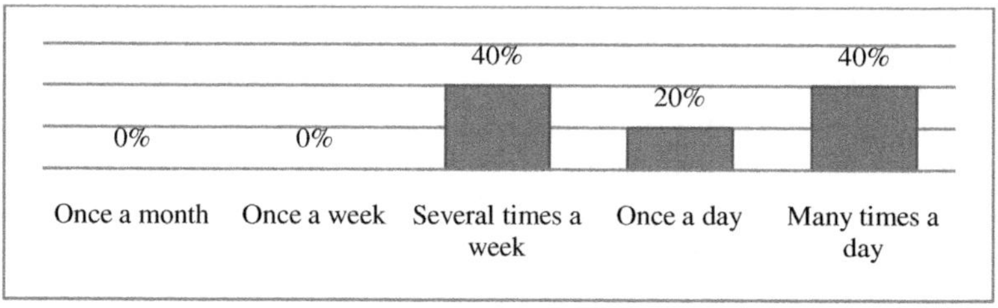

Fig. 2. Frequency of using Facebook

(Q3)How do you usually access Facebook? We asked respondents what types of devices they use to access the social network. All students answered that they used a personal computer (laptop or desktop) for this purpose; however, only one in ten respondents said that she used a mobile device to access Facebook. At the same time students do not use computers in the workplace, in the classroom and public places (such as a library or an Internet cafe) to access Facebook (Fig. 3).

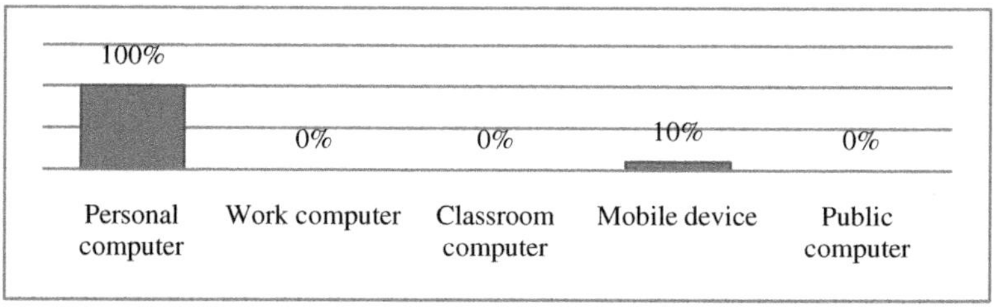

Fig. 3. Types of equipment to accessing Facebook

(Q4)Have you ever used your mobile phone/device to access Facebook? In our study, we tried to determine whether students have used mobile devices (such as mobile phones, smartphones, Tablet PCs or other devices) to access Facebook. Half of the students responded affirmatively. But at the same time, the other half replied that they have never used mobile devices for this purpose. Nevertheless, the responses indicate that students are ready to use mobile devices to access social networks. This can greatly facilitate the access at any time and any place to Facebook (Fig. 4).

(Q5) Have you ever used Facebook to learn something? Previously, we have mentioned that the students have already studied one session on the Facebook group "Educational Design". Nevertheless, we asked respondents whether they used the

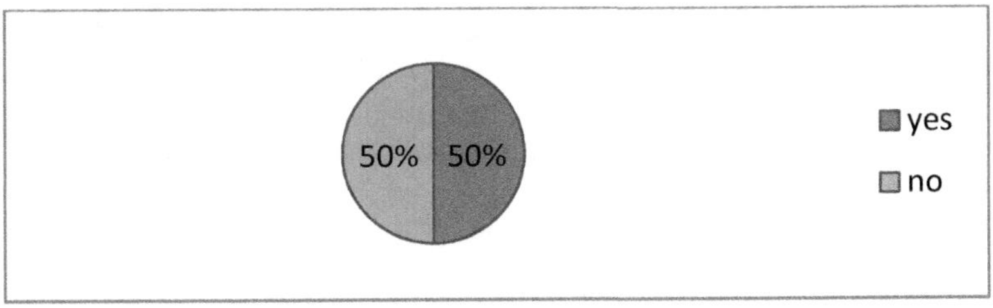

Fig. 4. Experience of using mobile devices to access Facebook

social network for learning. Three in ten students responded positively. However, seven in ten of students answered that they never had used Facebook for learning. This means that only a small number of students have experience using Facebook for educational purposes (Fig. 5).

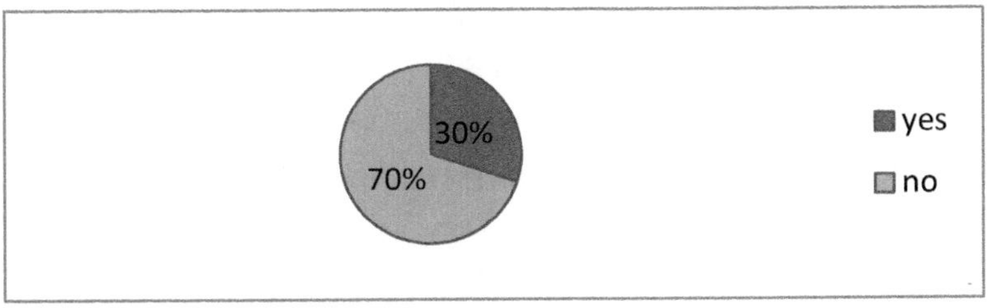

Fig. 5. Using Facebook for learning

(Q6) How active are you in the Facebook group "Educational Design"? We asked students to identify their active participation in the online learning course. Half of the students noted a rather low activity. Three of the ten students indicated some degree of activity. Only one student had an active part during the online course and one student had moderate activity. Nevertheless, it is important to note that students participated in low levels of activity in the Facebook group (Fig. 6).

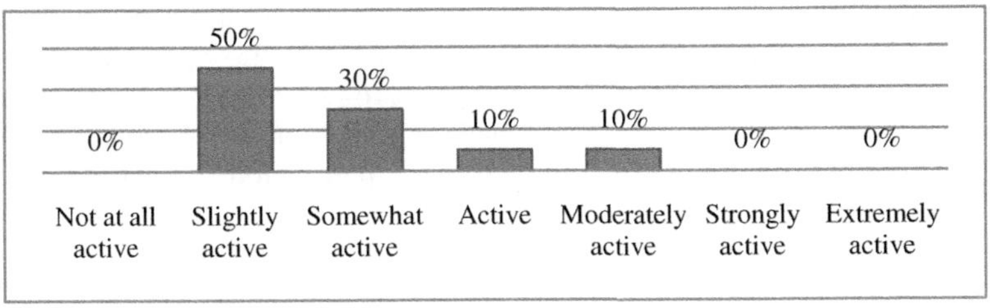

Fig. 6. Activity of students in Facebook educational group

(Q7) To what extent do you agree or disagree with using a Facebook group: "I develop more effective relationships with other students in the class." One of the central questions in our study was to determine how students have developed a relationship with each other by using Facebook in an online course. We have tried to figure out how effective the use of Facebook is for educational purposes. Three in ten respondents answered neutrally. Meanwhile, 40 per cent of students agreed with the opinion that Facebook is developing more effective relationships. In particular, three students slightly agree, and one student mostly agrees. On the other hand 30 per cent of participants said they did not agree that the social network can develop effective relationships in the classroom. In particular, two students noted slight disagreement and one of the ten students strongly disagreed with the statement in question. Nevertheless, the majority of students noted the positive role of Facebook in the development of closer relationships in the classroom (Fig. 7).

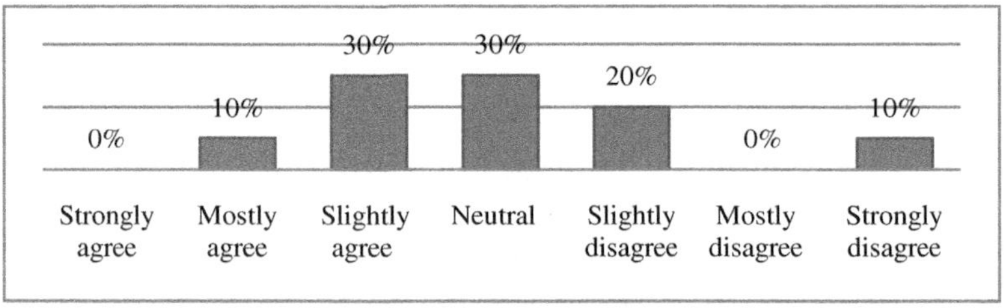

Fig. 7. Developing effective relationships by Facebook

(Q8) What would you like to share about your experience using the Facebook group "Educational Design"? At the end of our survey, we asked students to tell about their experiences in using Facebook for learning. Most of the students were dissatisfied with the organization and forms of using the social network as a part of the online course. For example, one student wrote, "Facebook as a teaching platform was an incomprehensive and disorganized way to learn" and another noted, "I think it was disorganized and it should be more optional." One respondent remarked, "I like share my comments, but I think I didn't have enough competences to criticize correctly and give positive comments about others students." We also received the following answers: "I think Facebook is for enjoying free time, but not for study. I think email would be better", "I do not like to share my opinions on Facebook." One student notably mentioned that: "Educational ideas that appear in this webpage are very useful to teach other people." It is important to note that this may have been the first encounter the students may have had with the use of a social network for learning. This could cause a generally negative perception in using Facebook for educational purposes.

4 Conclusion

The findings of our small study showed that students generally have a negative perception of using Facebook in learning. We specifically integrated into the online course our Facebook closed-group so that the students had the opportunity to compare advantages and disadvantages of the use of the social network in education. It is important to note that some of the students in our closed-group firstly used as Moodle and Facebook as educational platforms. While some students reported that it was easy to use Facebook to comment on texts or tasks, other students did not like the constant change of location of posts when they were updated. We were able to define that students from different countries have enough Facebook experience to freely use it in learning. Basically, students use personal computers for accessing Facebook, and in some cases they use their mobile devices. However, only one student in our group said that she used a mobile device to access Facebook. We tried using Facebook to facilitate access to learning materials by different types of students' devices. In general, students were not active users of the closed education group, generally most of their activities consisted of reading learning materials and writing comments. In spite of the small population size in our student survey we plan to do other work that will include surveys with larger populations. We understand that the survey was done with 100% females and in future work we will try to find differences if the survey sample contains males only or a mix. It will likely help us to indicate new result and findings. Our limited experience in integrating two different platforms such as online learning systems and social network systems showed that students were dissatisfied with the forms and methods of implementation. We hope that further research will help improve in the future.

References

Bunus, P.: The Social Network Classroom. In: Lytras, M.D., Ordonez De Pablos, P., Avison, D., Sipior, J., Jin, Q., Leal, W., Uden, L., Thomas, M., Cervai, S., Horner, D. (eds.) TECH-EDUCATION 2010. CCIS, vol. 73, pp. 517–524. Springer, Heidelberg (2010)

Dylak, S.: Developing teachers' critical thinking through educational designing (2011), `http://amu.edu.pl/en/year-at-amu/a-year-at-amu/amu-pie/offer/amu-pie-offer-20122013-winter-semester/developing-teachers-critical-thinking-through-educational-designing` (retrieved April 23, 2012)

Grosseck, G., Bran, R., Tiru, L.: Dear teacher, what should I write on my wall? A case study on academic uses of Facebook. Social and Behavioral Sciences 15, 1425–1430 (2011)

Junco, R.: Too much face and not enough books: The relationship between multiple indices of Facebook use and academic performance. Computers in Human Behavior 28, 187–198 (2012)

Lampe, C., Wohn, D.Y., Vitak, J., Ellison, N.B., Wash, R.: Student use of Facebook for organizing collaborative classroom activities. International Journal of Computer-Supported Collaborative Learning 6, 329–347 (2011)

Odell, A., Nevin, P., Roberts, H.: Education in your Face(Book)! In: Proceedings of the 7th European Conference on e-Learning, pp. 231–239. Academic Publishing, UK (2008)

Reid, J.: "We don't Twitter, we Facebook": An alternative pedagogical space that enables critical practices in relation to writing. English Teaching-Practice and Critique 10, 58–80 (2011)

Roblyer, M.D., McDaniel, M., Webb, M., Herman, J., Witty, J.V.: Findings on Facebook in higher education: A comparison of college faculty and student uses and perceptions of social networking sites. Internet and Higher Education 13, 134–140 (2010)

Shambare, R., Mvula, A.: South African students' perceptions of Facebook: Some implications for instructors. African Journal of Business Management 5, 10557–10564 (2011)

Selwyn, N.: Faceworking: exploring students' education-related use of Facebook. Learning Media and Technology 34, 157–174 (2009)

Shiu, H., Fong, J., Lam, J.: Facebook – Education with Social Networking Websites for Teaching and Learning. In: Tsang, P., Cheung, S.K.S., Lee, V.S.K., Huang, R. (eds.) ICHL 2010. LNCS, vol. 6248, pp. 59–70. Springer, Heidelberg (2010)

Vivian, R.: University Students' Informal Learning Practices Using Facebook: Help or Hindrance? In: Kwan, R., McNaught, C., Tsang, P., Wang, F.L., Li, K.C. (eds.) ICT 2011. CCIS, vol. 177, pp. 254–267. Springer, Heidelberg (2011)

Wood, E., Zivcakova, L., Gentile, P., Archer, K., Pasquale, D.D., Nosko, A.: Examining the impact of off-task multi-tasking with technology on real-time classroom learning. Computers & Education 58, 365–374 (2012)

Social Network Sites and e-Learning Adoption

Ramón Rufín Moreno[1] and Cayetano Medina Molina[2]

[1] Universidad Nacional de Educación a Distancia, Spain
rrufin@cee.uned.es
[2] Centro Andaluz de Estudios Empresariales, Avda Leonardo da Vinci Ed. CEADE, Spain
cmedina@ceade.es

Abstract. The use of social network sites (SNSs), and the improvements gained from new technologies through e-learning platforms are two of the main topics that are currently discussed in the area of higher education. Both issues converge if what is being considered is the hypothetical effect that SNS use can have on e-learning adoption. Given the fact that there is no general consensus at this point, the present work addresses the moderating role that SNS use could potentially have on e-learning adoption. Our findings suggest that SNS use has a moderating effect on the relationship between the intention to use the platform and its posited antecedents. Furthermore, among these three antecedents only effort expectancy and social influence have a significant effect on the intention to use an e-learning platform.

Keywords: e-learning, social network sites, UTAUT, Web 2.0. learning strategy, technology adoption.

1 Introduction

Information and communication technology (ICT) dematerializes, delocates, and globalizes information, leading to a *digitization* process that changes the main format in which knowledge is conveyed, and this, in turn, changes the way people think and behave. Students now entering the university system have different skills from those students had in the past, and they attribute a key role to ICT insofar as it offers them new potential for developing their competences (Burkle, 2011; Cole, 2009). All of these factors, added to emerging trends in education, lead the potential of online technology to be constantly analyzed with the aim of creating flexible learning environments in higher education.

In addition to many other benefits, Web-based learning fosters development of the skills associated with the European Higher Education Area (EHEA), which includes a change in methodology that promotes students' *active participation*, initiative, and critical thinking, with a fundamental shift in focus from teaching to learning (Cole, 2009; Hsie & Cho, 2011; López-Pérez, Pérez-López, & Rodríguez Ariza, 2011).

The most widespread application of this concept is the use of e-learning platforms, even though at present they are primarily being used to complement face-to-face teaching through what is referred to as blended learning.

The success of e-learning depends on student participation, involvement, and social interaction. Since that is what will lead students to share knowledge, and since e-learning systems contribute to the development of virtual communities that provide

K.C. Li et al. (Eds.): ICT 2012, CCIS 302, pp. 69–79, 2012.

an active, collaborative audience for creating content, it is important to consider the following question: Will students' use of SNS — this use being considered as a personal attribute of students rather than an additional element of the e-learning platforms — have an effect on their use of e-learning platforms?

2 Technology and Higher Education

Introducing ICT into the educational process does not guarantee an improvement in its effectiveness or efficiency, nor does it in and of itself lead to educational innovation unless it goes hand in hand with changes in the learning process (Chen, 2011; Duart, 2011; Mazman & Usluel, 2010; Rodríguez, 2010). These goals are made more accessible by using Web 2.0, the basis for a new educational model in which the teacher's role shifts from the sole source of knowledge to that of its facilitator (Amat, 2011; Burkle, 2011; Collis & Moonen, 2011). Identifying the key technology trends in education calls for analyzing the implications associated with using Web 2.0 social environments, viewed as the ensemble of technologies focused on creating resources whose quality users then control together as part of a collaborative effort. These tools enable the appearance of social venues and the development of skills related to a new kind of critical, collaborative, creative technological literacy (Bruns & Humphreys, 2005; Perez Tornero, 2008).

Web 2.0 use in higher education offers countless opportunities for creating personalized, student-centered learning environments and for implementing two current learning approaches: constructivist and collaborative (Cole, 2009; Deng & Yuen, 2011). Furthermore, given that most of the key competences for lifelong learning are closely related to the skills generated by using 2.0 tools, it is essential to analyze the implications that are identified for some of their most widespread applications in terms of their effect on higher education (Ortega, 2011).

In the case of *wikis*, there are certain reservations as to their use in university settings, since they are perceived differently from their ordinary use (Cole, 2009). Blogs enable interaction and collaborative learning through the exchange of knowledge and teamwork. Blog use in university settings reinforces reflection among students, reinforcing their analysis and assessment skills (Deng & Yuen, 2011). Given that students complain about the lack of opportunities for establishing real communication, integrating SNS into educational practices has become a key element for achieving more robust learning opportunities (Collis & Moonen, 2011; Mazman & Usluel, 2010). The success of 2.0 learning systems is based on interactive and collaborative learning and in the development of online educational communities (Wang & Chiu, 2011).

SNSs are defined as all the applications that increase group interaction, shared collaborative spaces, social connections, and information exchanges in a Web-based environment. These sites brings people with common interests together and are particularly effective in promoting communication and collaboration, hence being quickly adopted in educational settings (Ajjan & Hartshorne, 2008; Mazman & Usluel, 2010; Wang & Chiu, 2011; Zhan, Xu, & Ye, 2011).

Some of the benefits offered by working SNSs into the educational context are related to fostering socialization in a safe, practical environment; enabling inclusive education; reinforcing informal learning processes; supporting knowledge acquisition through subliminal learning processes; facilitating immersion in foreign language environments; reducing knowledge gaps; and contributing to boost and build a digital identity (Ajjan & Hartshorne, 2008). However, if we wish to associate SNSs with the learning process, we must bear in mind the existence of certain factors that could determine its success (Cole, 2009; Jones, Blackey, Fitzgibbon, & Chew, 2010).

In higher education circles, the advisability of linking SNS to e-learning platforms is a subject of debate. Despite overall acceptance of their being essential at this point, results differ when the impact of SNS on the educational process is subjected to an empirical analysis. Among those who report a positive outcome, Ajjan and Hartshorne (2008) confirm that SNSs reinforce collaborative learning, involve participants in critical reasoning, and boost communication and writing skills. Heirberger and Harper (2008) suggest a positive correlation between SNS use and student involvement as predictors of academic success, as well as also helping students to adapt to the university's culture (Kuh, 2009). Against this, other authors suggest that SNSs can have a negative effect on school work when they are perceived differently in the educational and personal contexts (Cole, 2009; Junco & Cotton, 2011).

3 Use of Social Networks as a Moderating Factor in e-Learning Platform Acceptance

One of the most widespread theories in technology acceptance analysis is the Unified Theory of Acceptance and Use of Technology (UTAUT) (Venkatesh, Morris, Davis, & Davis, 2003), which posits the existence of four key elements for technology acceptance and use. It states that performance expectancy, effort expectancy, and social influence affect intention of use, while intention of use and facilitating conditions are what determine how the technology is actually used. According to previous theories, the main determinant of behavior is the intention to carry it out; in other words, actions are based on individual attitudes. Thus consumers are rational decision-makers who behave (actual use) according to the value attributed to the results of their behavior and to the expectations they have regarding that behavior in terms of achieving those results (intention of use). Since motivation for using an e-learning system is very different from that of using generic information systems, if one wishes to apply it to technology acceptance in higher education, one has to study the matter in greater depth (Chen, 2011).

- Several studies confirm that perceived usefulness, one of the components from which *performance expectancy* is drawn, has a positive effect on intended and actual use of an e-learning platform (Liu, Li, & Carlsson, 2010; McGill & Klobas, 2009; Van Raaij & Schepers, 2008).
- Since users' beliefs and attitudes evolve according to the level of experience they acquire, so will the determinants for e-learning acceptance. Individuals who are scarcely familiar with e-learning will need more time to develop the skills required

for its use. Hence perceived ease of use has a stronger impact on attitude and intention of use, whereas perceived usefulness has an influence among more experienced users (Lin, 2011). Since some e-learning applications are still in their initial stages, *effort expectancy* will be critical in determining its intention of use (Sánchez, Martín, & Villarejo, 2007; Wang, Wu, & Wang, 2009). However, in some cases it has been posited that its effect on e-learning adoption is only indirect, through perceived usefulness (Van Raaij & Schepers, 2008).

- The potential impact of *social influence* on the intention to use e-learning, on the other hand, has been questioned, as it has been observed that social norms have a significant effect on intention of use when that use is mandatory, particularly in the early stages of experience (Van Raaj & Schepers, 2008).

Several studies have analyzed e-learning platform adoption based on the UTAUT model. While Teo (2009) concludes that the elements influencing behavior are limited to facilitating conditions and social influence, McGill and Klobas (2009) hold the opposite view, stating that none of the listed components determine the intention to use e-learning. More recently, Chen (2011) has confirmed that performance expectancy and facilitating conditions influence behavior intention, whereas effort expectancy and social influence do not. In keeping with prior studies, this author also confirms that behavior intention determines e-learning platform acceptance (Liao, & Lu, 2008; Toral, Barrero, & Martínez-Torres, 2007).

Studies that include additional variables in the model agree on highlighting the role of performance expectancy, effort expectancy, and even playfulness as antecedents to the intention to use e-learning, although Terzia and Economides (2011) add the perceived usefulness variable, while Wang, Wu, and Wang (2009) include social influence and self-management of learning.

In other words, we cannot consider there to be a consensus as to e-learning adoption and use — not among the studies based on the initial UTAUT model formulation nor among the studies that include the roles of new variables in their considerations. However, what remains to be confirmed is whether the relationships between the variables included in the models may be moderated by certain features found in users. Hence a need has been perceived to include moderating variables in new research in order to move ahead in the study of technology acceptance (Venkatesh et al., 2003).

It is important to remember that although e-learning platform acceptance may depend on students' involvement and social interaction, without which it is doubtful whether the necessary exchange of knowledge could occur (Ma & Yuen, 2011), SNSs are ideal for providing an active, collaborative audience for content development by enhancing communication and cooperation between students (Harrinson & Barthel, 2009; Jones, Lanfgraben, & Morris, 2006; Wang & Chiu, 2011; Zhan, Xu, & Ye, 2011). Therefore, we have to ask ourselves whether students' use of SNSs actually has a moderating effect on e-learning tool adoption, which would suggest the following hypotheses:

H_1: SNS use has a moderating effect on the relationship between the antecedents of the intention to use an e-learning platform and that intention itself.

H_2: SNS use of has a moderating effect on the relationship between the antecedents of actual use of an e-learning platform and that actual use.

4 Methodology

4.1 Development of the Model

This study is based on the classic formulation of the UTAUT model (Venkatesh et al., 2003), including the role of frequency of social network use (Fig. 1).

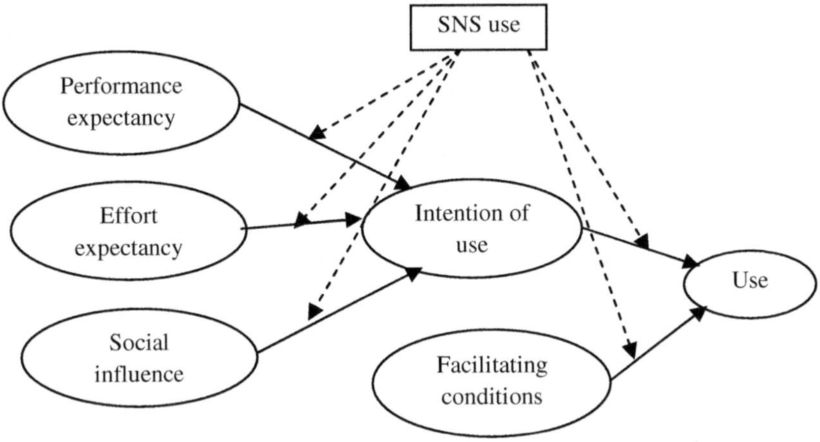

Fig. 1. Model used

The scales used for measuring the performance expectancy, effort expectancy, social influence, and facilitating conditions constructs are drawn from Chan et al. (2010), whereas intention of use and actual use are drawn from Wang and Shih (2009), all of them through three items. Lastly, frequency of social network use is measured according to one single item. Seven-value Likert scales are used throughout.

4.2 Field Work

Since the aim of this study was to measure the intention to use an e-learning platform, the questionnaire was personally handed out to students from the four undergraduate classes, to avoid a sample selection bias, and 155 valid questionnaires were obtained. As stated previously, SNS use is a personal attribute of students and not an additional element of the e-learning platforms, most of them actually using Facebook for that purpose.

When we analyzed the profile for the sample, gender parity was apparent, with only a slight bias towards male gender (56% of the survey respondents). We also observed that most of the survey respondents' ages were comprised between 20 and 22, followed by those of ages 23 to 25 (25%). As far as their respective classes, first-year (39%) and third-year students (41%) were most represented, but these differences were far smaller when we viewed them from the perspective of the cycles these students belonged to. First-cycle students accounted for 52% of the survey respondents, whereas the second cycle accounted for 48%. There were 65% who claimed to use the platform with an average frequency, whereas 28% claimed to do so very often. Only 7% claimed to use it very occasionally. Lastly, we must add that 62% of the survey respondents had prior experience in using similar e-learning platforms.

The scales initially proposed for performing the statistical analysis were adaptations of scales that had been validated in several previous studies, and whose content we therefore could assume to be valid. The statistical behavior of the constructs included in the model was analyzed by developing the Structural Equations Model (SEM) with SmartPLS 2.0.M3 (Ringle, Wende, & Will, 2008). The purpose of PLS modeling is to predict dependent variables. This aim leads to an attempt to maximize explained variance (R^2) of the dependent variables. Compared to covariance-based methods, PLS adapts better to prediction and theory development applications, although it can also be used for theory confirmation. One of the reasons for using PLS modeling is that it is more appropriate for small and medium-sized samples, such as the 155-case sample in this study.

4.3 Results

Since the factor loading for the items in terms of the construct they belong to are higher than 0.707 and above the required significance level, we chose to maintain the initial loadings we had considered. Convergent validity was established by analyzing the Average Variance Extracted (AVE), having stated that the AVE values must be higher than 0.5. In the case of our study, they were well above that value, and therefore the convergent validity of the related constructs in the structural model could be accepted. To establish the discriminant validity, the AVE value must be higher than the variance shared by the construct and the other represented constructs, and that condition was met in our study. In addition, all the items have a higher loading for the construct they belong to than for any other, and this result again confirms the discriminant validity of the items we used.

4.4 Structural Model

An analysis of the structural model enables us to conclude that social influence (path = 0.1454, t-value = 0.2162) and effort expectancy (path = 0.3775, t-value = 2.7966) are the determinants for the intention to use the e-learning platform, whereas the effect of performance expectancy on that intention is not significant (path = 0.0817, t-value = 0.5071). Meanwhile, both facilitating conditions (path = 0.3149, t-value = 3.7213) and behavior intention (path = 0.3151, t-value = 3.1457) have a significant effect on e-learning platform use.

4.5 Multigroup Analysis — Interaction Effect

To confirm whether students' use of SNS had an effect on e-learning platform adoption, we proceeded to analyze the interaction effect. According to Rigdon,

Schumacker, and Wothke (1998), it is the most straightforward method for analyzing moderating effects, and its use is recommended whenever possible. Our findings suggest that students' use of SNSs moderates the relationships between performance expectancy, effort expectancy, and social influence on behavior intention. However, it does not moderate behavior intention's and facilitating conditions' relationships to actual use of the e-learning platform, and this is hence rejected. The value offered by the test shows that the higher the frequency of SNS use, the lower the impact of expected performance, expected effort, and social influence on behavior intention.

4.6 Quasi-Moderated Relationships

Analysis of moderating relationships focuses on the impact that the moderating variable has over the dependant variable. If this relationship appears to be significant, what we have is a case of quasi-moderation, and accordingly, one can consider that the relationship between the independent and the dependent variable will be influenced by the value of the moderating variable (Brown & Chin, 2004). Therefore, and based on the data included in the table above (Table 1), we can assume that SNS use has a significant effect on intention of use, even though it may not be the case for actual use.

Table 1. Quasi moderation analysis

Dependent variable	Variable	Impact on dependent (t-value)
Intention of use	Performance expectancy	0.872095 (3.488310)
	Effort expectancy	0.872095 (699108)
	Social influence	0.539944 (2.197469)
Use	Intention of use	–0.872095 (093045)
	Facilitating conditions	–0.872095 (076486)

4.7 Analysis of the Results

The first hypothesis to confirm was the one that analyzed the potential moderating effect on the relationship between intention of use and its antecedents. As we can see from the interaction effect, SNS use among students has a moderating effect on the relationship that performance expectancy, effort expectancy, and social influence have on intention of use, leading us to accept H_1. The resulting value shows that the greater the use of social network sites, the lesser the influence of these variables, although in the structural model performance expectancy does not appear to have a significant effect on the intention to use an e-learning platform.

Our second hypothesis aimed to determine whether SNS use was related to e-learning platform use. Our findings lead us to reject H_2, since this moderating effect did not appear in any of the relationships that intention of use and facilitating conditions had with actual use of an e-learning platform.

5 Conclusion

5.1 Confirmation of the Relationships Posited in the Model

The present study establishes that students' intention to use an e-learning platform is determined by effort expectancy and social influence, but not by performance expectancy. In keeping with previous studies (Van Raaij & Schepers, 2008), we found that social influence had a strong effect on intention of use because, even though that use was not mandatory, use of the platform examined in our study was in its initial stages. In keeping with Wang, Wu, and Wang (2009), effort expectancy is a critical determinant for the intention to adopt e-learning. Contrary to what some authors have argued (Liu, Li, & Carlsson, 2010; McGill & Klobas, 2009), performance expectancy not only does not have a determining influence on behavior intention, but does not even have a significant effect on it.

In order to further pursue the interpretation of Lin's approach (2011), according to which effort expectancy plays a more prominent role among inexperienced users, the experience that users of these platforms have ought to have been explicitly quantified. In other words, although according to the students' own responses in some cases they are indeed experienced, it is difficult to determine the source of this experience. Although some respondents may have acquired it at other universities, it seems like a reasonable assumption that a large percentage of these students would lack that experience.

Finally, in keeping with prior studies, we found that intention of use and facilitating conditions determine university students' actual use of e-learning platforms (Liao & Lu, 2008; Teo, 2009; Toral et al., 2009).

5.2 The Moderating Role of SNS Use in e-Learning Adoption

According to Ma and Yuen (2011), the success of e-learning depends on students' participation, involvement, and social interaction, which could be reinforced by SNS use, this use being considered as a personal attribute of students and not an additional element of the e-learning platforms. SNS use is thus independent from the educational institutions promoting the e-learning platforms. The present study concludes that SNS use moderates the relationship between the antecedents for behavior intention and that very intention, but not the effect of behavior intention and facilitating conditions on actual resulting use of the platform.

SNS use leads performance expectancy, effort expectancy, and social influence to have a weaker effect on behavior intention. Greater SNS use may imply that the student is familiar with the technology, and therefore, as posited in previous studies (Lin, 2011; Wang, Wu, & Wang, 2009) the greater the user's experience is, the weaker the impact of effort expectancy will be. Getting students involved in active interaction based on SNS can be one of the ways, along the lines proposed by Swan (2001), to change users' perceptions so as to have the lesser impact on effort expectancy that we mentioned earlier.

The socialization and enculturation of young people in virtual environments, and the development of certain technological literacy-related skills pertaining to SNS use with a clearly critical, collaborative, and creative character (Bruns & Humphreys, 2005; Perez Tornero, 2008) lead to differing behavior of the relationship between social influence and the intention to use an e-learning platform, which results in social influence having a lesser impact on intention of use as its use increases. It is important to bear in mind that, according to our findings, SNS use has a positive effect on of the intention to use e-learning platforms.

The relationships that remain unaffected are those that relate the antecedents for intention of use to actual use. In other words, the significant effect of intended use and facilitating conditions on actual use of an e-learning platform is not dependant on students' SNS use.

5.3 Implications for Universities

If universities wish to benefit from the advantages of adopting and using their e-learning platforms, whether they only intend to use them occasionally or as support for their face-to-face classroom experiences through blended learning, they must bear in mind the role of SNS use among their students.

First of all, it is important to consider that both effort expectancy and social influence have an effect on the intention to use e-learning platforms. This means that universities must take two factors into account: on the one hand, they must clearly convey the platform's ease of use; on the other, they must explain that, given the relevance of social influence, the associated benefits of bringing new students on board are exponential. However, given that the rate of SNS use is expected to remain stable or even increase, it is possible that the impact of these variables will be weaker in the future.

Meanwhile, actual e-learning platform use will be determined by intention of use and facilitating conditions. In other words, it will be essential for students to perceive that the institution has the necessary technology and staff to provide help if they should need it. Although these relationships do not depend on SNS use, it is important to remember that SNS use will have a direct influence on the intention to use an e-learning platform. The relevance of facilitating conditions had already been addressed in previous studies that suggested that the main challenge for ICT use in higher education environments was associated with the learning process and its difficulties (Ricoy & Fernández, 2013).

Therefore, we believe that universities can be expected to benefit from their students' use of SNS over time, since it will lead them to actively participate in creating content and using e-learning platforms, thus enabling institutions to optimize both e-learning and blended learning alike.

References

Ajjan, H., Hartshorne, R.: Investigating faculty decisions to adopt Web 2.0 technologies: Theory and empirical test. The Internet and Higher Education 11(2), 71–80 (2008)

Amat, A.F.: Usando la web 2.0 para informarse e informar. Una experiencia en educación superior. Teoría de la Educación [Theory of Education] 12(1), 145–166 (2011)

Brown, S.P., Chin, W.W.: Satisfying and Retaining Customers Through Independent Services Representatives. Decision Sciences 35(3), 527–550 (2004)
Burkle, M.: El aprendizaje on-line: oportunidades y retos en instituciones politécnicas. Comunicar [Communicate] 37(19), 45–53 (2011)
Chen, J.L.: The effects of education compatibility and technological expectancy on e-learning acceptance. Computers & Education 57, 1501–1511 (2011)
Cole, M.: Using Wiki technology to support student engagement: Lessons from the trenchs. Computers & Education 52(1), 141–146 (2009)
Collis, B., Moonen, J.: Flexibilidad en la educación superior: revisión de expectativas. Comunicar [Communicate] 37(19), 15–25 (2011)
Deng, L., Yuen, A.H.K.: Towards a framework for educational affordances of blogs. Computers & Education 56, 441–451 (2011)
Duart, J.M.: La Red en los procesos de enseñanza de la Universidad. Comunicar [Communicate] 37(19), 10–13 (2011)
Harrinson, T.M., Barthel, B.: Wielding new media in Web 2.0 explaining the history of engagement with the collaborative construction of media products. New Media & Society 11(12), 155–178 (2009)
Heirberger, G., Harper, R.: Have you facebooked Akin lately? Using technology to increase student involvement. In: Junco, R., Timm, D.M. (eds.) Using Emerging Technologies to Enhance Student Engagement. New Directions for Students Services, vol. (124), pp. 19–35. Jossey-Bass, San Francisco (2008)
Hsie, J.J., Cho, V.: Comparing e-Learning Tools' Success: The Case of Instructor-Student Interactive vs. Self-placed Tools. Computers & Education (2011), doi:10.1016/j.compedu.2011.05.002
Jones, N., Blackey, H., Fitzgibbon, K., Chew, E.: Get out of MySpace. Computers & Education 54, 776–782 (2010)
Jones, P.R., Launfgraben, J.L., Morris, N.: Developing an empirically based typology of entering students toward participation in Learning communities. Assessment & Evaluation in Higher Education 31(3), 249–265 (2006)
Junco, R., Cotton, S.R.: Perceived academic effects of instant messaging use. Computers & Education 56, 370–378 (2011)
Kuh, G.D.: What student affairs professionals need to know about student engagement. Journal of College Student Development 50(6), 683–706 (2009)
Liao, H.L., Lu, H.P.: The role of experience and innovation characteristics in the adoption and continued use of e-learning websites. Computer & Education 51(4), 1405–1416 (2008)
Lin, K.M.: E-Learning continuance intention: Moderating effects of user e-learning experience. Computers & Education 56, 515–526 (2011)
Liu, Y., Li, H., Carlsson, C.: Factors driving the adoption of m-learning: An empirical study. Computers & Education 55, 1211–1219 (2010)
López-Pérez, M.V., Pérez-López, M.C., Rodríguez-Ariza, L.: Blended Learning in higher education: Students perceptions and their reaction to outcomes. Computers & Education 56(3), 818–826 (2011)
Ma, W.W.K., Yuen, A.H.K.: Understanding online knowledge sharing: An interpersonal relationship perspective. Computers & Education 56, 210–219 (2011)
Mazman, S.G., Usluel, Y.K.: Modeling educational usage of Facebook. Computers & Education 55, 444–453 (2010)
McGill, T.J., Klobas, J.E.: A task-technology fit view of learning management system impact. Computers & Education 52, 496–508 (2009)
Ortega, M.C.: Las nuevas tecnologías como instrumentos innovadores de la educación a lo largo de la vida. Revista Española de Pedagogía [Spanish Journal of Pedagogy] 69(249) (May-August 2011)
Perez Tornero, J.M.: Teacher Training Curricula for Media and information literacy. Report of the International Expert Group Meeting. UNESCO House, París (2008)

Ricoy, M.C., Fernández, J.: Contribuciones y controversias que genera el uso de las Tic en la educación superior: un estudio de caso. Revista de Educación [Journal of Education] 360 (January-April 2013), doi:10-4438/1988-592X-RE-2011-360-125

Rigdon, E.E., Schumacker, R.E., Wothke, W.: A comparative review of interaction and nonlinear modeling. In: Schumacker, R.E., Marcoulides, G.A. (eds.) Interaction and Nonlinear Effects in Structural Equation Modeling, pp. 1–16. Lawrence Erlbaum, Mahwah (1998)

Ringle, C.M., Wende, S., Will, A.: SmartPLS 2.0 (Beta) [Computer Software] (2008), `http://www.smartpls.de/` (retrieved)

Rodríguez, R.M.: El imapacto de las tics en la transformacón de la enseñanza universitaria: repensar lso modelos de enseñanza y aprendizaje. Teoría de la Educación [Theory of Education] 11(1), 32–68 (2010)

Sánchez, M.J., Martín, F.A., Villarejo, A.F.: El modelo TAM y la enseñanza superior. Una investigación del efecto moderador del sexo. Revista Española de Pedagogía [Spanish Journal of Pedagogy] 238 (September-December 2007)

Swan, K.: Virtual interaction: Design factors affecting student satisfaction and perceived learning in asynchronous online courses. Distance Education 22(2), 306–332 (2001)

Teo, T.: Modelling technology acceptance in education: a study of pre-service teachers. Computers & Education 52(1), 302–312 (2009)

Terzis, V., Economides, A.A.: The acceptance and use of computer based assessment. Computers & Education 56, 1032–1044 (2011)

Toral, S.L., Barrero, F., Martínez-Torres, M.R.: Analysis of utility and use of web-based tool for digital signal processing teaching by means of a technological acceptance model. Computers & Education 49(4), 957–975 (2007)

Van Raaij, E.M., Schepers, J.J.L.: The acceptance and use of a virtual learning environment in China. Computers & Education 50(3), 838–852 (2008)

Venkatesh, V., Morris, M., Davis, G., Davis, F.: User acceptance of information technology: toward a unified view. MIS Quarterly 27(3), 425–478 (2003)

Wang, H.C., Chiu, Y.T.: Assessing e-learning 2.0 system success. Computers & Education 57, 1790–1800 (2011)

Wang, Y.S., Shih, Y.W.: Why do people use information kiosks? A validation of the United Theory of Acceptance and Use of Technology. Government Information Quarterly 26, 158–165 (2009)

Wang, Y.S., Wu, M.C., Wang, H.Y.: Investigating the determinants and age and gender differences in the acceptance of mobile learning. British Journal of Educational Technology 40(1), 92–118 (2009)

Zhan, Z., Xu, F., Ye, H.: Effects of an online Learning community on active and reflective learners' learning performance and attitudes in a face-to-face undergraduate course. Computers & Education 56, 961–968 (2011)

An Effective Tool to Support Teaching and Learning of Modular Programming

Fu Lee Wang, Reggie Kwan, and Kenneth Wong

Caritas Institute of Higher Education, Hong Kong SAR, China
{pwang,rkwan,kfwong}@cihe.edu.hk

Abstract. Computer programming is one fundamental skill to cover in a computer science program. A number of computer aided teaching/learning systems have been developed to support effective teaching and learning of computer programming. An electronic submission system, which allows students to submit, compile and test their computer programs, has been developed. Surprisingly, we find the system an effective tool to help students to learn modular programming. It addresses a number of issues in teaching and learning of computer programming. The system allows students to work on individual modules of a programming project at same time. Hence, the software can be developed much faster. It also helps students to develop teamwork skills. Moreover, the system helps students to develop a number of good practices in modular programming. Questionnaire survey and focus group study results show that the system has a number of advantages. The system is highly evaluated by the students.

Keywords: computer aided learning, electronic submission system, computer programming.

1 Introduction

Traditionally, computer programming is the first course that computer science major students study in the first year of their undergraduate studies. It is one of the most important fundamental skills required for study of computer science. As a lot of courses are developed based on the knowledge acquired in this course, the students cannot further their studies in this area without a solid training in computer programming.

Unfortunately, a computer programming course is usually bounded by a number of constraints, such as number of contact hours, deviation of working habits and asynchronous learning paces among students (Du Boulay, 1986; Sleeman, 1986; Wang & Wong, 2008). These constraints affect the effective teaching and learning of computer programming in a traditional computer programming course. Some students find it difficult to study computer programming and it becomes a barrier to their further studies of computer science.

A number of computer aided teaching/learning systems for computer programming were developed in the literature (Anderson & Skwarecki, 1986; Stoffa, 2003). These systems aim to help the students to learn computer programming language more effectively. Efforts have also been devoted in research of design of programming

K.C. Li et al. (Eds.): ICT 2012, CCIS 302, pp. 80–90, 2012.

exercises with computer aided teaching/learning systems (Wang & Wong, 2008). Related studies show that these systems have a positive influence to students' learning. However, a number of difficulties faced by the students have not yet been addressed. Educators are still searching for an effective model for teaching of computer programming.

Instead of developing a computer aided teaching/learning system, a different approach is adopted in this project. An electronic submission system for computer programming courses have been designed and implemented. The students submit their computer programs or modules to the system. The system will compile the programs or modules and then test the final program against test cases which were provided by the instructor previously.

A number of electronic submission systems were developed (Dawson-Howe, 1995; Luck & Joy, 1999; Macpherson, 1997). A typical electronic submission system provides a platform to collect assignments and programming exercises from students. More advanced electronic submission systems with automatic assessment feature were developed (Cheang, Kurnia, Lim, & Oon, 2003; Choy, Lam, Poon, Wang, Yu & Yuen, 2007). These systems provide instant feedback to the students to provide better learning experience. However, these assessment systems do not intend to help students to develop good programming practices or understand programming concepts.

The system proposed in this paper provides a collaborative programming environment to a team of students in addition to electronic submission with automatic assessment feature. Each team member focuses on one module of a large programming project. The center of our system is to help students to under the concept of modular programming and help them to develop good programming practices. Results of questionnaire survey and focus group interview show that the electronic submission system is an effective tool in teaching of modular programming.

The following parts of this paper are organized as follows. Section 2 will discuss some difficulties in teaching and learning of computer programming languages. Section 3 will describe the design of the electronic submission system. Section 4 will present the evaluation results of the system. Section 5 will give some concluding remarks.

2 Difficulties in Teaching and Learning of Computer Programming

Even though computer programming skill is very important in study of computer science, a lot of undergraduate students find it difficult to study computer programming. Selected instructors and students in computer programming courses have been interviewed. The section below illustrates a number of difficulties faced by the students.

In Hong Kong, an undergraduate course typically carries three credits. Usually, there are three hours of contacting time between the instructors and the students per week for a three-credit course. Excluding the two hours of lecture, only one hour is remained for laboratory session. Because the duration of laboratory session is relatively short, students usually work on short programming exercises in laboratory sessions. As a result of insufficient practices of large programming exercises, some students are incapable of developing large programs to solve complex problems.

Students usually work alone on short programming exercises by themselves. As a result, some students lack teamwork skills to work in a team project. They fail to work as a team effectively for a large project. This will greatly reduce their employability after their graduations. In recognition of this problem, we intentionally give large programming projects to students. Students are divided into teams. Each team works on a project. Each team member works on individual modules. At last, the modules are integrated together to create a program. Due to the time constraint in the laboratory sessions, students work on their projects after the contact hours. However, the arrangement of team projects is not satisfactory. A number of complaints have been received from the students about the team projects.

The most common complaint is that some team members do not fully test their modules. Sometimes, some functions have not yet been implemented in their modules. After the students passed their modules to other team members, their team members fail to integrate the modules together. Occasionally, some team members need to rewrite the modules for other team members in order to integrate their modules together.

Sometimes, the overall quality of a project is significantly affected by bad programming practices of one team member. For example, some team members prefer to use variables at application scope. It saves their time in developing their modules. However, it makes it difficult for other members to debug the program. In some extreme cases, some team members would change the codes in other team members' modules in order to accommodate their modules. It leads to conflicts among team members and also increases the difficulty level of maintenance.

Typically, the learning paces for a team of students are not perfectly synchronized. Usually, fast learners complete their modules very quickly. However, the slow learners need much longer time to develop their modules. Subsequently, the fast learners need to waste a lot of time to wait for the slow learners to develop their modules before they can do a complete testing of the program as a whole. In some cases, some fast learners simply exclude the slow learners from the project, so that their overall grades will not be affected. Exclusion of team members from the team indeed violates our original intention to give team project.

On the other hand, team members of one project team may have different working habits. They may prefer to work at different time and different locations. Sometimes, the team members fail to identify a common time slot to work on the project. The difference in their working habits makes them difficult to cooperate with each other in a team project.

Finally, the team members update their modules from time to time. Version control of modules is another major concern in team project. Sometimes, some team members may test their modules with old version of modules provided by their teammates, which lead to problem of incompatibility.

Because teaching and learning of computer programming faces a number of difficulties, it is not effective to teach computer programming in a traditional computer programming course.

3 Electronic Submission System

To support effective teaching and learning of computer programming language, a number of computer aided teaching/learning systems for computer programming have been developed (Anderson & Skwarecki, 1986; Stoffa, 2003). Related studies show that these systems help students to learn computer programming languages more effectively.

In our project, a different approach is adopted. An electronic submission system for computer programming courses has been designed. The students can submit, compile and test their programs/modules in the system. Fig. 1 illustrates the operation of the electronic submission system.

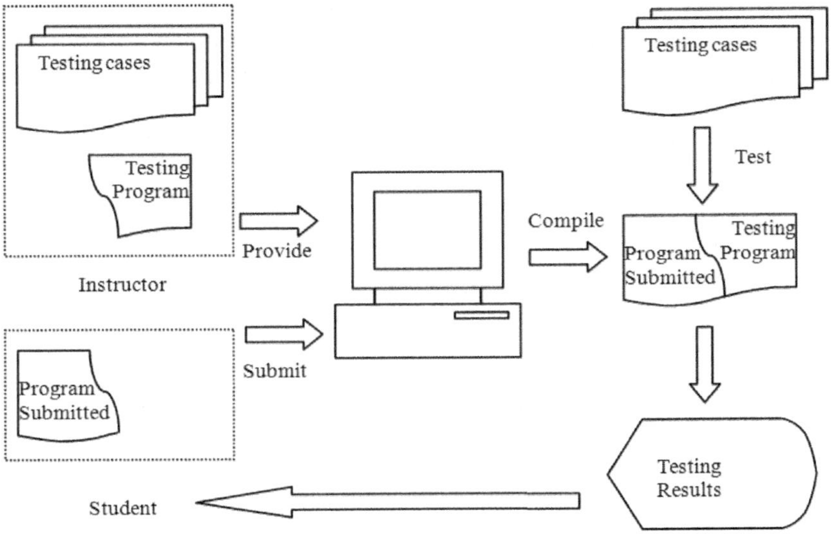

Fig. 1. Operation of the Electronic Submission System

The electronic submission system has a number of functions to support teaching and learning of computer programming. The basic functions of the system are listed below:

- The instructor can create programming exercises in the system.
- The instructor must provide a testing program for each programming exercise.
- The instructor must provide a set of test cases with inputs and corresponding outputs for each programming exercise.
- The students submit their computer programs to the system to solve one programming exercise.
- The system compiles the program submitted by the students together with the testing program provided by the instructor.

- The system uses the testing cases to test the correctness of the programs submitted by the students.
- The system shows the testing results to the students to provide instant feedbacks.

When the students go out to work in the workplace, they usually work in a team. In order to simulate the workplace environment that the students will face in the future, the system provides a collaborative working environment to the students to develop a large programming project.

The instructor first divides the students into teams to solve one programming exercise. Members in a team develop different modules of one computer program. The instructor assumes the roles as a program architect. He defines common interfaces between modules and provides specifications about each module. To facilitate an effective learning environment, the instructor provides a standard solution and driver program for each module.

The team members are assigned to work on individual modules. After a member develops his solution for one module, he/she will submit the module to the system to test with the driver program. Fig. 2 shows the submission screen of a team project. The student can choose to test his module with the driver program or with the modules submitted by his teammates.

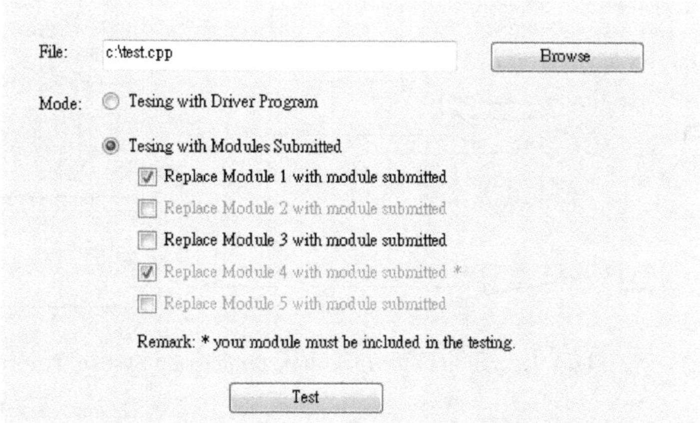

Fig. 2. Submission Screen for a Team Project

Fig. 3 illustrates the operation of the system for the team project shown in Fig. 2. As shown in the figures, there are five modules in the program. The student shown in the figure is currently working on Module 4 which must be included in the testing, hence the Module 4 provided by the Instructor is disabled (Fig. 3). Module 1 and Module 3 have been submitted by the student's teammates. However, Module 2 and Module 5 have not yet been submitted. For the modules which have already been submitted, the student can choose whether to include the modules in the testing. If a module is not included or not submitted, the system will automatically include the standard module provided by the instructor to give a complete solution. Then, the

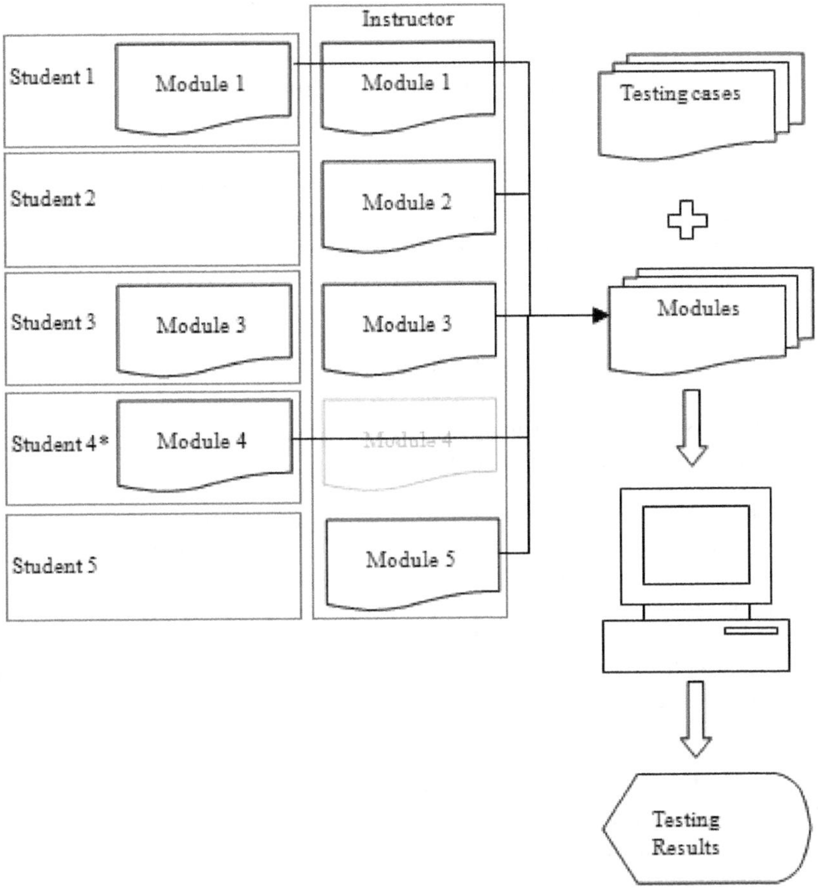

Fig. 3. Operation of the System for a Team Project

system compiles and tests the program with test cases in a similar way as individual programming exercise.

Our system provides a collaborative programming environment to a team of students. The team members are working on individual modules for a large project at same time. Because a set of standard modules are provided by the instructor, the progress of one member is not affected by other members.

The system also supports some more advanced features, for example, the system stores all modules submitted by the students in a library. The students can easily retrieve and reuse the modules stored in the libraries in the project which they are currently working on. The system also allows the students to share selected modules in their libraries with their classmates. The other teams can plug the modules shared by their classmates into their projects to test the functions provide by their classmates' modules. However, they are not allowed to read the source codes submitted by their classmates.

4 Evaluation and Discussion

The electronic submission system has been test run in an undergraduate computer programming course. The system is well accepted by the students. It helps students to understand the concept of modular programming. The system also addresses a number of issues in teaching and learning of computer programming. It helps students to develop a number of good practices in computer programming. Focus group interview and questionnaire survey have been conducted to evaluate the effectiveness of the system.

4.1 Difficulties Addressed by the System

The system has a lot of advantages. It addresses a number of issues found in a traditional computer programming course.

Large Programming Project. The most significant contribution of the system is that it supports the use of large programming projects. Traditionally, students work on short programming exercises because of time constraint of laboratory sessions. The system allows the instructor to divide a large program into several modules. In each laboratory session, the student work on one module only. Later on, the module will be integrated with other modules developed in other laboratory sessions or even with modules developed by their classmates to create a large project. This practice helps students to understand the modular approach in a large programming project.

Difference of Working Habits. With support of the system, a team of students are working together in a project. However, it is not necessary for the team of students to work together physically. The system will help them to link up their modules together. As a result, the collaboration among team members with different working habits will not be a serious problem. Nevertheless, students are encouraged to work together inside the computer laboratory to improve interpersonal communication and enhance their collaborations.

The system helps students to overcome geographical and time barriers. There is great potential for future extension of this system. For example, it can be used for courses which the students are spread over multiple campuses.

Asynchronous Learning Pace. As the instructor provides a set of standard modules in the system, the fast learners need not to wait for the modules developed by the slow learners before they can test the program. Some fast learners may be so keen to develop the entire solution. They can work individually for all modules. However, the slow learners can still work on their learning paces to develop their modules. This novel approach avoids potential conflict between teammates. The number of complaints received decreases significantly.

Version Control. The system keeps a record of the submission history of each module. When a student includes a modules submitted by his teammates, the system automatically retrieves the latest version of modules which have successfully passed the tests with driver programs and test cases. In other words, the system helps the team of students to manage version control of modules.

4.2 Good Practices of Computer Programming

On the other hand, the system helps students to develop a number of good practices in computer programming.

Understanding Requirement and Architecture. When the students receive a project description, they carefully study the specifications and requirements of modules. By studying these materials, students learn the system architecture of the project by implicit learning (Cleeremans, 1997). At the end of this course, the students acquire the skills to divide a complex program into small modules. Most students manage to give a good design of the functions of modules.

Modular Approach. The system forces students to focus on their modules. Students would have a very clear concept of modular programming approach. Students read the specifications of their modules carefully to ensure that they have implemented all functions. At the same time, the students examine the modular interfaces provided by the instructor and investigate how to pass data between modules by using the parameters specified by the instructor. This step helps students to reinforce the concept of data-passing between modules.

As all variables are declared locally within their modules, students are unable to use variables at application scope and modify the modules submitted by other team members. This greatly enhances the maintainability of their programs. On the other hand, students work on modules independently. It significantly speeds up the development of software. Moreover, the system helps students to understand reuse of modules in modular programming.

Software Testing. The system provides a good testing environment to students. After they develop their modules, they first test their modules with the driver programs and standard modules provided by the instructor. Then, the module is integrated with other modules submitted by the teammates to create a large project.

Before each module is submitted and stored in the system, it must undergo a serious proper testing step. The teammates can only access to the modules which have been properly tested. The procedure of serious testing strengthens students' attention to programming test.

4.3 Evaluation

A focus group interview has been conducted to get further information about the effectiveness of the system. A set of interview questions are designed by professionals in education development. The students enrolled in the course are interviewed by independent interviewers without presence of lecturer or personnel involved in system design. All students have positive evaluation with the system.

They believe that the system help them to develop good programming practices. Few responses from students are extracted as examples:

Student 1: *"The system is fantastic! It would be nice if we have similar system for other courses."*
Student 2: *"I don't need to wait until midnight to test the program. It is so good that I have some standard modules provided by Dr. X."*
Student 3: *"It is very useful to test each module separately before they are combined together."*
...

The preliminary results of the focus group interview show positive feedback from the students in this pilot. In order to get a more quantitative measurement for the system, a questionnaire survey has been conducted to get an evaluation of the system. The results are summarized as Table 1.

Table 1. Questionnaire Survey Results

No.	Item	Score
1	The system has a good use interface.	6.8
2	The system has a good response time.	9.1
3	The driver programs are useful.	8.4
4	The standard modules provided by instructor are useful.	9.2
5	The modules shared by classmates are useful.	8.1
6	The system helps me to have comprehensive testing of programs.	8.2
7	The system enhances my collaboration with my teammates.	8.1
8	The system helps me to control my learning pace.	6.5
9	The system fits my learning pace.	8.3
10	The system is useful to my study of computer programming.	8.5

The students in this survey give a score to each item on an integer scale from 0 to 10 inclusively, where a score of 10 indicates the highest satisfaction and a score of 0 indicates the lowest satisfaction. Around 100 students participate in the questionnaire survey. As shown in the table above, the system is highly evaluated by the students. Summing up the above, the system is an effective tool to teaching and learning of computer programming.

4.4 Post-course Observation

For the students involved in this project, their performances are traced in other programming related courses when they are promoted to senior years. Students have developed a good sense of modular programming approach in the course. They knew how to divide a large project into small modules in a top-down approach and develop the solution gradually in other courses.

The students' awareness of the importance of software testing is significantly enhanced. Even though it is not required in other courses, the students write simple driver programs to test their modules before they pass the modules to their teammates. On the other hand, the students keep libraries of modules which they have developed. As the student reuse the modules in the future projects, it speeds up the development cycle of programming projects.

Unlike other students in similar courses, students involved in this project seldom use variables in application scope. The collaboration among students in a team project is also enhanced. Those slow learners develop a module with fewer functions to their teammates for their initial testing purpose first. They continue to work on their modules before the modules are passed to teammates for final integration and testing.

5 Conclusion

This paper presents an electronic submission system which allows students to submit, compile and test their programs or programming modules. The system addresses a number of issues in teaching and learning of computer programming, such as, time constraints of laboratory sessions, difference in working habits, and asynchronous learning paces. The system provides a collaborative environment for a team of students to work on a large programming project. It helps students to develop concepts of modular programming. The system has been test run in an undergraduate programming course. The system is highly regarded by the students in this pilot. In conclusion, the preliminary results show the system is an effective tool in the learning of modular programming.

References

Anderson, J.R., Skwarecki, E.: The automated tutoring of introductory computer programming. Communications of the ACM 29(9), 842–849 (1986)

Cheang, B., Kurnia, A., Lim, A., Oon, W.C.: On automated grading of programming assignments in an academic institution. Computers & Education 41(2), 121–131 (2003)

Choy, M., Lam, S., Poon, C.K., Wang, F.L., Yu, Y.T., Yuen, L.: Design and Implementation of an Automated System for Assessment of Computer Programming Assignment. In: Leung, H., Li, F., Lau, R., Li, Q. (eds.) ICWL 2007. LNCS, vol. 4823, pp. 584–596. Springer, Heidelberg (2008)

Cleeremans, A.: Principles for implicit learning. In: Berry, D.C. (ed.) How Implicit is Implicit Learning?, pp. 196–234. Oxford University Press, Oxford (1997)

Dawson-Howe, K.M.: Automatic submission and administration of programming assignments. ACM SIGCSE Bulletin 27(4), 51–53 (1995)

Du Boulay, B.: Some difficulties of learning to program. Journal of Educational Computing Research 2(1), 283–299 (1986)

Luck, M., Joy, M.: A secure on-line submission system. Software - Practice and Experience 29(8), 721–740 (1999)

Macpherson, P.A.: A technique for student program submission on UNIX systems. ACM SIGCSE Bulletin 29(4), 54–56 (1997)

Sleeman, D.: The Challenges of teaching computer programming. Communication of the ACM 29(9), 840–841 (1986)

Stoffa, V.: Computer-aided learning of programming. In: Proceedings of the 4th International Conference on Computer Systems and Technologies: e-Learning, pp. 727–732. ACM, New York (2003)

Wang, F.L., Wong, T.-L.: Designing Programming Exercises with Computer Assisted Instruction. In: Fong, J., Kwan, R., Wang, F.L. (eds.) ICHL 2008. LNCS, vol. 5169, pp. 283–293. Springer, Heidelberg (2008)

A Mobile Application to Enhance Teaching and Learning in Classroom Environment

Sin-Chun Ng, Andrew Kwok-Fai Lui, and Dennis Siu-Fung Tsui

School of Science and Technology, The Open University of Hong Kong,
Hong Kong, SAR China
scng@ouhk.edu.hk

Abstract. Taking attendance in a large class is not accurate and efficient. The current attendance-taking approach uses up some unnecessary time in a lesson. The administrative work of the quizzes, marking and inputting results are of much heavier workload for lecturers and tutors. As a result, there arises the concern as to whether the efficiency and effectiveness of learning in classes would be affected. This paper presents a mobile application developed for a large class to enhance teaching and learning in a face-to-face environment. The mobile application includes two major tasks – real-time attendance taking and online quiz management. The paper makes use of the mobile phone technique to reduce the time spent on non-academic duties. It is intended to improve the efficiency and the effectiveness of face-to-face teaching in a classroom environment.

Keywords: mobile application, attendance taking, online quiz management.

1 Introduction

This paper introduces a mobile phone application for lecturers and students to be used in a large classroom. The application is intended to improve the efficiency and effectiveness of learning in a classroom environment. Attendance-taking in a large lecture class is often proved to be troublesome as the process is time-consuming and not practical. Tools could be developed which allow students to use their mobile device to signify their presences. There are two main parts of this mobile phone application, namely real-time attendance taking and online quiz management system.

Firstly, for the attendance recording, it has been initiated by the Nursing Department that the attendance of students is very important for the future career and development of prospective nurses. The attendance has to be reported to the Nursing Council for nurse registration. In order to make sure that students have really attended the classes, the lecturers have to take the attendance after each of the students proceeded to the in front of the class in order to allow the lecturers to take their attendance one after another. With a class size of more than 200 students, lecturers have to spend more than five minutes of each lecture to take the attendance register. The current attendance-taking approach used up some unnecessary time in a lesson. This issue can be solved by the mobile phone application which provides a fast and

K.C. Li et al. (Eds.): ICT 2012, CCIS 302, pp. 91–101, 2012.

accurate method for attendance taking. Students can take the attendance using their mobile phones directly.

Secondly, for the quiz management, a lecturer may conduct quizzes or surveys during the lesson in order to monitor the students' learning progress and provide interaction during the lessons. It is time-consuming to distribute and collect the quizzes (in hardcopy format) in a large class. It takes up much of the lecturers and tutors' time to mark the quizzes as well. After marking, the lecturers also have to input the quiz's results of the students in the spreadsheet or database as a record. The quizzes are mainly in the format of multiple choices. Therefore, some of the quizzes can be replaced by using a mobile phone application. The application provides a platform for the lecturers to set up the quizzes. Marking and recording of the results can be done automatically. Students can also check their quizzes' answer and grades with the display after the quizzes. Lecturers and tutors do not need to spend time on marking and inputting data. It helps greatly reduce the time spent on administrative work. This facilitates the general efficiency of teaching and learning. Also, lecturers can make use of the quiz system to conduct real-time surveys. Teachers can ask some questions during the lesson through this quiz system and the student can log-in and answer the questions simultaneously. The results will then be analyzed and sent back to the lecturers after a specified time. It enhances the interactions between teachers and students; hence the effectiveness of learning can be improved.

2 Attendance Record Management

Traditionally, there are two ways of attendance taking in a large class. One is by calling roll, and the other is by passing around sign-up sheets. However, they have their potential shortcomings as low efficiency and low accuracy (Forsyth, 2003; Green, 2007). A review about attendance management system by Shibata (2005) suggested that in order to prove the fact of the attendance in a class, students must present peculiar evidence that can be obtained only in the class. The author defined the evidence consists of three pieces, that is, i) person, ii) place and iii) time. That is to say, a student must be personally in the classroom during the class hours. Neither the method of using attendance cards nor roll-calling can guarantee the evidence of person, because, as denoted before, a student is able to act as somebody's proxy. A course management system does not always guarantee the evidence of person or place. If a student takes the risk to ask someone else to take up his/her own UserID, this person can act as the student's proxy. If students are allowed to gain access to a course management system from the outside of a class, the evidence of place cannot be guaranteed. Shibata suggested a method to solve the problems. All students should take a picture of the lecturer in class using their mobile phones and send the picture to the faculty through e-mail. After the class, the faculty receives the e-mail and then, checks the sender's identification and students' name, the date and time of message arrived and the contents of the picture. The sender's identification and student's name guarantee the evidence of the person. The date and time of message arrived guarantee the evidence of time. The contents of the picture guarantee the evidence of place and of time. To check the attendance more precisely, for example, to find out a transferred picture from somebody else, may check the date and time of the message sent, the size of the file of the picture, the date and time of the picture taken, the make of the mobile phone, and the model of the mobile phone. These data can be obtained by investigating the properties of the picture file.

However, this method is not quite feasible as it involves many extra administrative works. Although the author can guarantee the correctness that he has suggested, his method wastes a lot of human resources and time to do the administration works. Another approach is to use face recognition for attendance system (Swaty, 2009). Again, the matching process of face recognition may be too slow to record the attendance of a large class in real-time.

To cope with the above three pieces of evidence to show students' presence in class, i) person, ii) place and iii) time. Two technologies are used in the paper – the MAC address and the GPS technique of the mobile phone.

'MAC address' stands for 'Media Access Control address' is a unique code assigned to every piece of hardware that connects to the Internet. The MAC address will be unique to every device, even two devices of the same type. The MAC address is used by the Media Access Control of the Data Link Layer of TCP/IP or OSI model. It will be unique for every device connected to the network.

GPS technique stands for Global Positioning System (GPS). It is a global navigation satellite system deployed by the US Department of Defense and maintained by the US Air Force. GPS is a space based radio navigation system that provides accurate location and timing services to anyone with a GPS receiver. This service, made available to civilians in 1996 for navigation purposes, is free of charge, can support an unlimited number of users, and functions anywhere in the world. Most of today's smartphones are equipped with fully functional GPS receivers and supporting applications (Whipple, Arensman, & Boler, 2009).

3 Online Quiz Management

In a large class, it is also time consuming to distribute and collect the quizzes in paper. Lecturers need to spend a lot of time in distributing and collecting the papers to and from students. Grading the quizzes is also time-consuming. Recently, an online real-time quiz system was proposed by Okada, Tarumi, & Kambayashi (2000). The authors outlined the process of on-line quiz which process ideas to be used in the project. They suggested that for a teacher, the process of on-line quiz consists of the following three steps. The teacher does on-line quiz along these steps. The teacher prepares problems of online quiz based on his educational strategy, before class or at lecture. The teacher gives the quiz to students at appropriate points of the lecture. Students answer to this quiz. After the quiz, students' answers are gathered and marked. Results of on-line quiz are presented for the lecturer's easy reference. This makes the analysis and comparison of students' progress a simpler task. For students, the process of on-line quiz is convenient and quick. A student only has to take an on-line quiz and wait for the guidance from the lecturer. The on-line quiz function consists of the following four components– preparation of the problems, giving out the quiz, announcing the answers for each student, review and analysis of results. The quiz system comprises of these four components is suitable and applicable to the mobile learning applications. Our online quiz management system was developed based on these four components.

The mobile phone application provides a platform for lecturers to create the quiz. When the quiz begins, the questions will be released to students' mobile phones at the same time. When the students submitted the quiz, the answer will be sent to the server for marking. After that, the students can review their results and the model answer of the quiz. The lecturer can get back the statistics and review the student performance.

4 Methodology

The project was developed for iPhone Operating system (iOS) platform. The mobile application is developed on iOS platform. The reason for choosing iOS platform is that, every nursing student will be given an iPod Touch at the beginning of the semester.

The programming language for iOS is Objective-C. Besides that, the PHP hypertext pre-processor (PHP) is used in the project as a server-side programming language. It is a server side programming language that can create the dynamic websites. MySQL, a database management system is also used in this project. The server for the project is multi-threaded. When the lecturer and students open their application, there are two functions available for them to choose from. They are attendance taking and quiz system.

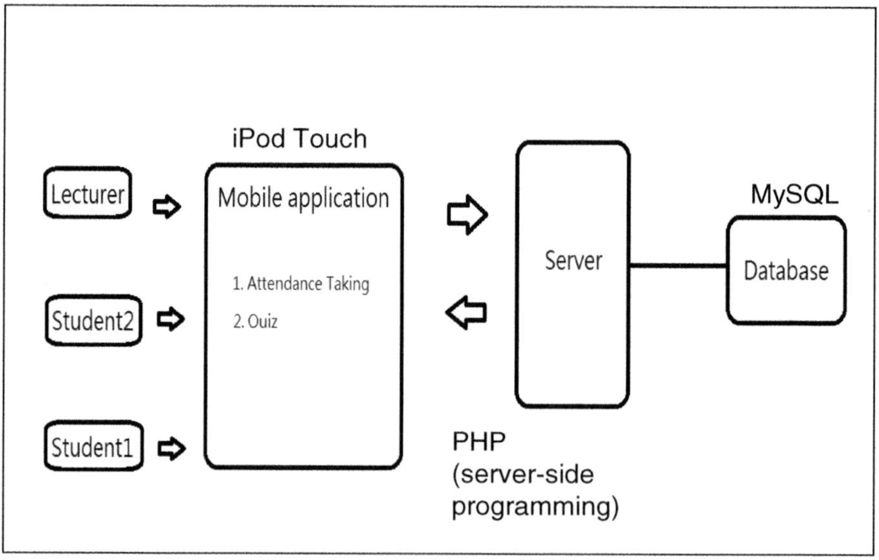

Fig. 1. Overall System Architecture of the Mobile Application

Fig. 1 shows the structure of the mobile application. The database stored all the data, which includes Student login ID, password, attendance record, quiz result, quiz questions and answer. The database is created by MySQL. And it is connected by a Multi-threaded server which is written with PHP server-side programming language.

When the students use the mobile application, the login screen will be displayed. A student has to enter his or her studentID and password to login the application. After that, a navigation bar is available in the menu. There are major functions such as, 'Attendance Taking System', 'Quiz System'.

For the attendance taking system, the students can make use of their iPod Touch to take attendance at the beginning of the lesson. The attendance will be recorded and sent to the database (MySQL). Students no longer have to approach the lecturer anymore. However, the identity confirmation will become another problem that has to be dealt with. Three validation approaches will be used to make sure a particular student has come to the lesson and take the attendance by himself or herself.

The first validation approach is 'Checking student's mobile phone MAC Address'. The MAC address will be unique to every device. The MAC address of each student's iPod touch will be recorded during the first time when they logged in. One student can only have one unique MAC address that is specific to his or her own iPod touch. If the students want to change their iPod touch, they have to report to the lecturer to renew the MAC address. When a student log in to the server to take the attendance, the server will check the MAC address to find out if it matches with the iPod touch or not. If not, then the attendance taking fails.

The second validation approach is 'Location checking'. With the use of the GPS of the students' iPod touch, it can confirm whether the students are within the campus or not. The GPS of the iPod touch connects to google map server, and the google map server sends the latitude and longitude back to the devices. If the latitude and longitude are within the range of the campus, it shows that the student is situated within the campus. If the location shows that the student is not within the campus, then the attendance taking will be failed.

Knowing that the student is inside the campus is not accurate enough, the third approach 'password validation' is used. At the beginning of each lesson, the lecturer's iPod Touch will receive a password from the server. The lecturer will key in the password to the desktop computer or projector or write it down on the whiteboard inside the lecture hall. Students have to enter this password in order to complete the attendance registration. If the MAC address, locations, password entered and the request time of the student are all valid, the attendance taking will be completed. These three approaches can ensure that the students have come to class and take their attendance by themselves. The lecturer can begin with the lesson right after he or she has announced the password to students.

For the quiz system, this mobile application provides a platform for lecturers to create the quiz. Lecturers can make use of the create-quiz-form of the application to set up the quiz. Lecturers can choose the information of the quiz, such as the date, time length, questions, marks, the answer of the multiple choices, etc. All data will be stored inside the database. Before doing the quiz, students have to login to the server which is the same technique as that of attendance taking to make sure the student has come to class and do the quiz by himself. When the quiz begins, the quiz questions from the server will be released to students' iPod Touch at the same time. When the quiz is over, all the answer from each student will be sent to the server for marking. The quiz result of the students will be stored to the database automatically. After that, the server will transfer some data back to students' device. Students will then receive their grades and the model answer of that quiz.

5 Results

Fig. 2 shows the structure of the application. There are two major functions in the application, namely 'Attendance Taking System' and 'Quiz System'.

Under the 'Attendance Taking System', there are two sub-functions. The first one is 'Attendance Taking'. It is for the student to take their attendance. The second sub-function is Attendance Record. Students can view their attendance record status of the whole semester. Besides that, there are 5 further sub-functions under the 'Quiz System'. They include 'Quiz', 'Quiz Result', 'Survey System', 'Create-Quiz-Form' and 'Quiz Settings'.

The first two functions are designed for students. Students can complete their quizzes during the class and they can view the respective results. 'Survey system' is for both lecturers and students. Lecturers can make a survey or raise questions during the class, after a specified time, the server will analyze the result, which will then be displayed for users' reference. The last two sub-functions allow lecturers to create quizzes and set out related information about the quizzes, such as the time of quiz commencement and the grade will be sent to the students.

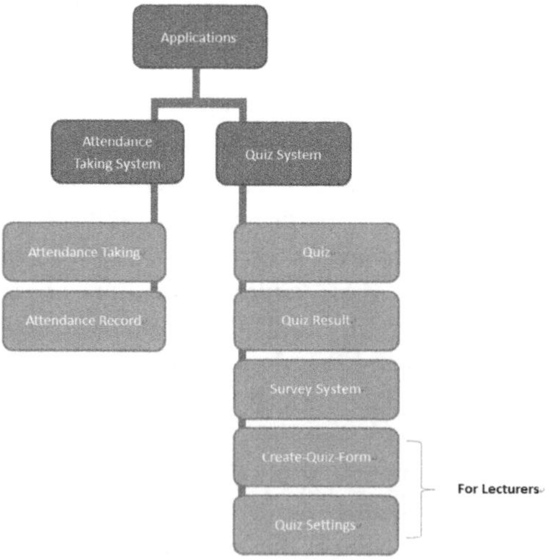

Fig. 2. System Functions

5.1 Login to the Mobile Application

When a user opens the applications, he/she will see a Login page (Fig. 3). User can input his/her student ID and password and press the login button. At the left bottom of the Login page, there is a shortcut which is linked to the website of OUHK.

Fig. 3. Login page of the mobile application

After logging in, a menu page will be displayed. There are two menu pages, one is for lecturers and the other is for students. On the students' menu, there are 5 functions. They are 'Attendance Settings', 'Attendance Record', 'Quiz System', 'Quiz Result' and 'Survey'. Lecturers' menu has two additional functions, 'Create Quiz' and 'Quiz Settings' (Fig. 4).

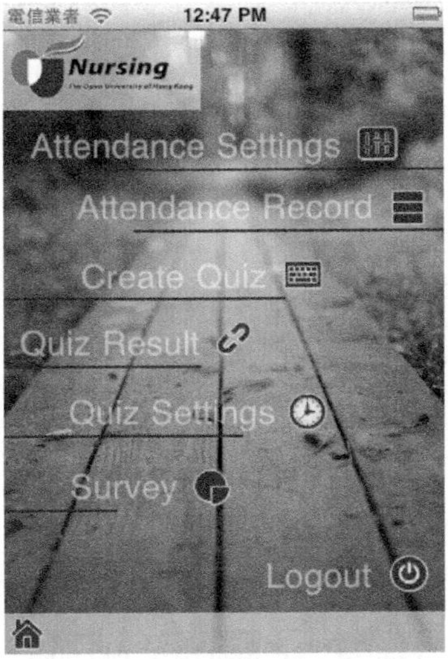

Fig. 4. Main Menu for Students

5.2 Real-Time Attendance Taking and Management

When a student clicks 'Attendance Taking', he/she will see his/her iPod touch's MAC address on the screen in the area of the first Validation approach. S/he has to locate his/her location using the GPS on the second approach. S/he then inputs the password and the course ID on the third approach (Fig. 5). After entering all the information, s/he clicks the 'submit' button to send the information to the server. If the MAC address, location, password and the request time are all valid, the attendance will be taken. Otherwise, the attendance-taking fails (Fig. 6).

Fig. 5. Screen for Attendance Taking

Fig. 6. Failed case for attendance taking

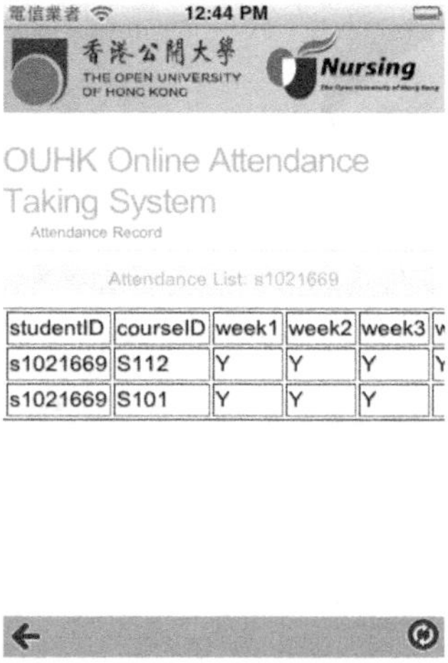

Fig. 7. View Record of Attendance

For the ‘Attendance Record’, students can view his or her attendance record of the whole semester (Fig. 7).

5.3 Online Quiz Management

For the ‘Quiz’ function, students can do the quiz during the lesson. When there was a quiz available at that time, the mobile device will be allowed to show the screen of the quiz as shown in Fig. 8. Questions will be shown at the bottom part and students can answer the question one by one and then click the submit button after finished. Since the quiz can be done in real-time, the lecturer does not need to pass the hardcopy quiz to the students and collect them afterwards.

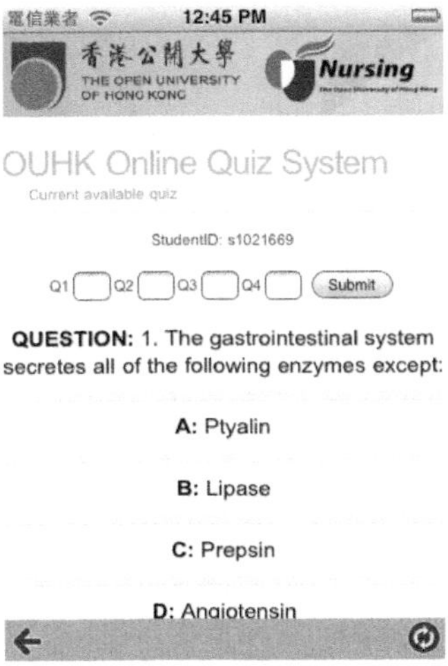

Fig. 8. Quiz system

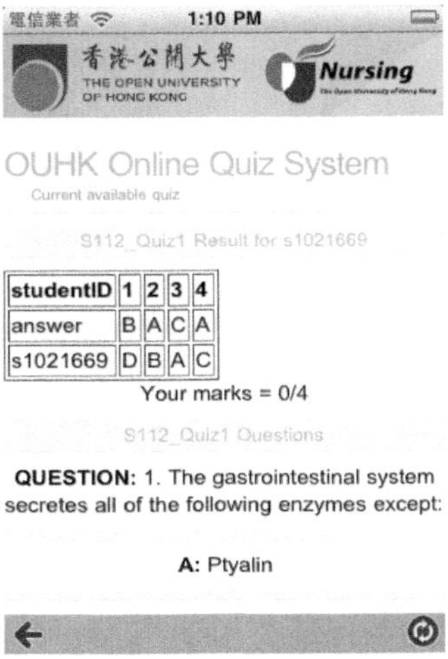

Fig. 9. Quiz Result

For the ‘Quiz Result’ function, once the lecturer released the Quiz result, students can view their marks and Quiz result that he/she has done before (Fig. 9).

For the ‘survey system’, the lecturer can ask a question in class and the students can answer the survey. The data will be analyzed in the server, after a certain period, the result will be shown on the screen (Fig. 10).

The Create-Quiz-form is used by the lecturers (Fig. 11). The lecturer can fill in the information about the quiz, such as the questions and multiple choice answer, marks, etc. The quiz XML file will be generated and uploaded to the server automatically. For the ‘Quiz settings’, it is also used by the lecturers. When a lecturer wants to start the quiz in the class, he/she can click the quiz-release-button to release the quiz to the students’ iPod touch. And also if the lecturer wants to release the marks and result to the students, he/she can click on the ‘result-release-button’.

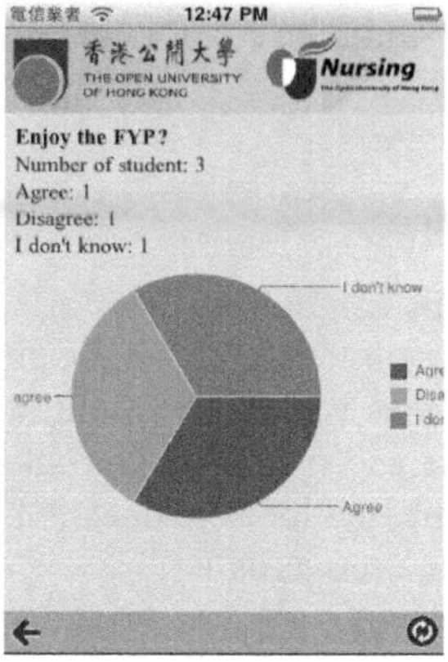

Fig. 10. Result of Survey

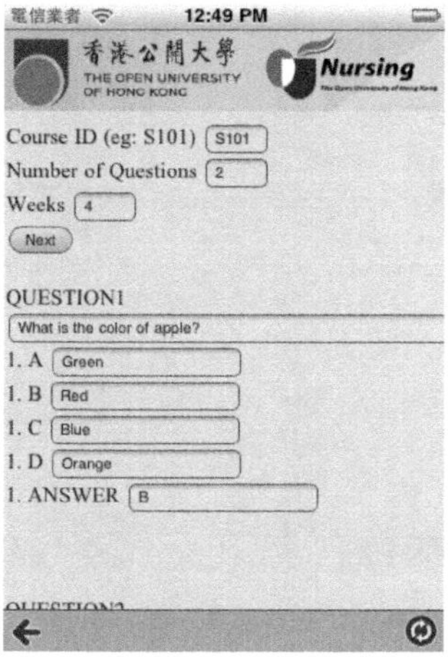

Fig. 11. Create-Quiz-Form

6 Conclusions

A mobile application for iOS platform has been successfully developed. The mobile application includes two major functions, namely real-time attendance taking and online quiz management systems, which help relieve the burdens on lecturers, and ultimately improve the teaching and learning in a face-to-face classroom environment. The system could capture the identity of the students accurately with a short period of time. It includes an identification process that reduces the possibility of fake identity. The system allows lecturers to upload questions to the database, distribute quizzes (or surveys) in multiple choices and collect quiz (or surveys) results on the web which could promote interactions in the class effectively and efficiently.

References

Forsyth, D.R.: The professor's guide to teaching: Psychological principles and practices. American Psychological Association, Washington, DC (2003)

Green, R.J.: On Taking Attendance. APS Observer (2007), http://www.psychologicalscience.org/observer/getArticle.cfm?id=2121 (retrieved April 14, 2012)

Shibata, H.: An Attendance Management System Using Mobile Phones. In: Proceedings of IEEE Pacific Rim Conference on Communications, Computers and Signal Processing, pp. 590–592 (August 2005)

Swaty, A.: Check the Compatibility of Face Recognition Time Attendance System with Organization's Requirements (2009), http://www.1888articles.com/check-the-compatibility-of-face-recognition-time-attendance-system-with-organization-s-requirements-098532.html (retrieved April 14, 2012)

Whipple, J., Arensman, W., Boler, M.S.: A Public Safety Application of GPS-Enabled Smartphones and the Android Operating System. In: Proceedings of the 2009 IEEE International Conference on Systems, Man, and Cybernetics, pp. 2059–2061. IEEE Press, Piscataway (2009)

Okada, A., Tarumi, H., Kambayashi, Y.: Real-Time Quiz Functions for Dynamic Group Guidance in Distance Learning Systems. In: Proceedings of the First International Conference on Web Information Systems Engineering, vol. 2, pp. 188–195 (June 2000)

Design and Development of Multi-subject Item Bank in an M-Learning System

Hui Ye, Zuyuan Wang, Qing Luo, and Yuanyuan Hu

Department of Physics, Tongji University, China
{11_yehui,zuyuanwang}@tongji.edu.cn

Abstract. As mobile technology changes day-by-day, learning through mobile phones is becoming fashionable and also proves to be feasible. Our research team is working on developing an m-learning system and has recently finished part of the development of a Short Messaging Service (SMS). This paper introduces the design and the development of another part of the m-learning system which is a multi-subject item bank. Bearing in mind the unavoidable weaknesses of the mobile phone, such as the limited capacity of the screen and the complex operations required of users, this research avoids some main shortcomings of the mobile phone and constructs an item bank with choice questions as the main method and combines with the advantages of multidisciplinary, detailed analysis, random sequencing options and mistake collection based on the Browser/Server(B/S) mode.

Keywords: m-learning, item bank, multi-subject, mistakes collection, B/S mode.

1 Introduction

When the first mobile learning project commenced around 2001, few people knew about the concept of mobile learning, let alone envisaging the potential of mobile devices for learning. However, in 10 short years mobile learning has developed greatly and is now being utilized in many large projects in schools, workplaces, museums, in both cities and rural areas around the world. The popularity of wireless communication and mobile technologies has provided the opportunity for learners to learn anywhere (Hwang, Tsai, & Yang, 2008). Studies have shown the evidence of the value of incorporating mobile devices in teaching and learning (McFarlane, Triggs, & Yee, 2009). A new learning style is rising rapidly all over the world.

With the rapid cost reduction of mobile phones, the mobile phone user group is becoming larger and larger. Based on the statistics of the Chinese Ministry of Industry and Information Technology, the number of mobile phone users in China has reached 975 million. The use of mobile phones for learning, however, is not common, and this is probably because the design and development of m-learning is still in its infancy. From the hardware perspective, the small screen and the complex operations required for some functions limit the development of m-learning. From the software

K.C. Li et al. (Eds.): ICT 2012, CCIS 302, pp. 102–112, 2012.

perspective, it is obvious that there are very few resources which are suitable for m-learning.

At present, there are many existing Web-based item banks. According to published papers, some item banks are used in online examinations (Guohong, Xiaodong, Yubin, & Guofang, 2012; Mengde & Rui, 2010), some are used for homework system (Zerr, 2007; Zhu & Wang, 2010), and some are for special purposes such as for the assessment of depression in persons with mental illnesses and physical diseases (Forkmann et al., 2009; Zerr, 2007). However, almost all of these existing item banks are catered for personal computers. Item banks designed for mobile phones are quite rare.

Its small and exquisite design is one of the main advantages of the mobile phone. However, its small size is also the main barrier for the development of m-learning resources, especially item banks. This study considers the main disadvantages of the mobile phone as it applies to m-learning, and constructs an item bank based on the B/S mode. And we choose multiple choice questions as the main method in this item bank to avoid requiring complex operations from learners – they can finish all the steps by simply selecting the radio button or the checkbox.

2 Design Concept

2.1 User Experience

User experience is one of the most important but easily ignored aspect indesign, especially educational products. Without the offer ofgood user experience, even the most powerful product will rapidly turn users away (van Schaik & Ling, 2008). The same is true for item banks. A website that participants feel is aesthetically pleasing may have a positive effect on trust (Karvonen, 2000), so for this reason, the color collocation of the pages was well considered. This frontpage of the item bank has title which stands out and avoids inclusion of inconvenient functions. The operation method in answering a question is also friendly to users as it requires only a tap and no laborious input. Users need not guess which button to press, because the navigation is straightforward.

2.2 Core Ideas

Value for Learners. Providing true value to learners should be the first aspect consideration of an education product. This item bank aims at helping learners consolidate the subject knowledge they have learned. And it can also help learners prepare for examinations. Using this system, learners will find their 'blind' area of the subject, and with the help of the collection o mistakes, the blind area will be cleared effectively. This bank allows learners to learn at the time of their choosing so learners learn more effectively.

Learners Willingness to Use. True value for learners is a main reason why learners are willing to use it. As well, this item bank is convenient to use as only one step – a tap on a button – is all that is needed to answer a question. We believe this will increase learners' willingness to use the item bank. We have also developed a user friendly function that allows learners to set a specific number of questions to work on for a session, which can meet the time available by specific learners' at any situation, for example, for learning at time periods such as queuing time for buses or lifts, commuting time and before sleep.

3 System Design

3.1 Database Design

This system includes a subject question database and a mistake collection database. The subjects question database is used for storing questions, classified by subject, and the mistake collection database is used for storing wrongly answered questions provided by users.

Table 1. The subjects question database

No.	Field name	Type	Note
1	Type	Varchar	Item type
2	Item	Varchar	Question
3	Option1	Varchar	Option 1
4	Option2	Varchar	Option 2
5	Option3	Varchar	Option 3
6	Option4	Varchar	Option 4
7	Answer	Varchar	Answer
8	Analysis	Varchar	Analysis
9	Chapter	Int	Chapter
10	Section	Int	Section

Table 2. The mistake collection database

No.	Field Name	Type	Note
1	Type	Varchar	Item type
2	Item	Varchar	Question
3	Option1	Varchar	Option 1
4	Option2	Varchar	Option 2
5	Option3	Varchar	Option 3
6	Option4	Varchar	Option 4
7	Answer	Varchar	Answer
8	Analysis	Varchar	Analysis
9	Chapter	Int	Chapter
10	Section	Int	Section
11	RightTimes	Int	Right done times

3.2 Question Group Generation Subsystem

The number of chapters of questions is X , and each chapter includes Y sections. The total number of selected questions N is set by the user. Then the system will generate C questions, which is the least common multiple number of N and X, from the relevant chapters or sections of the item bank picked by that user, and randomly selects C/N questions from each section. Then these selected questions are put into an array, from which N questions are randomly picked to make up the question group. (X, Y, N, C = 1, 2, 3, …)

3.3 The Mistake Collection Subsystem

After completing all the questions, learners can access the results, and add or delete the wrongly answered questions or questions which contain unclear concepts, to the mistake collection subsystem as they wish. This is explained in more detail in the methodology section.

4 Architecture

The background architecture of the item bank system can be seen in Fig. 1 while the foreground architecture is shown in Fig. 2.

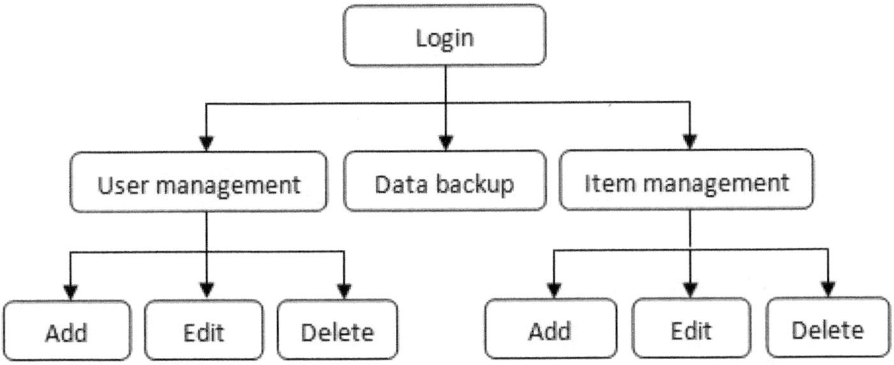

Fig. 1. The background architecture

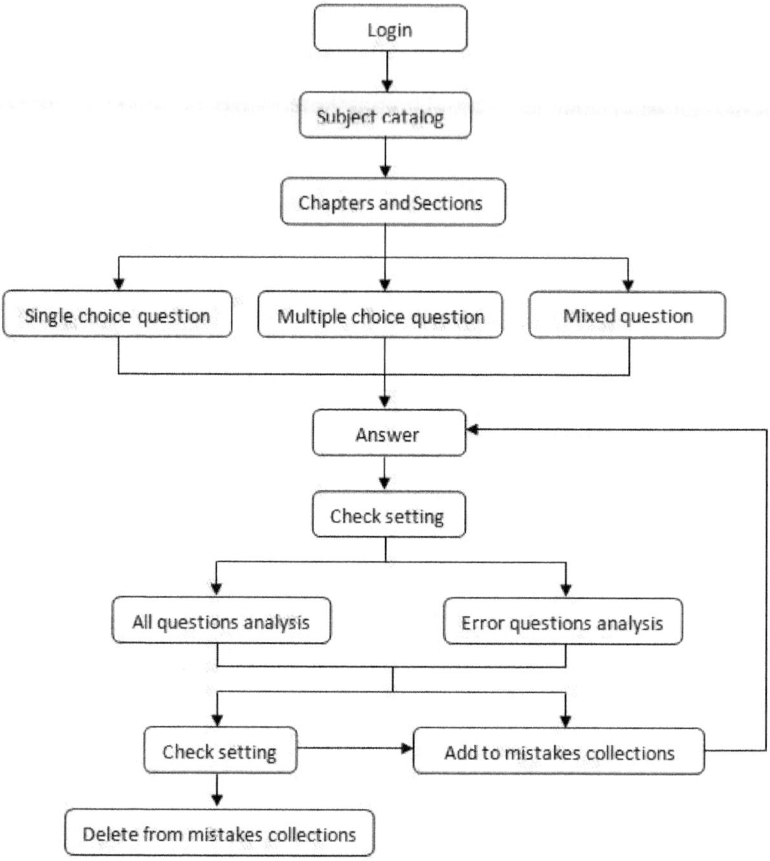

Fig. 2. The foreground architecture

5 Methodology

5.1 Techniques

The techniques used in the item bank include WAP2.0, Java EE, Mysql, Tomcat, Apache. WAP2.0 is the protocol used to create webpages. Compared with WAP1.0, WAP2.0 has many advantages such as supporting both WML and XHTML, and controlling the layout of pages by CSS. Java EE is used to create dynamic webpages and the support database. Mysql is used to build a database system for the item bank. Our m-learning system is based on the Web servers of Apache and Tomcat. The only work to construct the Web server for the item bank is to build a virtual directory.

5.2 Operation of the Item Bank

When a freshman uses the item bank for first time, his/her first step is to register, before login. As for registered users, the first step is to login. After logging in, it comes to the homepage, namely, the subject catalog page (Fig. 3). There is a **Setting** button at the top right corner of every page, and tapping it will open the setting page (Fig. 4). This item bank supports the selection of a specific number of questions for each group, setting the conditions of deleting questions from the mistake collection and displaying question analysis. Tapping **OK** after finishing choosing the setting will bring the user back to the previous page.

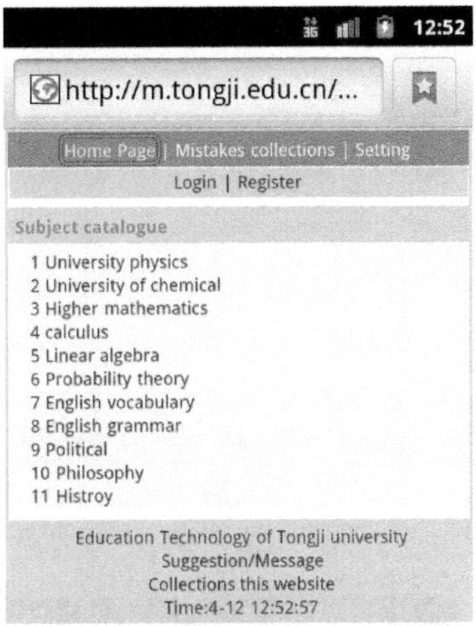

Fig. 3. Subject catalog

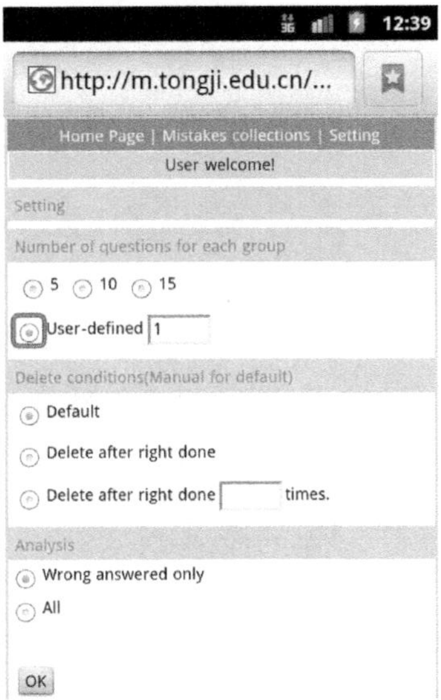

Fig. 4. Setting page

Learners can then select a subject and enter the chapters and sections catalog (Fig. 5). They can choose one of the question type, which includes single choice questions, multiple choice questions and mixed questions. Learners can choose any combination of chapters and sections. After that, they can tap on **OK** and start to answer.

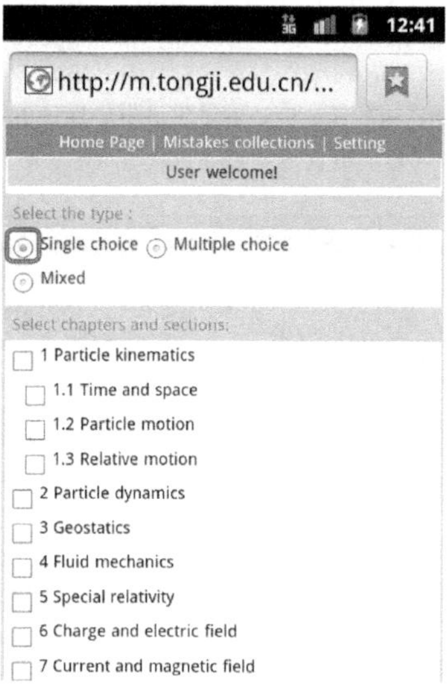

Fig. 5. Chapters and sections catalog

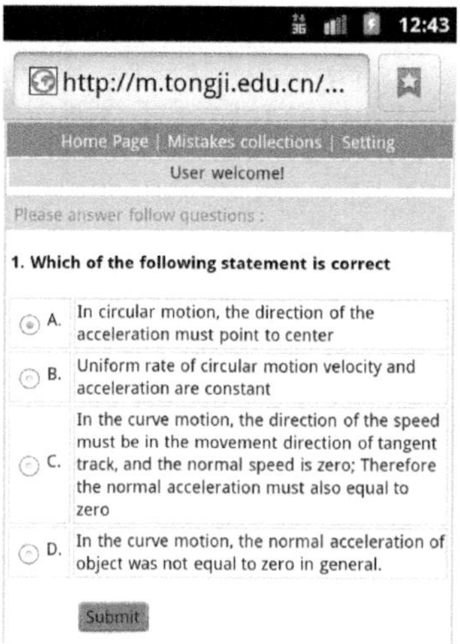

Fig. 6. Answer page

The questions displayed on the answer page are randomly chosen from the database of the selected chapters and sections, and the quantity of the questions depends on your selection (Fig. 6). For the single choice question, radio buttons are provided, while for the multiple choice question, there are checkboxes. All answer

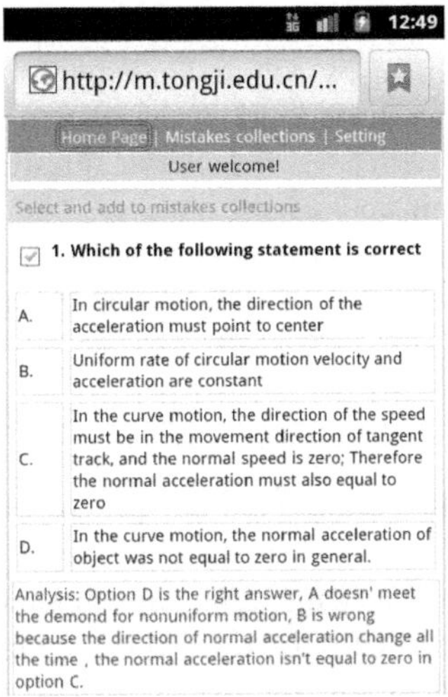

Fig. 7. Analysis page

steps will be carried out with taps, and no text input is necessary. After answering all the questions, students will tap **Submit** at the bottom of the page to finish.

Then the question analysis page (Fig. 7) will appear. This page displays the analysis of the error questions or all questions according to the settings (in red) below the questions. If learners cannot understand a question, they can select the checkbox before the title and tap **Submit** to add them to the mistake collection. The same question won't be added twice.

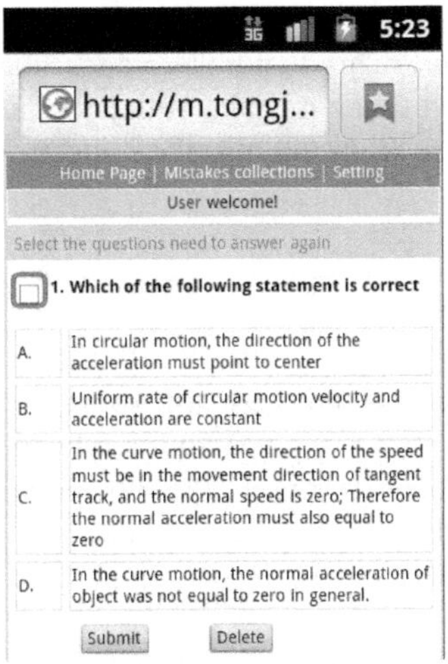

Fig. 8. Mistakes collections

Tap the **Mistakes collections** button on the top of every page to enter the mistake collection page which is named by subject and managed like a document. Choose a subject and tap to open it, to display all of the questions of this subject which have been added by the learner (Fig. 8). Select the questions which the user wants to answer again and tap **Submit** and start to answer. The system will judge whether or not to delete the correctly answered questions from the document based on the settings. The user can also directly manually delete the question.

6 Advantages

Some advantages of this item bank have been mentioned above. The following is a summary of all advantages.

Multi-subject. This feature makes the item bank suitable for more groups.

Choice question form. It is usually difficult to do complex work on a mobile phone, this system simplifies the operation and makes them pleasing to use for learners.

Free to set expected number of questions. It is usually at abnormal time periods when learners use mobile phones to study. Through this, learners can make full use of free time.

Random sequencing options. Questions put in fixed order require that learners remember which questions they have finished working on in an earlier sesssion. The random sequencing option solves this problem effectively.

Detailed analysis. Only excellent questions with excellent analysis can really help learners to consolidate the knowledge point.

Select and combine chapters and sections according to demands. This feature meets the demand for different purposes such as unit testing in which a learner usually selects one chapter or several sections or a final examination which the student should select all chapters.

Intelligent mistake collection. This feature provides that the questions that have not been mastered will be added to the mistake collection automatically or manually. The questions also can be deleted from the mistake collection in the same way after being correctly answered.

7 Existing Problems

The research is still in progress, and there still some problems that need to be solved. The following are some main problems encountered which will be solved later.

Content is not abundant enough. For now, there is only one subject — college physics — which contains an appreciable number of questions and is still increasing. Other subject questions will be added after the whole m-learning system has been finished and tested.

Browser base is not convenient to manage. Learners are required to input the link address to enter the item bank system and login to use it every time unless the browser cache still keeps it. The m-learning system will potentially be developed into application software in the future to solve this problem.

Lack of practice test evaluation. The testing of this item bank will start after further improvement. As a part of the m-learning system, the evaluation result will be given out together with other parts after the whole system has been finished.

8 Conclusion

Nowadays, in universities, almost all students have one or more than one mobile phone. Furthermore, the functions of mobile phones are more and more powerful. This provides a good environment for m-learning. Item banks are nearly a blank area in m-learning research at present. This study is a new attempt and it tries to provide a reference to follow-on research work in this area.

Even though the design of the item bank is simple, it is quite suitable for m-learning. This idea also can be used to construct other item banks such as the driving test item bank or the civil service exam item bank which use choice question as the main method.

This paper presents the design and development of the item bank of an m-learning system. While it also considers some disadvantages of the mobile phone; meanwhile, it also introduces many advantages of the item banks, such as multi-subject, random sequencing options and detail analysis. Currently, we have established the basic functions, and more functions need to be improved and added. With further improvement, we will step into the trial process. After finishing the whole m-learning system, a test evaluation report will be provided. In the near future, the m-learning system will be built as an application software.

References

Forkmann, T., Boecker, M., Norra, C., Eberle, N., Kircher, T., Schauerte, P., Mischke, K., Westhofen, M., Gauggel, S., Wirtz, M.: Development of an item bank for the assessment of depression in persons with mental illnesses and physical diseases using Rasch analysis. Rehabilitation Psychology 54(2), 186–197 (2009)

Guohong, L., Xiaodong, W., Yubin, Q., Guofang, L.: Design for Item Bank in Exam System Based on Network. In: Wu, Y. (ed.) Advanced Technology in Teaching - Proceedings of the 2009 3rd International Conference on Teaching and Computational Science (WTCS 2009). AISC, vol. 116, pp. 633–639. Springer, Heidelberg (2012)

Hwang, G.J., Tsai, C.C., Yang, S.J.H.: Criteria, strategies and research issues of context-aware ubiquitous learning. Educational Technology & Society 11(2), 81–91 (2008)

Karvonen, K.: The Beauty of Simplicity. In: Proceedings of the 2000 ACM Conference on Unviersal Usability, Arlington, Virginia, pp. 85–90 (2000)

McFarlane, A., Triggs, P., Yee, W.C.: Researching mobile learning: overview. British Educational Communications and Technology Agency, UK (September 2006-September 2008) (2009), `http://dera.ioe.ac.uk/1473/1/becta_2009_mobilelearning_summary.pdf` (retrieved)

Mengde, D., Rui, L.: Research on Web-Based Test Item Bank System. Paper presented at the 2010 International Conference on Management and Service Science, Wuhan, China (2010)

van Schaik, P., Ling, J.: Modelling user experience with web sites: Usability, hedonic value, beauty and goodness. Interacting with Computers 20(3), 419–432 (2008)
Zerr, R.: A quantitative and qualitative analysis of the effectiveness of online homework in first-semester calculus. Journal of Computers in Mathematics and Science Teaching 26(1), 55–73 (2007)
Zhu, W., Wang, Y.: The application and practice of a Web-based Instruction Support System for the undergraduates. Paper presented at the 2010 3rd IEEE International Conference on Computer Science and Information Technology, Chengdu, China (2010)

An e-Learning System for Piano Instruction

Ruiheng Sun, Ningsheng Ma, Yuening Zhang, Qing Luo, and Hui Ye

Department of Physics, Tongji University, China
2011srh@tongji.edu.cn

Abstract. This paper exhibits an e-learning system that combines hardware and software in order to build a platform for piano instruction. Firstly, we set the e-learning system in contrast with traditional teaching. Then we analyse the composition of the piano instruction system, and describe its construction and functions. Then we put forward a new measure for learning piano. Finally, we discuss the evaluation of the system based on learner's behavior and cognition to complete the system, and show the superiority in the teaching by e-learning system and the revolution for piano instruction.

Keywords: e-learning system, electronic music, distributed learning, piano instruction, interactive program.

1 Introduction

Computer technology brings new vitality to e-learning piano instruction. Recently, the rapid development of e-learning systems has used the benefits from computer technology, electronic music, and former high-end electronic musical instruments to bring the music into the classroom and even the family home. Compared to traditional analogue electronic musical instruments, many electronic technologies have matured, especially in sampling, digital encoding, and digital processing. The sounds are beautiful compared with traditional piano touch keys. The music produced is truly revolutionary.

1.1 Background

As a musical instrument, the piano appeared more than 300 years ago. Arranging time and space to learn how to play the piano has been a challenge that every piano player has faced. From the literature and the data that can be found, obviously the main form of teaching is one-on-one among professional and amateur piano players. This situation continued throughout the 20th century. Technology has developed at a dramatic speed. As a philosopher of the Western scientific community said "Just as the industrial revolution replaced the amount of physical labor, computer and electronic products are rapidly assuming much more mental work, and are expanding the capabilities of the human brain in a variety of ways."(He, 2010)

K.C. Li et al. (Eds.): ICT 2012, CCIS 302, pp. 113–121, 2012.

Along with computer technology changing rapidly, digital audio sampling based on electronic musical instruments and digital processing technology has developed optimistically. Piano instruction based on an e-learning system has quickly been implemented in music teaching and learning to show its unique advantages and powerful vitality in music education. This article proves the superior performance of the e-learning system in the piano instruction practice.

1.2 Contrast Traditional Piano Learning with the e-Learning System

The traditional one-on-one teaching has defects that can't be overcome. For example: As Neil Miller (2006) points out in elementary piano teaching room, teachers repeat the same content to different students. This results into low efficiency and a large waste of time and resources. The accommodation of students is limited. Due to there being only a teacher and a student it's difficult to build a lively classroom atmosphere. This environment can't make students experience the real performance feeling. If there is more than one student, each person's voice will interfere with the other's.

An e-learning system for piano instruction provides a new music teaching form. Composite by a number of electronic keyboard musical instruments, demonstration software, and piano teaching systems, these elements integrate video, listening, and practice as a whole. This system changes the traditional mode of teaching, enriches the teaching content, enhances the students' interest, reduces teaching strength, and improves the quality of teaching. According to Nancy Faber and Randall Faber (1994), the core of the system is a controlled audio communication channel which can solve the problems of interface with communication problems. It can specify who speaks or listens, and controls the listening content. On this basis, the system also develops a series of functions making piano collective teaching simpler, easier, and efficient. This e-learning system launches piano instruction from the traditional analog era into the digital era.

2 Composition of the e-Learning System

Our e-learning system contains two parts: *hardware* provides several surfaces to the server, and *software* provides piano demonstration and teaching management.

2.1 Hardware

The hardware of this e-learning system's composition is several pianos with VGA screens connected through the hub to a server system. The system includes all computer components, professional audio equipment, piano, keyboards, pedals, cables, chips, professional interface digital audio servers and a terminal (Ballora, 2003). These components are not inferior to the necessary components of a piano in quality. The most important point among them is that through a USB cable and independent developed chips, the piano and computer can be interactive. This makes full use of the infinite Internet capabilities. We use USB 2.0 as a surface, and can connect up to 48 access points. The maximum transmission speed is 160 Mbps, which can realize the transmission delay less than 1/1000 per second. The surface of terminal use RJ45, signal to noise ratio is greater than 80 db, so that the digital quality can reach the level of CD (Smith, 2003). The pianos are connected with a display via a VGA interface so that the players or learners are able to fully enjoy the convenience brought by the interactivity. Music can be displayed on the screen. Whether it is preloaded in the organ or from the USB memory stick, it can be displayed. You can always follow the screen music (Strange, 1995). Multiple pianos are connected to the server through a coaxial cable to access the teaching management system.

Fig. 1. Digital audio server and terminal

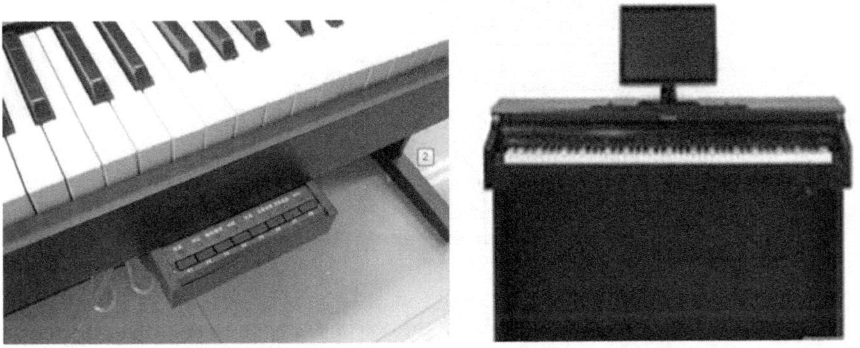

Fig. 2. Piano with terminal and VGA screen

2.2 Software for Demonstration

A demonstration system for piano technology content includes piano music and a piano technique demonstration. Piano demos can be completed by teachers or by computer software. As a result of the computer teaching software's applications, students can be exposed to a large number of different types and works of different styles. The number of demonstration teaching repertoire is substantially increasing (Akkoyunlu & Yılmazsoylu, 2008). As a result, the piano instruction is more vivid.

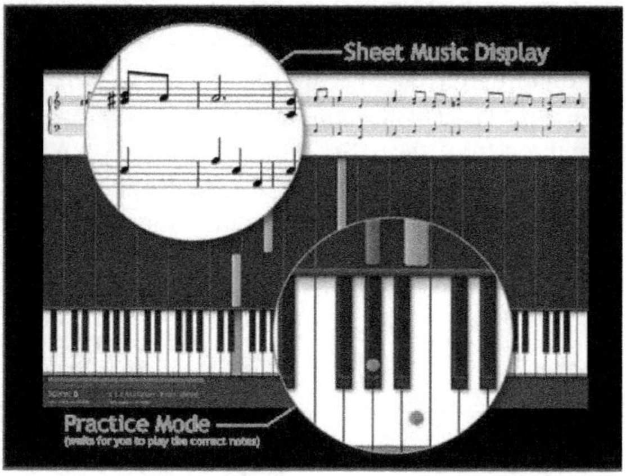

Fig. 3. Scoreboard of the demonstration program

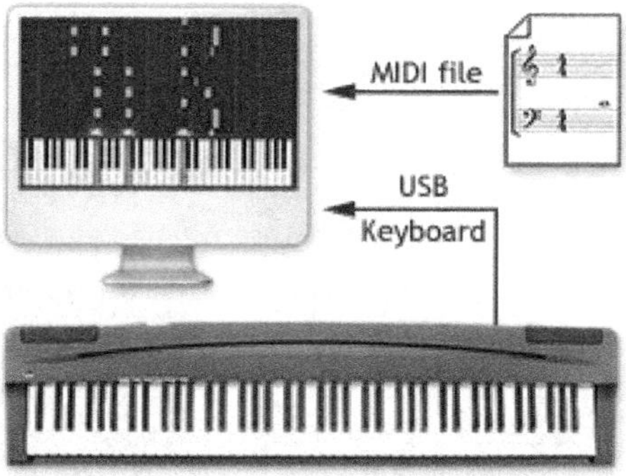

Fig. 4. Connection of the demonstration program

2.3 Software for Management

Instructing function: (1) Speech of e-learning teacher and teaching materials. When the switch is turned to the teaching state, the voice of the teacher's microphone will be sent to the class. The teacher can click Open in the dialog box on the panel of the player, select the file to play, and then click OK to open the audio file to play. (2) A single demonstration solo. Each student's seat is in the display area with the mouse cursor on the terminal. The teacher can let a student be in the demonstration and can click again to cancel the demonstration state. Any talking by the students in the demonstration state is sent to the whole class, and playing the keyboard is also transmitted to the whole class. When a teacher selects a student to demonstrate, the student plays the keyboard to the whole class who can watch on their screens. This becomes another method of demonstration teaching. (3) A demonstration ensemble. If the teacher wishes to choose an ensemble demonstration, the demonstration students can discuss with each other and answer the questions of the teacher and play together, the sound will be sent to the whole class. (4) Call. If a student presses the call button, the student's end call lights. The call icon will be displayed on the software interface, when the student presses the call button again, the student terminal calls the lamp, and the software interface on the call icon will disappear.

Self-study function: (1) Teachers' speech and teaching materials play. Teachers have no choice under the circumstances of any group, the teacher's speech is always transmitted to the whole class and sent to the class textbook play. When the teacher selects a group, the teacher's speech is only sent to this group, while the textbook play is sent only to this group of students. (2) Packet. A packet can be divided into a group of 1 2 1 4 1. A group of students can talk to each other. They can also hear each other play. To change the packet status a teacher can click on the grouping button. (3) Talk and listen. To simplify the operation, talk and listen are merged into one operation. When a teacher clicks on a grouping, the teacher can hear the speech of the grouping of students, and listen to the materials. The teacher does not speak during the monitoring function. If the teacher begins to speak, the content of the speech will be sent to the currently selected call group, this time for the call feature. (4) Issued textbooks. Teachers can send material to students to freely control practice. Tracks can be listened to repeatedly. Click the send materials button, select a textbook in the file dialog box that pops up the file, then click the OK button. At this time, students can use the F1–F6 keys to control the playback of the teaching materials.

Examination function: (1) Teachers' speech and teaching materials. In teaching status the content broadcast by the teachers' speech and teaching materials are sent to students in the class. (2) A separate call. Click on a student, the teacher and the student are in a separate call. (3) Exam recording. The teachers clicks the Start Recording button, and from this point onwards, the student's speech and keyboard playing will be recorded until the teacher clicks the stop recording button. The teacher clicks the Save Record button, the recording of all students will be saved to the student directory. (4) View the recording file. Click on the student icon in the upper right corner of the view button and a dialog box will pop up which displays all the audio files of the student. The teacher can listen to the contents of this file.

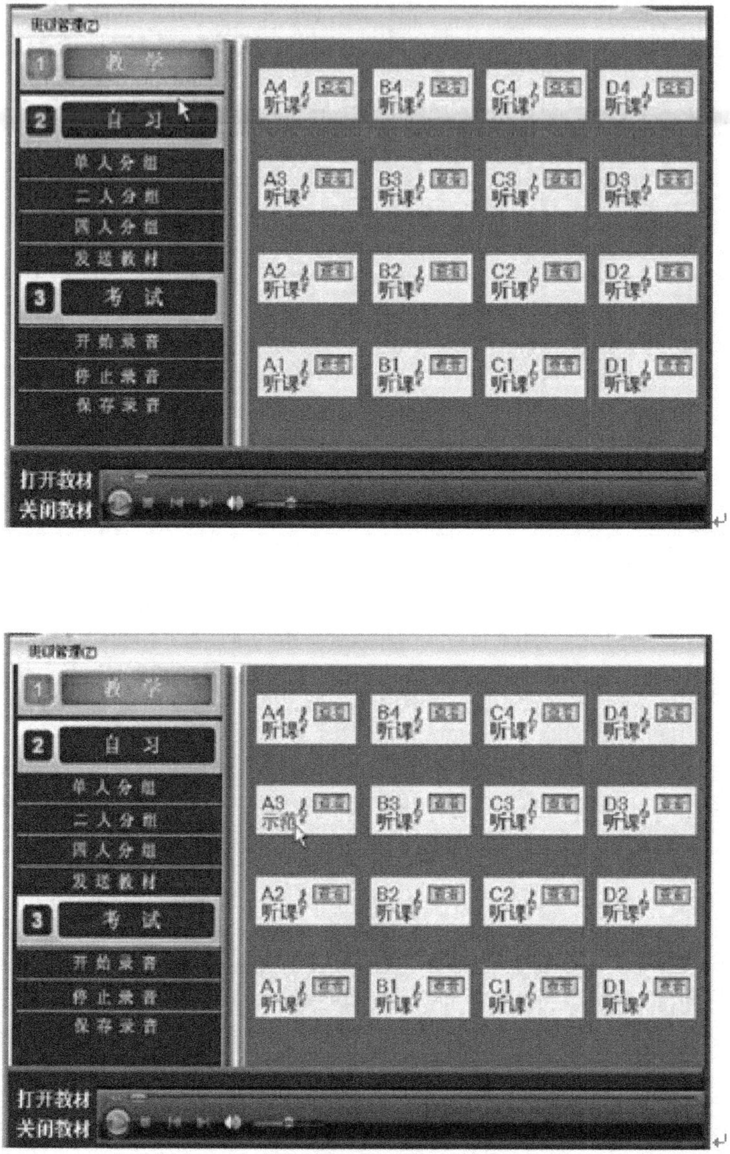

Fig. 5. The management panel of the system

3 Survey of the Teaching Effect

In the first part, we mentioned that we would show the advantages of the e-learning system. Here we will prove this according to a survey. We divided the learners into two parts: traditional artificial teaching and e-learning teaching. Both groups had 45 learning members. We recorded how much time they spent mastering a new song. The four songs are "One man's dream", "In the morning light", "The first snowflakes" and "Kiss the rain". Each group has practiced for three hours every day. This survey table takes the average time of all group members. The x-axis represents the number of days. The y-axis is the name of the tune. It is evident that e-learning system is more efficient than the traditional way.

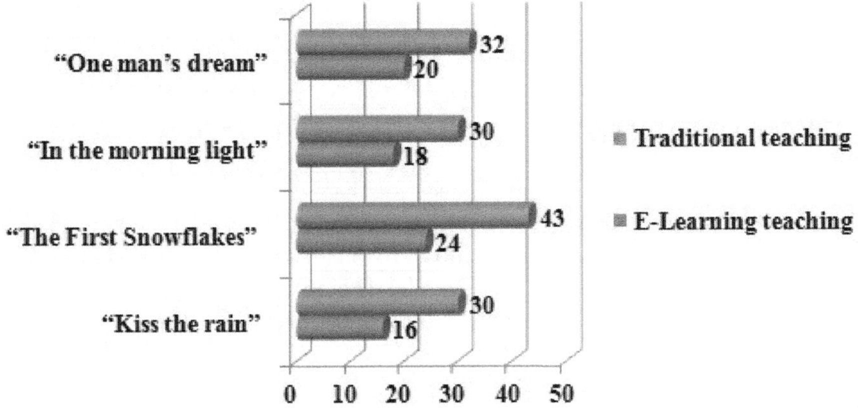

Fig. 6. The time of masting the same tunes under two ways

4 Improvements

An ideal e-learning system, in addition to a demonstration management system, includes the following parts (He, 2001): (1) A training system, mainly due to the electric piano equipment and connecting lines. (2) Audio system, select the appropriate configuration according to different requirements. (3) Remote controlled system of network equipment.

The demonstration system is responsible for the content of piano technology demonstration lectures. In addition to being personally played by teachers to complete the demonstrations of the piano, works can also use computer software to complete demonstrations. Due to the use of the computer presentation of educational software, to enable students to come into contact with a lot of different eras and different styles of work, the teaching track demonstration is substantially increased. Teaching scenarios are more vivid.

The management system provides effective communication between teachers and students. Teachers through computer-controlled video and audio equipment, a single observation and guidance for each student in real time, can also be guidance for all students. Communication between teachers and students can be separate, and can also be collective. In addition, students can also communicate with each other and encourage each other. Students in the classroom could either play solo or in ensemble.

In addition, you can also use many of the functions attached to the electric piano to practice such as the metronome function, transform sound functions, MIDI functions, recording functions, and so on.

The sound system can teach acoustics to achieve the perfect quality. Through the further processing of audio software, computing and transmission, students can improve their musical ear. It can also enable students to listen to and learn some different music which is a necessary foundation of knowledge. The course content can also be converted into computer files to be stored for student control or review use. Professional music training, the performance of the sound system plays a crucial role in the music teaching effectiveness.

The remote control system to connect to the network device is set for distance learning (Albano, 2008, p. 139–140). The use of computer networks, electronic pianos, and computer-based distance education has opened up a broad space for development. Through increased computer network transmission speed, distance education has made the electronic piano possible. Once all of the network has installed facilities, the electronic piano classroom, with students and teachers thousands of miles away from each other achieves the purpose of distance education.

5 Conclusion

In short, the electronic piano teaching system incorporates the full use of the computer and its outstanding achievements of electronic technology. Standing in the forefront of science and technology has played an unprecedented role in promoting the popularization and improvement of modern piano education. Electronic piano classroom software and hardware support, piano teaching form and content is more diverse, more colorful. We have reason to believe that as information and network technology continues to leap in the technological environment, the electronic piano teaching system will grow rapidly towards the direction of the network. An integrated region, the era of the province, country and even around the world, piano teaching resources will surely come.

References

Akkoyunlu, B., Yilmazsoylu, M.: Development of a scale on learners' views on blended learning and its implementation process. The Internet and Higher Education 11(1) (2008)

Albano, G., Ferrari, P.L.: Integrating technology and research in mathematics education: the case of e-learning. In: García Peñalvo, F.J. (ed.) Advances in E-Learning: Experiences and Methodologies, pp. 132–148. Information Science Reference (IGI Global), Hershey (2008)

Ballora, M.: Essentials of music technology. Prentice Hall, Upper Saddle River (2003)

He, K.: The functions of instruction system. Instructional Technology (2001)

He, L.: Modern computer industry revolution: Computer industry revolution and knowledge platform. Global Electronics China 11 (2007)

Strange, A.: Electronic music: System, Techniques, and Controls. W. C. Brown, Dubuque (1995)

Smith, J.O.: Mathematics of the discrete Fourier transform, with music and audio applications. W3K Publishing, Menlo Park (2003)

Faber, N., Faber, R.: The chromatic scale. In: Faber, N., Faber, R. (eds.) Piano Adventures: Theory Book, Faber Piano Adventures, US (1994)

Miller, N.: The piano lessons book: The piano student's guide for getting the most out of practicing. CreateSpace, US (2006)

Analysis of Experts' and Novices' Thinking Process in Program Debugging

Ching-Zon Yen[1], Ping-Huang Wu[2], and Ching-Fang Lin[3]

[1] Department of Mathematics and Information Education, National Taipei University of Education, Taiwan
yenk@tea.ntue.edu.tw
[2] Department of Electrical Engineering, Tungnan University, Taiwan
phwu@mail.tnu.edu.tw
[3] Department of Electronic Engineering, De Lin Institute of Technology, Taiwan
cflin112@yahoo.com.tw

Abstract. Program debugging is a complex cognitive process. Since it is an important step in programming, debug training not only improves learner's programming capacity, but also their problem solving capacity. For the purpose of this paper, three C language experts were invited; novices were represented by three third-year students. All six persons participated in a think-aloud experiment, where every person was given two programs to debug; each program was set up to contain three error types, i.e. syntax, semantic and logic.

The results showed that experts have a better grasp of feedback from the compiler. On the other hand, experts and novices have similar thinking process in syntax debugging. In semantic debugging, experts are able to comprehend the output results, but novices are rather confused; as to logic debugging, novices are less developed in logical structuring. This paper suggests student's debugging capacity must be reinforced in programming courses, particularly in semantic and logic debugging.

Keywords: C language, program debugging, think-aloud.

1 Introduction

The objective of programming is to facilitate the production of software that is appropriate, convenient and user-friendly for users to easily control the computer (Patterson, 2005). A conventional programming class is mostly lecture-based given by professors and accompanied by model demonstrations. This approach puts students in a passive learning mode deprived of active thinking. Since programming requires creative thinking, it is difficult to improve students' capacity and the learning outcome is often unsatisfactory. When students face new challenges, they are not equipped with solving capacity due to their deficiency in analysis, judgment, planning and decision making. With time, students will lose interest in programming and the teaching objective is deemed a failure.

Programming errors can be divided into three types, i.e. syntax, semantic, and logic. According to previous studies (Vessey, 1986; Carver & Risinger, 1987; Gilmore, 1991; Bisant & Groninger, 1993; Tsau, 1996; Bellows, 2005), syntax errors do not pose as bottlenecks in programming primarily because they can be corrected

K.C. Li et al. (Eds.): ICT 2012, CCIS 302, pp. 122–134, 2012.

by the compiler; a semantic bug cannot be found during compiling, so it is more difficult to be detected; the compiler cannot detect logic errors, but the program is still executed simply with incorrect output, making logic debugging the most difficult among all.

Program debugging is a complex cognitive process, and since it is an important step in programming (Gilmore, 1991; Mutschler, 2006), training will not only improve learner's programming capacity, but also their problem solving capacity. Bisant and Groninget (2003) suggest that debugging consists of two processes, i.e. comprehension process and fault location process. Xu (2006) believes that since program comprehension plays an important role in the development of programming, regardless of design or modification, programmers should start with program comprehension. Yoon and Garcia (1998) identified two debugging strategies that are recognized to help programmers debug with the use of tools. Uchida (2000), Ko & Myers (2003) propose that debugging is of the utmost importance in programming. Although the abovementioned studies have different takes on debugging, they all agree that the debugging process invariably help students better understand the error types and improve their programming capacity.

Owing to the booming advances in computing technology, computer skills are considered as an essential skill for college students. Software programming and hardware planning capacity are equally highlighted; therefore, the development in programming capacity is regarded as an important subject in the curriculum. The quality of programming relies on thinking, and think-aloud is a helpful method for gleaning into the thinking process. It is thus worthy to explore the think-aloud process and protocol analysis in programming to offer valuable insights into the curriculum design for programming courses.

A number of studies have shown that experts are more skilled than novices in the knowledge, competence and strategy for problem solving (Maria, 2007), yet the cause of this difference remains unclear. For educational purposes, if this difference is clarified, it would be possible to bridge the learning gap by devising teaching methods to quickly and efficiently help novices in learning. Think-aloud is able to elicit real behaviors of human, and is fitting for investigation into problem solving processes (Krutetskii, 1976; Newell & Simon, 1972), which can in turn shed light on the differences between experts and novices. When we perform problem solving, we are met with various situations that may require the repetition of problem solving cognitive activities, during which past knowledge and experiences are unquestionably utilized as the basis of problem structuring and problem solving.

The development of problem solving skills is an important subject nowadays, particularly in mechanical and electrical departments, thus a program debugging class acts as the perfect training for college students. In addition, there is much to be learned in this area, motivating this present study to further investigate this topic.

This paper attempts to study the three error types of programming, i.e. syntax, semantic and logic, by analyzing the think-aloud process to elucidate the differences in the debugging process and thinking process between experts and novices. We also aim to reveal the debug difficulty among the three types of errors by collecting data on the time spent on debugging, in a bid to offer suggestions for future improvement in programming teaching that would ultimately help professors better understand students' approach to programming and improve teaching methods for enhanced learning outcomes.

2 Literature Review

2.1 Implications of Debugging

Debugging is a series of process that involves seeking out the bugs in a program and correcting them. It is a complex cognitive process that requires not only familiarity of the program execution, but also a comprehensive understanding of the program structure, making it a challenging process in software engineering. Vessey (1983) and Gould (1975) conducted research into the cognitive aspects of debugging and characterized debugging as an iterative process of synthesizing, testing, and refining hypotheses about fault locations and repairs. Bisant and Groninget (1993) think that debugging is composed of two processes, i.e. comprehension and fault location. Various researchers (Carver & Klahr, 1986; Bisant & Groninger, 1993; Tsau, 1996; Xu, 2006; Mark, 2007) believe that the debugging process includes two steps —comprehension and correction —but it is not uncommon for debuggers to skip the comprehension step and go directly to correction whenever an error message appears. Xu (2006) thinks that comprehension plays an important role, no matter whether it is about program design or correction, hence the foremost fundamental for programmers is comprehension. Many studies have investigated program comprehension (Brooks, 1983; Letovsky, 1986; Letovsky & Soloway, 1986; Gill, 2007) and models have been proposed, e.g. "top-down" theory, where the programmer first accepts a hypothesis and tests it, and step-by-step check every sub-hypothesis. Yoon and Garcia (1998) proposed debugging tools to help programmers in error detection. Two strategies are identified —i.e. comprehension strategy and isolation strategy, where the former aims to search for the difference between the actual execution and anticipated outcomes, and the latter makes use of the programmer's hypotheses about the bugs which are employed to search for bug locations in the program. According to Katz and Anderson (1998), debugging strategy differs depending on whether the code is self-written or written by others. He points out that debugging self-written code can be performed through a simple flowchart and critical cognitive activity, as familiarity of the code allows a backward reasoning approach; on the contrary, when debugging unfamiliar program structures and algorithms written by others, a forward reasoning approach is more often chosen.

Regarding debugging speed, many reports show that experts are able to correct more errors than novices and locate the bug faster (Youngs, 1974; Wiedenbeck, 1985; Nanja & Cook, 1987; Goering, 2006; Lammers, 2006). As for the thinking process in program debugging, Tsau (1996) points out that there exist differences between syntax, semantic and logic error types.

Uchida (2000) suggests three steps to program debugging: program reading, bug location and bug correction. Ko and Myers (2003) suggest that most bugs are the results of problems arising from programmer's focus, language structure, algorithm and use of the function library.

2.2 Program Error Types

Program error types can be divided into syntax bugs, semantic bugs and logic bugs. Syntax errors do not pose as a bottleneck in programming primarily because they can be corrected by the compiler. Semantic bugs cannot be found during compiling, so they are more difficult detect. The compiler cannot detect logic errors, while the program is still being executed but with incorrect output, so logic debugging is the most difficult.

For a novice programmer, it is important to find the bugs and correct them. Miller (1974) found that a novice spends 1.58 times more time debugging than on actually writing the program. Allwood and Bjarhag (1990) also showed that debugging work takes up half of the time in the entire programming process.

Essentially, programming is a series of problem solving activities, a creative thinking process. Debugging, an intricate cognitive process, is an important and highly challenging step in programming, and merits adequate training to improve learner's programming concepts and structuring capacity for augmented learning outcomes.

2.3 Related Studies

Since debugging capacity is crucial to any programmer, Tsau (1996) examined students' debugging capacity from four aspects: knowledge, process, skill and strategy, where 18 students took part in a think-aloud experiment for Quick Basic language diagnosis. Of them, six second-year students were considered as novices, six fourth-year students as intermediates and six lecturers as experts. A total of ninebugs were set up in the program; three syntax, three semantic and three logic errors. Video recordings and protocol analysis showed that (1) during the debugging process, students are not stuck in syntax and semantic errors; (2) students have difficulties finding logic errors; (3) there is no significant difference in the students' debugging process for the three types of errors; (4) students are unable to understand the message from the QB interpreter; (5) students do not have the necessary skills to debug logic errors; and (6) students' debugging strategies are limited and inflexible.

In an investigation into programming strategy, Rezel (2003) divided students learning VB language into two groups for an experiment. The training group (N = 19) were trained in targeted self-explanation strategy, whereas the control group (N = 20) were asked to perform think-aloud without training of other learning strategies. All the students received three tasks that involved programming and coding. The result showed that there is no significant difference between the two groups in terms of completing the program. The success in completion is mainly attributed to prior programming experience. Protocol analysis from recordings showed that the successful students tend to adopt more strategies than their counterparts.

Ruthruff and colleagues (2005) examined program debugging from the think-aloud approach, where the programmer's debug skills are improved by means of interactions among programmers.

Studying the cognitive process of software engineering is conducive to understanding the software and making improvements. Xu (2006) developed a dialog-based protocol and self-directed learning theories to better understand the cognitive activities of programmers in software engineering. Dialog-based protocol is based on paired programmers working together in a think-aloud process. Self-directed learning theory is based on the constructivist learning theory and Bloom's Taxonomy. Singh (2006) also used think-aloud protocols in an Electromagnetics class, having students explain their understanding on symmetry, electric field and electric flux and the learning difficulties on these specific topics. The results, targeted at upperclassmen and graduate students, showed that students have significant learning difficulty in these areas.

3 Research Methods

3.1 The Experiment

First, three C language experts were invited; two university professors and another professor at an institute of technology, all of whom have taught C language. The novices consisted of three third year students who have studied C language. All six people participated in a think-aloud experiment. Before the experiment, they received think-aloud training. Every participant was given two debugging tests. During the think-aloud process, they were asked to express their thoughts verbally, while the researchers were involved into the process in the form of clinical interview. The think-aloud process was audio and video recorded. After the experiment, the recorded data were transcribed and used for protocol analysis. The researchers analyzed the protocols and discussed the questionable parts with the participants to clarify the content for insights into their debugging process.

Secondly, the researchers examined the time taken for debugging syntax, semantic and logic errors, respectively. A total of 15 third-year students participated in this experiment, where the debugging tests are the same as the previous experiment.

In addition to audio and video recording, Anicam, a computer-screen recording software favorable to data collection in think-aloud, was also used in this experiment. A program debugging test paper, debugging behavior categorization and think-aloud guidelines were compiled as follows.

3.2 C Language Debugging Program

For data collection, the researchers selected two programs for the debug test, one of which is the multiplication table and the other is the Fibonacci sequence. Each program consisted of three bugs (one synthetic error, one semantic error and one logical error), at a total of six problems to be tackled, as presented in Figure 1.

3.3 Debugging Behaviors

To study the debugging thinking process, several coding classifications were referenced (Vessey, 1986; Carver & Risinger, 1987; Gilmore, 1991; Bisant &

Groninger, 1993; Tsau, 1996). According to the characteristic of the programming language, related debugging theories, reasoning approaches and possible debugging behaviors, a categorized debugging behavior list was drafted. After discussions with other professors, conjecture and confirmation were added to make the finalized list as follows.

1 Understanding: understanding the meaning of the task, the meaning of the program, and the output results
2 Questioning: calling the bugs into question
3 Conjecture: guessing the correct program and the execution result
4 Execution: executing the compiler, the program, and step
5 Observation: observing the content of the program, error message, and the output results
6 Correction: adding program, inserting program, deleting program, and correcting program
7 Confirmation: describing the cause of error and correct coding

```
/******************
program 1
Multiplication table
******************/

# include <stdio.h>
# include <stdlib.h>

void main (void)
{
 int i, j;
 for (i=1; i <= 9; i++)
 {
  for (j =1; j <= 9 ; j ++)
 printf (" %d * %d = %d \
     t", i , j , i*j );
  printf( " \ n " );
```

```
/******************
program 2
Fibonacci sequence

******************/
# include <stdio.h>
# include <stdlib.h>

int Fib (int n) ;

/****  Fib ( )  ****/
int Fib ( int n )
{
  int n1=0 , n2=0 , sum=1 , i ;

if ((n==1)  ||  (n==0))
    return  n;
else
{
  for (i=2 ; i <=n ; i ++)
{
   n1=sum;
   sum=sum+n2;
   n2=n1;
  }
```

Fig. 1. C language debugging program

```
17   }
18  /* system ("pause"); */
19  }
```

```
26      return sum;
27    }
28  }
29
30  /****main ( ) ****/
31  void main (void)
32  {
33    int i ;
34
35  printf ("Fibonacci sequence:");
36  for (i=0 ; i <=25 ; i++)
37  {
38      if (i%8==0)
39         printf ("\n");
40       printf ("%d\t", Fib(i));
41  }
42  printf ("......\n");
43  /*   system ("pause");    */
44  }
```

Fig. 1. (*continued*)

3.4 Research Procedure

The steps are presented as follows:

1 Mapping out the research plan
2 Literature review
3 Setting up C language bugs, as follows:

Question 1：syntax error	%d changed to d	(line 15, program 1)
Question 2：syntax error	n==0 changed to m==0	(line 16, program 2)
Question 3：semantic error	i=1 changed to i=0	(line 12, program 1)
Question 4：semantic error	n2=n1 changed to n1=n2	(line 24, program 2)
Question 5：logic error	printf("\n") in line 16 moved to before line 15 (program 1)	
Question 6：logic error	else in line 18 moved to after line 20 (program 2)	

4 Categorization of debugging behaviors
This study adopted the coding classification framework put forward by Tsau (1996) in program debugging behavior and method analysis. The researchers, with their C language knowledge, invited other professors of C language expertise, to jointly formulate a C language program debugging behavior classification list, including 7 dimensions, i.e. understanding, questioning, conjecture, execution, observation, correction and confirmation.

5 Expert consultation and evaluation
6 Selection of the participants
7 Editing the think-aloud guidelines
8 Think-aloud experiment and audio/video recordings
During the think-aloud process, Anicam was utilized to capture screen images, while the participants were videotaped. Afterwards, the researchers transcribed the data for protocol analysis. Anicam was configured to activate the zip utilities to compress the recorded files into different image formats that served as the basis for the protocol analysis.
9 Protocol analysis
C language was chosen as the programming language used in this study, while the debugging involved syntax errors, semantic errors and logic errors. The think-aloud process required the participants to verbally express their thoughts and were recorded by Anicam, and complemented by clinical interview by the researchers. The participating professors were coded as T_1, T_2, and T_3; and the students coded as S_1, S_2, and S_3.
10 Data compilation

4 Research Findings and Discussion

Based on the experiment data and the protocol analysis, the findings are presented as follows.

4.1 Analysis of Program Debugging Time for Experts and Novices

Seven dimensions of C language debugging behaviors are defined in this paper: understanding, questioning, conjecture, execution, observation, correction, and confirmation.

Several findings can be observed from the frequency analysis of debugging behavior in Figure 2. First, the frequency of observation and confirmation was found to be higher among experts than novices. Further analysis showed that experts had more observations of syntax error compared to novices, where experts were also found to be more capable of describing the reasons behind the errors in the confirmation and offering the correct command. Second, novices exhibited a higher frequency of questioning than experts. Third, in terms of strategies, conjecture was more often adopted by novices, where they opted for trial and error as their problem solving approach when encountered with bottlenecks; in contrast, experts made more use of algorithms, demonstrating they were more familiar with the program structure principles, e.g. definition of program variables or command syntax. Fourth, there was no significant difference regarding the understanding, execution, and correction behaviors between experts and novices.

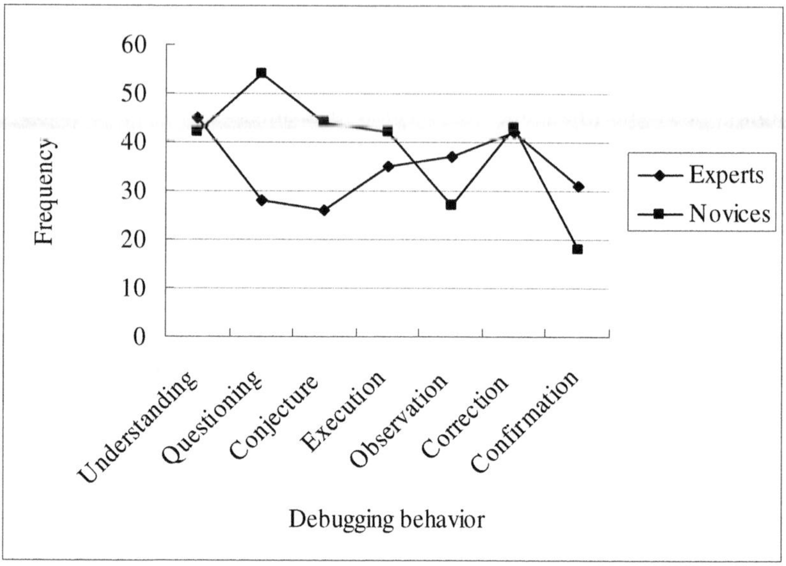

Fig. 2. The frequency analysis of debugging behavior

4.2 Analysis of Program Debugging Thinking Process in Experts and Novices

According to the protocol analysis, experts are quicker in semantic and logic debugging than novices. In terms of completion rate, experts are also more adept in semantic and logic debugging. The differences on syntax, semantic and logic debugging between experts and novices are as follows.

In the debug process, experts are able to quickly decipher the error messages from the compiler, regardless of error types. In contrast, novices are only capable of grasping syntax errors from the compiling result, and are at a loss when it comes to semantic and logic errors. Hence, novices take more time in debugging semantic and logic errors, and are often making conjectures as they are uncertain of the right steps to take for debugging.

Experts and novices have nearly identical thinking processes in syntax debugging. In semantic debugging, experts are able to comprehend the output results, while novices are perplexed. In logic debugging, novices are less developed in the logical structuring needed for programming. Experts mostly adopt forward reasoning method as their debugging strategy and novices opt for the backward reasoning method, attempting to solve the problem from the outcomes. Findings by Katz & Anderson (1988) and Larkin (Larkin, 1980) corroborated with our results.

4.3 Analysis of Student's C Language Debugging Time

To observe the time taken for syntax, semantic and logic error detection, 15 third-year students participated in the debugging experiment.

Table 1 shows that students spend more time in logic debugging than in semantic or syntax debugging. From table 2, the variance analysis of the three error types indicated that there is a significant difference between the three types ($F=92.64$, $p < 0.05$). In other words, time spent by students on debugging the three types of error was significantly different, prompting us to examine it further.

Table 3 illustrates the mean difference of debug time between syntax and logic error is significantly different (MD (I – J) = –651.242; $p < 0.05$); and also significantly different between semantic and logic error (MD (I – J) = –423.000; $p<0.05$). In contrast, the mean difference of debug time between syntax and semantic error is not significant (MD (I – J) = –197.507; $p>0.05$). Table 1 also shows that debug time for syntax and semantic errors are less than that for logic; there was no significant difference in debug times between syntax and semantic errors. From the statistical analysis, syntax debug has the highest completion rate (77%), followed by semantic (58%), and logic (36%). Figure 3 shows the debug time and completion rate for the three error types.

Table 1. Debug time for three error types in seconds (S), person-time (N)

	N	M	SD	SE	95% CI		Min	Max
					Lower	Upper		
Syntax	30	157.42	73.67	13.45	79.96	234.88	70	485
Semantic	30	299.24	143.78	26.25	155.22	443.25	115	820
Logic	30	554.02	266.08	48.58	246.38	861.66	200	1200
Total	90	336.89	274.17	28.90	127.86	590.04	70	1200

Table 2. Variance analysis for three error types

	SS	Df	MS	F	Sig.
Inter-group	1243255.0	2	621627.50	92.64*	0.042
Intra-group	583794.2	87	6710.28		
Total	1827049.2	89			

*p < 0.05

Table 3. Student's debugging time among three error types

Type(I)	Type(J)	MD (I – J)	SE	Sig.
Syntax	Semantic	–197.507	59.37	0.133
	Logic	–651.242*	59.37	0.025
Semantic	Syntax	197.507	59.37	0.133
	Logic	–423.000*	59.37	0.042
Logic	Syntax	651.242*	59.37	0.025
	Semantic	423.000*	59.37	0.042

*p<0.05

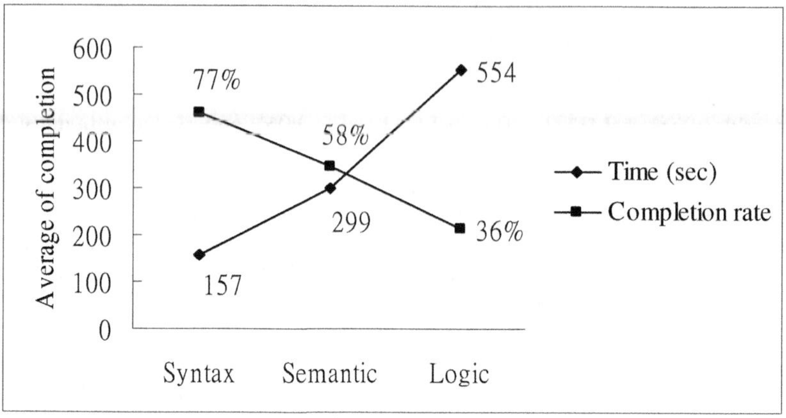

Fig. 3. Debug time and completion rate for three error types

5 Conclusions

In this study, debugging behaviors in C language include understanding, questioning, conjecture, execution, observation, correction, and confirmation, at a total of seven dimensions. In the frequency analysis of debugging behavior, the frequency of syntax error observations by experts was higher than that of novices. In addition, experts were able to better describe the reason for the errors and offer the correct command in the confirmation process, whereas novices had a higher frequency of questioning. In terms of strategy, novices were found to make more conjectures, meaning novices adopted trial and error as their means of problem solving in the face of bottlenecks. Further investigation found that experts were more capable of using algorithms to debug, suggesting they are more acquainted with program structure principles, such as the definition of program variables or command syntax. Therefore, understanding the definition of program variables, command syntax, or program structure principles is prerequisite to programming.

The differences in the thinking process of debugging syntax, semantic and logic errors between experts and novices are as follows. (1) Experts have a firmer grasp on the feedback message from the compiler. (2) The debugging and thinking process for syntax errors is more consistent between experts and novices. In terms of semantic errors, experts can better understand the output, while novices are often clueless about the debugging processe. In terms of logic errors, novices have poor and inadequate concept on the logical structure of programs. (3) In debugging tactics, experts tend to adopt forward reasoning problem-solving strategies, while novices tend to opt for backward problem-solving approaches.

The debugging time for syntax and semantic errors was both less than that for logic errors, while no significant difference was observed between syntax and semantic errors. Regarding the statistics of the three types of errors, syntax error had the highest completion rate, followed by semantic error, with logic error having the lowest completion rate.

Based on literature and findings in this study, program debugging serves as one of the best ways in fostering students' problem-solving ability. Hence, it is recommended that debugging capabilities should be highlighted in programming curriculums, particularly with emphasis on semantic and logic abilities. Program debugging activities allow students to think critically, thereby helping them to develop the necessary knowledge and skills for programming.

Acknowledgement. This project is partly supported by the National Science Council under NSC-98-2511-S-152-012.

References

Allwood, C.M., Bjorhag, C.G.: Novice's debugging when programming in Pascal. International Journal of Man-Machine Studies 33, 707–724 (1990)

Bellows, P.: High-visibility debug-by-design for FPGA platforms. Journal of Supercomputing 32(2), 105–118 (2005)

Bisant, D.B., Groninger, L.: Cognitive processes in software fault detection: a review and synthesis. International Journal of Human-Computer Interaction 5(2), 189–206 (1993)

Brooks, R.: Towards a theory of the comprehension of computer program. International Journal of Man-Machine Studies 18(6), 543–554 (1983)

Carver, S.M., Klahr, D.: Assessing children's LOGO debugging skills with a formal model. Journal of Educational Computing Research 2(4), 487–525 (1986)

Carver, S.M., Risinger, S.C.: Improving children's debugging skills. In: Empirical Studies of Programmer: Second Workshop, pp. 147–171. Ablex, Norwood (1987)

Gill, R.: VBA programming for Microsoft Office project, versions 98 through 2007. SciTech Book News 31(3) (2007)

Gilmore, D.J.: Models of debugging. Acta Psychologica 78, 151–172 (1991)

Goering, R.: Multicore design strives for balance: but programming, debug tools complicate adoption. Electronic Engineering Times 1416, 1–74 (2006)

Gould, J.D.: Some psychological evidence on how people debug computer program. International Journal of Man-Machine Studies 7(1), 151–181 (1975)

Katz, I.R., Anderson, J.R.: Debugging: an analysis of bug-location strategies. Human-Computer Interaction 3, 351–399 (1988)

Ko, A.J., Myers, B.A.: Development and evaluation of a model of programming errors. In: Proceedings of IEEE Symposia on Human-Centric Computing Languages and Environments, pp. 7–14 (2003)

Krutetskii, V.A.: The psychology of mathematical abilities in school children. The University of Chicago Press, Chicago (1976)

Lammers, D.: Debugger covers every embedded pin. Electronic Engineering Times 1436, 34 (2006)

Larkin, J., Dorothea, P.S., Herbert, A.S.: Expert and Novice Performance in Solving Physics Problems. Science 208(4450), 1335–1342 (1980)

Letovsky, S.: Cognitive processes in program comprehension. Empirical Studies of Programmers, 58–79 (1986)

Letovsky, S., Soloway, E.: Delocalized plans and program comprehension. IEEE Software 19(3), 41–48 (1986)

Mark, J.: British inventors develop chip debugging method. US Fed News Service, Including US State News, Washington, D.C. (2007)

Maria, S.: Competencies and tips for effective leadership: from novice to expert. Journal of Nursing Administration 37(4), 167–170 (2007)

Miller, L.A.: Programming by non-programmers. International Journal of Man-Machine Studies 6, 237–260 (1974)
Mutschler, A.S.: Ambric aims for massively-parallel programming. Electronic News 52(42), 21 (2006)
Nanja, M., Cook, C.R.: An analysis of the on-line debugging process. In: Empirical Studies of Programmers: Second Workshop, pp. 172–184 (1987)
Newell, A.J., Simon, H.A.: Human problem solving. Prentice-Hall, Englewood Cliffs (1972)
Patterson, D.A.: Reflections on a programming olympiad. Communications of the ACM 48(7), 15–16 (2005)
Rezel, E.S.: The effect of training subjects in self-explanation strategies on problem solving success in computer programming. Abstract retrieved from ProQuest-Dissertation, AAI3093148 (2003)
Ruthruff, J.R., Prabhakararao, S., Reichwein, J., Cook, C., Creswick, E., Burnett, M.: Interactive, visual fault localization support for end-user programmers. Journal of Visual Languages & Computing 16(1/2), 3–40 (2005)
Singh, C.: Student understanding of symmetry and Gauss's law of electricity. American Journal of Physics 74(10), 923–936 (2006)
Tsau, S.R.: College students' diagnostic capabilities in computer programming. Abstract retrieved from ProQuest-Dissertation, AAI9636605 (1996)
Vessey, I.: Expertise in debugging computer program: an analysis of the content of verbal protocols. IEEE Transactions on System, Man and Cybernetics 16(5), 621–638 (1986)
Vessey, I.: Expertise in debugging computer programs. International Journal of Man-Machine Studies 18, 459–494 (1983)
Wiedenbeck, S.: Novice/expert differences in programming skills. International Journal of Man-Machine Studies 23, 383–390 (1985)
Xu, S.: Cognitive aspects of software engineering processes. Abstract retrieved from ProQuest-Dissertation, AAI3210999 (2006)
Uchina, S., Monden, A., Linda, H., Matsumoto, K., Inoue, K., Kudo, H.: Debugging process models based on changes in impressions of software modules. In: Proceedings of International Symposium on Future Software Technology, pp. 172–184 (2000)
Yoon, B., Garcia, O.N.: Cognitive activities and support in debugging. In: Proceedings of 4th Annual Symposia on Human Interaction with Complex System, pp. 160–169 (1998)
Youngs, E.A.: Human errors in programming. International Journal of Man-Machine Studies 6, 361–376 (1974)

Student Teachers' Perception of the VBL System to Enhance Technology Integration Competencies

Ya-Fung Chang, Yi-Chin Chen, and Chia-Ling Hsu

Graduate Institute of Curriculum and Instruction, Tamkang University, Taiwan
yfchang@mail.tku.edu.tw

Abstract. The purpose of this study was to investigate student teachers' perceptions of the video-based case learning (VBL) system to enhance their technology integration competencies. A self-developed questionnaire was used to gather student teachers' perceptions regarding the system's main components and overall benefits. At the end of student teaching, ten participants were invited to complete the questionnaires and follow-up interviews. These results indicate that the VBL system combining video cases, guiding questions and discussion forums was able to promote in-depth thinking about technology integration in instruction. Moreover, student teachers perceived an increase in field observing skills. However, a higher increase in their abilities, willingness, and confidence of using technology in the teaching field did not appear. Furthermore, student teachers expressed a high expectation of video quality and efficient use of the system. Accordingly, recommendations and further research were provided so as to maximize the system's benefits.

Keywords: student teaching, technology integration, video-based learning, video cases.

1 Introduction

In today's information society, it is necessary for future teachers to know how to use technology effectively to facilitate student learning. In Taiwan, the Ministry of Education has specified "Instructional Media and Operations" a required course for pre-service teachers. In addition, many teacher education programs have offered an elective course "Computers and Instruction" so as to enhance pre-service teachers' technology competencies. In our teacher education program, students are required to take one of the two courses mentioned above. We, as teacher educators, have also developed and employed a Web system to promote our students' technology integration competencies and have obtained favorable results (Chang & Hsu, 2010; Chang, Hsu, & Kao, 2009). However, it turns out to be quite a different situation when these students finish their university coursework and participate in the internship program as student teachers in secondary schools. With insufficient field teaching experience, student teachers normally feel shocked when faced with such an authentic and complicated situation for the first time. In addition, the length of an internship for teacher preparation in Taiwan lasts only six months. Besides teaching,

K.C. Li et al. (Eds.): ICT 2012, CCIS 302, pp. 135–149, 2012.

student teachers need to practice many other skills, such as school administration, class management, and student guidance. Student teachers also have to prepare a national qualification examination usually held one month later after the internship program. Although the internship program with field teaching experience offers student teachers a good opportunity to examine theories learned from the university coursework as well as to put theory into practice (Dexter & Riedel, 2003; Hernandez-Ramos & Giancarlo, 2004), it becomes a real challenge for them to continue growth in technology integration competencies within the many constraints mentioned above.

To help student teachers' growth in technology integration, we have developed a video-based case learning (VBL) system based on previous research (Cannings & Talley, 2002; Harris, Pinnegar, & Teemant, 2005; Hsu, 2004; Rickard, McAvinia, & Quirke-Bolt, 2009). The system has the following characteristics: (1) the system collects video cases regarding technology integration into subject teaching from our former student teachers; (2) the system displays guiding questions for each case's video clip to stimulate reflection and discussion; (3) the system provides a discussion forum where student teachers can share as well as exchange ideas and opinions with their peers. We have also invited some student teachers to use the VBL system during the fall semester of 2011, and conducted an evaluation survey and follow-up interviews at the end of the internship. This study reports the evaluation results and accordingly provides relevant suggestions at the end.

2 The Internship Program

Having completed university coursework required for teaching certificates, our students need to succeed in internships in secondary schools before they are allowed to take the national teacher qualification examination. According to Taiwan's regulations, an internship program lasts six months, that is, either from August to January, or from February to July. During that period, student teachers practice in cooperating schools under the guidance of their mentors. Considering the internship program as a formal course, we require our students to return to our campus for 4-hour professional development courses every two weeks. Usually we offer five classes of the internship program in the fall semester. Each class has about 12 student teachers under the supervision of a university professor.

Our goal of the internship program is to assist student teachers in reflecting and exploring the relationships between theory and practice, and further developing their own teaching belief and feasible strategies. For the 4-hour campus course, student teachers meet with their class supervisor and share their field experience with other classmates. In addition, for professional growth in secondary subject teaching skills, there are group meetings arranged for student teachers who teach the same subject areas so that they can share their practical teaching experience as well as discuss their teaching problems. All together, there are only four blocks, that is, eight hours of group meetings, with each block lasting about two hours. Indeed, the number of subject teaching meetings is limited in contrast with 36 hours of a semester. However, it is difficult to allocate more meeting hours since the time schedule is quite tight.

In view of insufficient arrangement of professional development in subject teaching for the current internship program, we attempt to create a platform for student teachers so that they may have opportunities to extend their discussion about teaching practice beyond their meeting hours. Furthermore, we intend to use videos to capture authentic teaching so that student teachers can observe them repeatedly, and their discussion may be more focused and productive with supporting evidence (Santagata & Angelici, 2010; Shepherd & Hannafin, 2009). In addition, the focus of the videos selected is on technology integration in classrooms to encourage student teachers' use of technology in the teaching field. Finally, many studies have demonstrated the importance of reflection on internship experience to promote professional growth (Kaminski, 2003; Zeichner & Liston, 1987). Therefore, guiding questions are created besides the videos to engage student teachers in deep reflection.

3 The VBL System

To meet student teachers' urgent needs of practical knowledge on subject teaching as well as professional demands of reflection and collaboration, we have developed a Web system called the "video-based case learning" (VBL) system (Chang, Chen, Chang & Hsu, 2012). IThe focus of subject teaching is on technology integration into instructional practices. The system provides authentic teaching videos of a variety of subject areas for student teachers to observe, with guiding questions as a basis for discussion to promote their reflection. Fig. 1 shows the diagram of the VBL system, and Fig. 2 and 3 display computer frames of the title page and the login page.

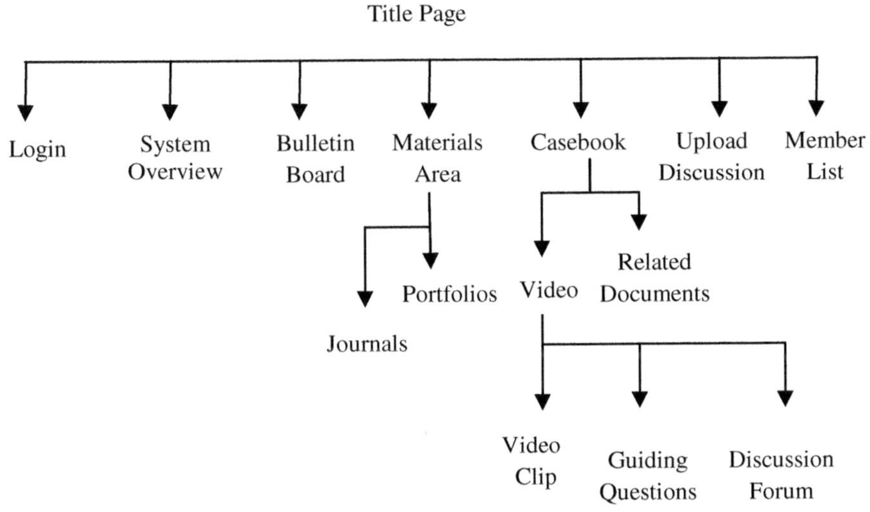

Fig. 1. Diagram of the VBL system

Fig. 2. The title page

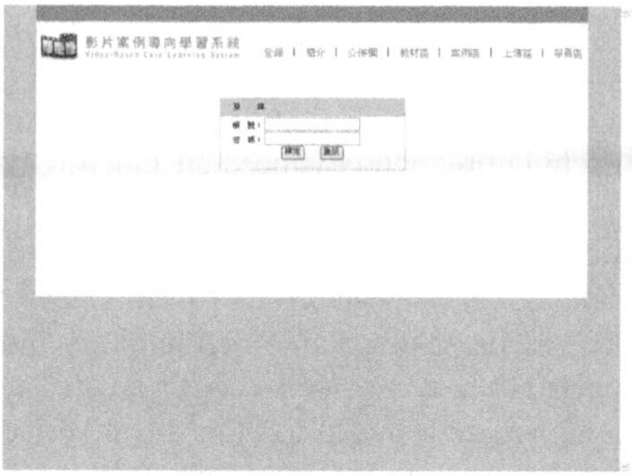

Fig. 3. The login page

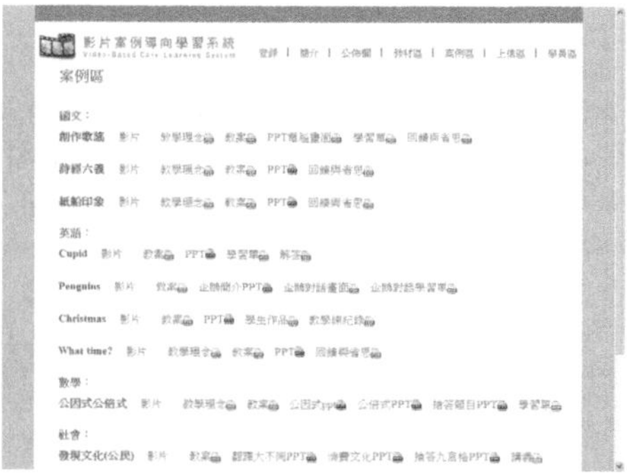

Fig. 4. The casebook page

Fig. 5. The video page

Fig. 6. The discussion forum

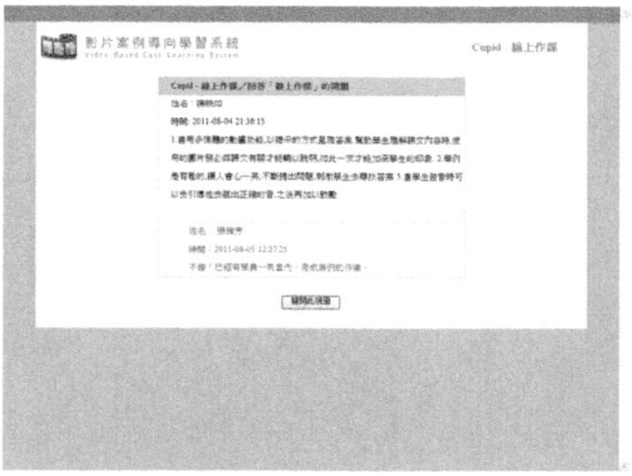

Fig. 7. Display of a topic in the forum

The cases in the casebook were collected from our former student teachers in field teaching for final evaluation at the end of their internships. We only selected the cases which demonstrated the use of technology in classrooms. The cases were categorized by content areas, as shown in Fig. 3. In addition to videos, the system also included related teaching documents for each case, such as teaching beliefs, lesson plans, slides, handouts, worksheets, feedback and reflection reports, and so on. These documents can be accessed by hyperlinks, as indicated in Fig. 4.

The video in a case originally lasts a class period. However, we only picked up three parts from the video according to different activities carried out in that period. That is, a case has three video clips. A clip lasts about 5 minutes. On the right side of the video player are three questions regarding the video clip to stimulate reflections. For example, the case "Christmas" is an English lesson for junior high schools, with three clips entitled "warm up", "guided reading", and "group competition". Fig. 5 shows the video page of the "Christmas" case. Below are questions for the "warm up" clip:

1 What are the characteristics of the PPT slides used in the video clip? Do you think it can be linked to the next activity of "guided reading" successfully?
2 What were good skills that the teacher demonstrated when she encouraged and prompted students to answer questions? What are other good skills that you suggest the teacher to use?
3 Please discuss other things that you observe, and put down your comments or reflections.

Just below the video player, there is a discussion forum for the video clip. Student teachers must log into the system before they can leave their comments in the forum, as shown in Fig. 6. Also they can view the content of a topic in the forum, and then write a response to it, as indicated in Fig. 7.

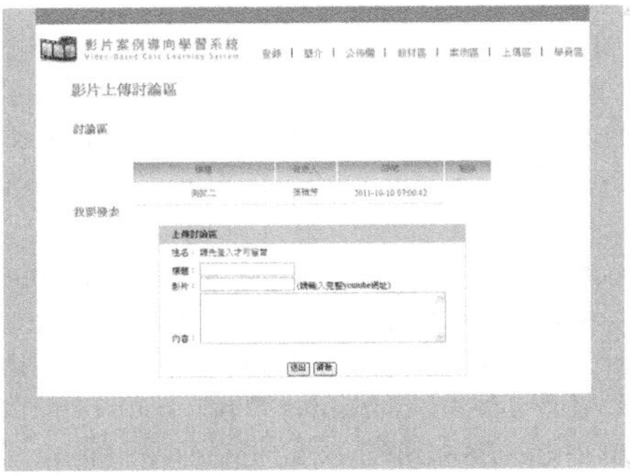

Fig. 8. The upload discussion page

Fig. 9. Display of a upload topic

For student teachers to upload their own teaching video, we recommended the YouTube system since it was popular, reliable and easy to operate. After student teachers had uploaded their video to the YouTube system, they then set its sharing function. In so doing, they could embed the video into our system by leaving a message in the upload discussion forum and specifying the location of the video. The message page not only displayed the text but also broadcast the video. Furthermore, a login member could write a response after watching the video. Fig. 8 and 9 demonstrate how it works. In short, our system intended to create an environment where student teachers could share their ideas with their peers who taught the same subject area. Moreover, their discussion was supported by evidence disclosed in videos and other teaching artifacts.

4 Design of the Study

4.1 Participants

Since the VBL system was not available until August 2011, our internship program schedule which was officially confirmed in June did not include the use of system by students. It was later decided that the system would be used by a small number of students. To reduce the effects of alteration to the internship program schedule to a minimum, we only asked two groups of student teachers to use the system. These two groups were under the supervision of the researchers. One group had 12 student teachers whose subject area was English; the other group had 15 student teachers who were in different subject areas including 6 in Business, 5 in History, 3 in Guidance and Counseling, and 1 in Civics. All together, there were 27 participants consisting of 20 females and 7 males. Furthermore, more than half of the participants were graduate students.

4.2 Instrument

A questionnaire was designed to measure student teachers' perception of the VBL system in terms of five facets: the casebook, the video clips, the guiding questions, the discussion forum, and the overall benefits. Table 1 displays the statements included in each facet. Using a 5-point Likert-type scale, the questionnaire contained 26 items and the score on each item ranged from 1 (mostly disagree) to 5 (mostly agree). A higher score indicates a more favorable perception of the system. In addition to those items, the questionnaire included six open-ended questions. The first five questions invited participants to provide opinions or suggestions regarding cases, teaching materials, videos, guiding questions, and discussion forums. The last question encouraged participants to write more about their personal experiences in using the VBL system. Ten participants completed the questionnaires at the final session of the internship program.

To gain more understanding about participants' perception of the VBL system, we also arranged follow-up interviews after the administration of questionnaires. The interviews encouraged participants to talk about 1. how they studied the cases, watched the videos, and wrote comments; 2. what features or functions should be added or modified regarding the VBL system; 3. how the system should be implemented in internships to maximize its benefits; and 4. what they had learned or obtained from using the VBL system.

4.3 Procedure

Since it was late when we decided to include the VBL system in our internship schedule, we had to find extra time for its implementation. As mentioned before, to minimize such disturbance, only 27 student teachers participated in the study. Our plan was to have them stay for about fifty-minute longer after the first three sessions when they returned to the university campus. In other words, participates had nearly three more hours of meetings in subject teaching than the rest of student teachers. The implementation process of the VBL system was as follows:

1. At the end of the first session, we invited two groups of participants to stay behind the class and introduced the VBL system to them. Then we asked the English group to study the English case and the other group to study the Civics case, and then to write comments in the discussion forum before our next meeting.
2. In the next session, we again asked the 27 students to stay behind the class, and separately led the group discussion of the specific case designated last time. The third session followed the same pattern as the previous one.
3. As scheduled in the internship program guide, in the fourth session we invited student teachers to express their teaching beliefs and strategies about their subject area.
4. In the following three sessions, participants took turns showing their field teaching demonstrations by using videos, as scheduled.
5. At the end of the final session, we asked participants to complete the questionnaires of the VBL system as well as participate in the follow-up interviews.

5 Results

Since not every participant was enthusiastic about the VBL system, we only selected those with a higher degree of involvement to report their perception of the system. As a result, ten participants completed the questionnaires and interviews. Their subject areas were six English, two Business, and two History.

5.1 Results from the Questionnaire

About the Casebook. As indicated in Table 1, the overall score of the first section was 4.04. The mean scores on most items were equal to or above 4.00. For example, participants reported that the casebook's screen design and its operation were good. Furthermore, the participants had a positive attitude towards the cases and their documents, and thought that they were valuable resources. A participant stated that "the video cases exhibit a lot of good teaching demonstrations. I think it is great!" The lowest score appeared on item 4. This shows that the participants did not feel that the number of cases was adequate. Many statements in the open-ended questions also asked for more cases with various topics and diverse applications, or even with in-service teachers' demonstrations.

Table 1. Descriptive data of the evaluation questionnaire

Items	Mean	SD
1 The Casebook	**4.04**	**.92**
1.1 Its screen design is easy to understand.	4.00	.94
1.2 It is easy to operate.	4.00	.94
1.3 The hyperlinks are accurate.	4.40	.97
1.4 The number of cases is adequate.	3.60	.84
1.5 The teaching subjects included are proper.	4.20	1.03
1.6 The cases are valuable resources.	4.10	.74
1.7 The cases' related documents are comprehensible.	3.80	1.03
1.8 The cases' related documents are valuable resources.	4.20	.92
2 The Video Clips	**3.94**	**.89**
2.1 Its screen design is easy to understand.	4.00	.94
2.2 It is easy to manipulate the video.	4.20	.79
2.3 The video runs smoothly.	4.10	.32
2.4 The video has high clarity	3.10	1.10
2.5 The videos are valuable resources.	4.30	.67
3 The Guiding Questions	**4.05**	**.68**
3.1 The questions are easy to understand.	3.90	.88
3.2 The questions match the focus of the video.	4.20	.63
3.3 The questions are helpful for video observation.	4.10	.57
3.4 The questions are helpful to stimulate reflection.	4.00	.67
4 The Discussion Forum	**3.98**	**.95**
4.1 It is easy to operate.	3.80	1.03
4.2 It is easy to read the messages in the forum.	3.60	1.07
4.3 Leaving messages in the forum promotes reflection.	4.20	.63
4.4 Reading other's messages helps inspire various ideas.	4.30	.95
5 The Overall Benefits	**4.02**	**.68**
5.1 The system can increase my abilities of applying technology in the teaching field.	3.80	.79
5.2 The system can increase my willingness of applying technology in the teaching field.	3.90	.57
5.3 The system can increase my confidence of applying technology in the teaching field.	3.70	.67
5.4 The system can increase my field observation abilities.	4.30	.67
5.5 The system can help me think deeply how to integrate technology into my instruction.	4.40	.52

About the Video Clips. As indicated in Table 1, the overall score of the second section was below 4.00. In fact, the participants said that the video clip's screen design and its operation were good. The participants also considered the video clips valuable resources. The lowest score appeared on item 4, the video quality. In the open-ended questions, many participants also pointed out such problems. For example, the frame size of the video player was quite small, and a lot of video clips were taken by long shots. Sometimes, it was difficult to figure out what the teacher was doing in the classroom. Many complained about the video's unclearness and noises. Some suggested increasing the length of a video clip as well as the number of clips.

About the Guiding Questions. As indicated in Table 1, the overall score of the third section was 4.05. That indicates the participants considered the guiding questions relevant to the focus of the video clip. In addition, participants said that these questions were helpful for video observation or reflective thinking. Many comments to the questionnaire also indicate that the guiding questions were understandable and useful in catching the point of a video clip. However, a participant suggested that the questions be more open-ended to stimulate more discussions.

About the Discussion Forum. As indicated in Table 1, the overall score of the fourth section was below 4.00. Although the participants rated the discussion forum high in terms of inspiring various ideas and facilitating reflective thinking, the forum's display format and its operation received lower scores. Some participants complained in the questionnaire that it was inconvenient to read the messages in the forum since the screen jumped to another page when a topic was chosen. A participant further suggested that the system adopt the facebook format and allow the user to go straight reading and responding in the forum without screen change.

The Overall Benefits. As indicated in Table 1, the overall score of the last section was about 4.00. Item 5 had the highest score 4.40. That means the participants highly agreed on the system's benefit of helping them think deeply about how to integrate technology into instruction. Another benefit, with a higher rating of 4.30, was an increase of field observation abilities. A participant pointed out in the questionnaire that "Generally speaking, the system is meaningful. For teachers, they do not only obtain professional knowledge but also engage themselves in self reflections." Another participant expressed that "By observing the video cases, I have acquired many skills in using instructional media because I really lacked teaching experience prior to student teaching. Video-observing makes me think and seize some good ideas from the cases to be used in my own teaching." However, the other three benefits were all rated below 4.00, namely, in the abilities, willingness, and confidence of using technology in the teaching field. A participant suggested adding in-service teachers' demonstrations to the casebook so as to increase student teachers' confidence of using technology in the future.

5.2 Results from the Interviews

Experience with the Cases. It was found that one participant strictly followed the process of reading the lesson plan, examining the PowerPoint slides, viewing the video clips, and then studying the guiding questions. Most participants went directly to view the videos and read the guiding questions so as to get an overall view of the teaching procedure. Then they went back to read the lesson plan and download the PPT slides. Some participants admitted that they would skip the lesson plan or other materials if they were busy. Still a participant stated that since she was teaching English, she selected the cases of English teachers and read their teaching beliefs and personal reflections.

Suggestions about the VBL System. In addition to a suggestion to increase the cases and to upgrade the video quality, a participant suggested a setting up a procedure for the user to follow so as to get a more comprehensive picture of a case. Another participant proposed to add a brief introduction to each case's video demonstration, and believed that the guiding questions should be read before video observing. As for the "upload" function, a participant spoke frankly that it was too tedious to edit our teaching video, upload it to the YouTube system, make a connection to the VBL system, and then write a statement explaining what was going on in the video. It was much easier just bringing the teaching video to the class and play the video segments you want to show. At the same time, we could provide explanations as needed, and respond directly to the questions from the classmates.

Suggestions about System Implementation. As for the best time to introduce the VBL system, a participant indicated that the sooner the better. He suggested using the system at the beginning of student teaching to help them grasp authentic situations in the teaching field earlier. In fact, they did not have much time to use the system later on. However, another participant had a different point of view. She said that before the class began in September, student teachers were busy with school administrative affairs. Therefore, observing the videos did not make a lot of sense to them. After student teachers entered the classroom and watched the teacher teaching, they then had a good sense of these teaching videos.

As for the low participation rate of the discussion forum, some indicated that the poor design of the forum led to inconvenience of leaving messages. Another participant assumed that the topics or issues to be discussed were the key. She explained that if the topics met student teachers' need, such as problems of using media in the classroom or unexpected occasions while using technology in teaching, more discussions would take place. Some suggested a good introduction of a case was important, such as its background or some key points to be noticed so as to join in a discussion more easily. Some proposed students observe and discuss cases at the same time in class meetings so that everyone got a chance to talk. Consequently more ideas would be gathered. However, a participant pointed out that some ideas just would not come out until you read the same case a second or third time. Therefore, she believed a need of some incentives to encourage student teachers' participation in the forum.

Personal Growth Using the VBL System. Some participants expressed that they had learned a lot from the discussion forum by discovering different points of view and obtaining various ideas and strategies. In short, these video cases were considered as good learning models to them. A participant further shared her personal experience illustrating how useful the video cases were. While using the VBL system, she happened to see a video showing a student teacher getting stuck in his teaching since a period of time was needed for a projector to warm up. Cleverly the teacher asked the students to read some paragraphs in the textbook instead of merely waiting and doing nothing. The participant did the same thing when she found an equipment problem of sound playing in the middle of her teaching demonstration. Such period of time was just long enough for other people to fix the problem, and she successfully performed all the activities as planned.

6 Discussion

The results of our study indicate that the video cases are valuable and useful to student teachers. These results are in agreement with previous research that video cases show teaching reality in authentic classrooms and provide pre-service teachers with vicarious learning (Chang & Hsu, 2010; Ertmer, Deborah, & Judith, 2003; Perry & Talley, 2001). Such teaching reality is very important especially to student teachers since they will soon teach in authentic classrooms and yet of them lack field teaching experience. Furthermore, these videos were teaching demonstrations by their predecessors in our cooperating schools. With a lot of similarity, student teachers may get a realistic picture of teaching in the field. Student teachers also recognized the benefits of the discussion forum to stimulate many ideas and different point of views. Hence, they acquired a variety of teaching skills and strategies useful for their teaching. Student teachers also acknowledged the importance of guiding questions to promote reflections as well as pinpointing the direction of video observing. These results are consistent with the studies by Chang (2011) as well as Santagata and Angelici (2010). One reason for providing questions is that a video contains such rich messages that a viewer may get lost easily. Another reason is that student teachers had few teaching experiences in the field, let alone using technology. Therefore, clear and specific guiding questions were considered as a scaffold. However, to avoid narrowing student teachers' perspectives, there were only two questions for each video. The third question was used to encourage them to discuss other things observed in the video.

Taking into consideration the video cases, guiding questions, and discussion forums, student teachers highly agreed that the VBL system helped student teachers think deeply how to integrate technology into instruction. Similarly, student teachers perceived that their field observing skills had improved after using the video cases. These results are consistent with the studies by Chang and Hsu (2010) as well as Rosaen, Lundeberg, Terpstra, Cooper, Fu and Niu (2010). The reason might be that the system offered student teachers opportunities to practice their observing skills with the aid of guiding questions. In contrast, student teachers' perceptions of the other three benefits were weaker. They were student teachers' abilities, willingness, and confidence of using technology in the teaching field. These results are in agreement with the studies by Chang, Hsu and Chen (2011) as well as Fitzgerald, et al. (2009). These studies claim that vicarious experience cannot replace direct experience, and experiential learning is especially important for teaching. Hence, the use of video cases is necessary but not sufficient for professional growth in technology integration in teaching. What practical activities to be accompanied with the VBL system that fits well student teachers' developmental stages of using technology suggested by Taylor (2004) need further study.

Since student teachers perceived the video cases as valuable resources, they certainly would welcome more cases with different subject areas, topics, and applications to be included in the VBL system. Hence they would like to find more useful materials whenever necessary. Furthermore, student teachers also had high expectations of the video quality and did not find the video were of good enough quality. For video data reduction, we converted all the videos into the FLV format. Accordingly, the video's quality was affected. In addition, the videos were taken in real classrooms. It was difficult to get rid of noises or other interferences. Finally, the person in charge of video recording in the classroom usually lacked professional techniques or experience, and occasionally needed to take care of other things at the same time. As a result, video quality varied. There are two ways to make up for the problem of poor quality. One is to adopt another video format with higher resolution; the other is to use video editing packages to remove noises and add subtitles (Chang et al., 2009).

It is relatively easy to deal with the technical problems such as improvement of video quality and modification of display format of the discussion forum. However, it is much more complicated when the focus shifts from "state of the art" to so called "state of the actual" (Miller, 2009; Selwyn, 2011). From the interviews, it is easy to find that "time" was a great concern to many student teachers. For example, participants would go directly to view the video and left a message without examining related materials if time was short. A clear introduction for each video case was suggested to save case exploration time, and case discussion was recommended to be performed directly in class meetings instead of the system's forum to gather more ideas immediately. Similarly under the time pressure, student teachers hesitated to use the upload function since it would take too much time and effort. Therefore, besides "perceived usefulness" of the system, efficient use of the system is expected since student teachers are often occupied with so many things that they need to get things done easily and quickly. In other words, we should take "efficiency" into serious consideration while designing and implementing the system for student teachers.

To increase student teachers' use of the VBL system in such pressured situations, some suggestions are provided based on the evaluation report:

1. Modify the casebook's display format so that the user can get familiar with a case in a short time. For example, add a brief description of a case besides its title, and reorder its documents into the following sequence: teaching belief, lesson plan, video, PPT slides, worksheet, feedback and reflection so as to direct the user to read important information prior to video observation.
2. Introduce the VBL system early in the orientation meeting held in the middle of June so that student teachers can have more free time to use the system before the internship program begins in August and before secondary school courses start in September.

3. Invite the professors in charge of the "subject teaching practicum" courses to post key issues as well as to lead discussion in the forums so as to encourage more participation. Student teachers need to complete the "subject teaching practicum" course before going to the internship program. Therefore, they know the professor quite well and the professor is able to identify these student teachers' current needs in subject teaching.
4. Encourage the university supervisors in the internship program to monitor their student teachers' participation in the VBL system and to include the system's case discussions in group meetings of subject teaching.
5. Provide incentives for student teachers' more enthusiastic participation in the VBL system, i.e. to use the system actively and effectively during the internship period.

7 Conclusion

Our study investigated student teachers' perceptions of the VBL system to enhance their technology integration competencies. We found that the system consisting of video cases, guiding questions and discussion forums is able to promote in-depth thinking about technology integration in instruction. Firstly, the video cases of former student teachers' teaching demonstrations may make up for their insufficient experience of field teaching, and increase their observing skills in the field. Secondly, the guiding questions seem helpful to student teachers for grasping the main points of the video. Finally, the discussion forum offering good opportunities to exchange ideas can stimulate different views and self reflections. Therefore, we believe such system is beneficial to student teachers.

We also found a high expectation of video quality and efficient use of the system. We recommend a careful editing and handling of the teaching demonstration videos to clearly reveal the teaching processes. Furthermore, we think time is a big concern for student teachers to use the system. Accordingly, relevant suggestions are provided regarding system design and implementation so as to increase the use rate of the VBL system and at the same time, to engage student teachers in deep learning. More empirical studies are needed to investigate the effects of such modifications.

Finally, the VBL system alone is not able to produce a higher increase in student teachers' abilities, willingness, and confidence of using technology in the teaching field. Opportunities should be provided for student teachers to practice their technology use in the classroom. Accordingly, more issues need to be addressed. For example, what activities are suitable? When is the best time to perform? How are these activities integrated into the VBL system? In short, more challenges occur when a system is actually implemented in real settings.

Acknowledgement. This study was supported by a grant from the National Science Council, Taiwan, Republic of China, under Contract No. NSC 100-2410-H-032-055.

References

Cannings, T.R., Talley, S.: Multimedia and online video case studies for preservice teacher preparation. Education and Information Technologies 7(4), 359–367 (2002)

Chang, Y.F.: An empirical study of applying online video cases in a technology course for pre-service teachers. Journal of Educational Media and Library Science 48(4), 589–615 (2011)

Chang, Y.F., Chen, Y.C., Chang, M.F., Hsu, C.L.: Development of a VBL system to enhance student teachers' technology integration competencies. Paper presented at International Workshop on Information Science and Education Technology (WISET 2012). The Institution of Engineering and Technology, Xiamen (2012)

Chang, Y.F., Hsu, C.L.: The effects of applying a VCS system on pre-service teachers' competencies for technology integration. In: Abas, Z.W., Jung, I., Luca, J. (eds.) Proceedings of Global Learn Asia Pacific 2010, pp. 1394–1401. AACE, Penang (2010)

Chang, Y.F., Hsu, C.L., Chen, Y.R.: Effective use of online video cases in a technology course for pre-service teachers. In: Zhang, Y. (ed.) Proceedings of 2011 3rd International Conference on Education Technology and Computer, vol. 3, pp. 49–53. IACSIT, Changchun (2011)

Chang, Y.F., Hsu, C.L., Kao, C.H.: Development of a VCS system for pre-service teachers to support technology integration into classrooms. In: Proceeding of 2009 International Conference on ICT in Teaching and Learning, pp. 50–60. Springer, Hong Kong (2009)

Dexter, S., Riedel, E.: Why improving preservice teacher educational technology preparation must go beyond the college's walls. Journal of Teacher Education 54(4), 334–346 (2003)

Ertmer, P.A., Deborah, C., Judith, L.: Increasing preservice teachers' capacity for technology integration through the use of electronic models. Teacher Education Quarterly 30(1), 95–112 (2003)

Fitzgerald, G., Koury, K., Mitchem, K., Hollingsead, C., Miller, K., Park, M.K., Tsai, H.H.: Implementing case-based instruction in higher education through technology: What works best? Journal of Technology and Teacher Education 17(1), 31–63 (2009)

Harris, R.C., Pinnegar, S., Teemant, A.: The case for hypermedia video ethnographies: Designing a new class of case studies that challenge teaching practice. Journal of Technology and Teacher Education 13(1), 141–161 (2005)

Hernandez-Ramos, P., Giancarlo, C.A.: Situating teacher education: From the university classroom to the 'real' classroom. Journal of Computing in Teacher Education 20(4), 121–128 (2004)

Hsu, S.: Using case discussion on the web to develop student teacher problem solving skills. Teaching and Teacher Education 20, 681–692 (2004)

Kaminski, E.: Promoting pre-service teacher education students' reflective practice in mathematics. Asia-Pacific Journal of Teacher Education 31(1), 21–32 (2003)

Miller, M.J.: Talking about our troubles: using video-based dialogue to build preservice teachers' professional knowledge. The Teacher Educator 44(3), 143–163 (2009)

Perry, G., Talley, S.: Online video case studies and teacher education: A new tool for preservice education. Journal of Computing in Teacher Education 17(4), 26–31 (2001)

Rickard, A., McAvinia, C., Quirke-Bolt, N.: The challenge of change: Digital video-analysis and constructivist teaching approaches on a one year preservice teacher education program in Ireland. Journal of Technology and Teacher Education 17(3), 349–367 (2009)

Rosaen, C.L., Lundeberg, M., Terpstra, M., Cooper, M., Fu, J., Niu, R.: Seeing through a different lens: what do interns learn when they make video cases of their own. The Teacher Educator 45(1), 1–22 (2010)

Santagata, R., Angelici, G.: Studying the impact of the lesson analysis framework on preservice teachers' abilities to reflect on videos of classroom teaching. Journal of Teacher Education 61(4), 339–349 (2010)

Selwyn, N.: Schools and Schooling in the Digital Age: A Critical Analysis. Routledge, London (2011)

Shepherd, C., Hannafin, M.: Beyond recollection: Reexamining preservice teacher practices using structured evidence, analysis, and reflection. Journal of Technology and Teacher Education 17(2), 229–251 (2009)

Taylor, L.: How student teachers develop their understanding of teaching using ICT. Journal of Education for Teaching 30(1), 43–56 (2004)

Zeichner, K., Liston, D.: Teaching student teachers to reflect. Harvard Educational Review 57(1), 23–48 (1987)

Citizenship Education via an Online Peer Discussion Blended Learning Approach: Lessons Learned

Khe Foon Hew and Wing Sum Cheung

National Institute of Education, Singapore
{khefoon.hew,wingsum.cheung}@nie.edu.sg

Abstract. Many countries view citizenship education as one of the main obligations of formal schooling. In this paper, we describe a case study involving a Singapore primary school (two primary five classes) to foster primary school students' affective commitment to their country. We describe a blended learning approach that combined the use of an asynchronous online peer discussion forum, persuasive cases, reflection, face-to-face classroom discussions, and teacher presentations. We discuss the theoretical foundations of the blended learning approach. We share insights of the blended learning approach based on students' data (e.g., online postings, questionnaires, reflections, and interviews), as well as our own reflections. The results of our study suggested that the blended learning approach was able to instill a positive student affective commitment to their country. Finally, we discuss several important lessons learned that could inform the design of future instructional strategies in implementing blended learning for the purpose of citizenship education.

Keywords: citizenship education, asynchronous online discussion, elementary education, affective domain, peer learning.

1 Introduction

Citizenship education has often been considered as one of the essential obligations of public education in every country and society (Sears & Hughes, 1996; Sim & Print, 2005). Although citizenship education can take many forms, there is a general agreement among scholars that it focuses on the development of a national identity, geopolitical and civic knowledge, as well as a sense of belonging, commitment or allegiance to one's country (Banks, 2001; Barrett, 2007; Kerr, Cleaver, Ireland, & Blenkinsop, 2003; Kerr, Lines, Blenkinshop, & Schagen, 2002; Sears & Hughes, 1996; Sim, 2008; Torney-Purta, Lehmann, Oswald, & Schulz, 2001).

Notwithstanding the fact that citizenship education may occur through various means (e.g., family), formal schooling remains the primary source of citizenship education for many students (Sim & Print, 2005). In most countries, textbooks remain the major resources underpinning the instruction and learning of citizenship education (Kerr, 2000). However, there is a growing move in some countries to increase the range of resources available to teachers to support citizenship education, particularly

K.C. Li et al. (Eds.): ICT 2012, CCIS 302, pp. 150–164, 2012.

through the use of blended learning that utilizes the use of information and communications technology (ICT) (Kerr, 2000). Several scholars have suggested that blended learning can offer a higher level of interaction among students than commonly experienced in face-to-face courses (Dziuban, Hartman, & Moskal, 2004; Wingard, 2004).

In this paper, we describe a blended learning approach that combined the use of an asynchronous online peer discussion forum, persuasive cases, reflection, face-to-face classroom discussions, and teacher presentations in an attempt to foster primary school students' affective commitment to country. This paper is organized as follows. We first begin with a brief overview of citizenship education in Singapore, attitudes and beliefs, as well as the theoretical framework that informs the design of our blended learning approach. We then describe the citizenship education project. This is followed by the findings, and a discussion of several important lessons learned related to the use of blended learning for the purpose of citizenship education.

2 Background

Ever since Singapore attained self-government in 1959, citizenship education in Singapore has appeared in many forms. There have been, perhaps, seven major forms of citizenship education in Singapore throughout the years. Citizenship education was originally taught as Ethics between 1959 and 1966; it was later replaced by Civics in 1967; Education for Living in 1973; Being and Becoming and Good Citizens in the late 1970s; Religious Knowledge and Confucian Ethics in 1982; Civics and Moral Education in 1992; and, National Education in 1997 (Sim & Print, 2005).

Probably some of the most extensive changes to citizenship education have been related to National Education (Han, 2000). The primary objective of National Education is to develop both positive knowledge and attitudes of Singapore's young citizens (Sim & Print, 2005). There are in total six main National Education messages (Ministry of Education, 2007): (a) Singapore is our homeland; this is where we belong, (b) We must preserve racial and religious harmony, (c) We must uphold meritocracy and incorruptibility, (d) No one owes Singapore a living, (e) We must ourselves defend Singapore, and (f) We have confidence in our future.

In this paper, we focus on the first National Education message — Singapore is our homeland; this is where we belong. Specifically, we investigated a particular dimension of citizenship — i.e., students' affective commitment toward Singapore. Affective commitment, which may be conceptualized as a form of attitude, refers to the sense of attachment to the nation state. There is a growing body of educational research that examines this very issue. These studies include Torney-Purta, Lehmann, Oswald, and Schulz's (2001) study of nearly 90,000 14-year-old students' (from 28 countries) feelings about their own country, Kerr, Lines, Blenkinshop, and Schagen's (2002) analysis of 3,043 14-year-old United Kingdom students, Lee's (2003) work on 4,997 grade 9 students in Hong Kong, among others. For example, Torney-Purta et al. (2001) found that 87% of students subscribed to feelings of love for their country. A majority of students (77%) indicated that they would not want to live permanently in another country. Kerr et al. (2002) reported that although slightly over half (59%) of respondents agreed and strongly agreed that they had love for their country, 19% indicated that they would prefer to live permanently in another country. Lee (2003) reported that 82% of respondents loved their country; however, almost half of the respondents (45%) agreed and strongly agreed that they would prefer living permanently elsewhere, instead of Hong Kong.

3 Theoretical Framework

3.1 Attitudes, Beliefs and Persuasion

Nurturing a desirable attitude (sense of attachment) among students toward their country is a very important task; however, this is not easy to achieve. Even though attitudes are not easily changed, this does not mean they cannot change.

Although many researchers tend to use attitudes as a term which includes beliefs (Eleftherios & Theodosios, 2007), a clear distinction between these two terms would better serve our purpose in this paper. Attitudes have been described by psychologists as evaluative judgments about a given entity, object or event (Crano & Prislin, 2006; Gawronski & Bodenhausen, 2006). In other words, attitudes can be defined as feelings that indicate whether a person likes or dislikes something (Havelka, 2003; Simpson, Koballa, Oliver, & Crawley, 1994). In the context of our citizenship education project, student attitudes toward Singapore may be conceptualized as students liking or disliking Singapore.

Beliefs, on the other hand, can be defined as premises or suppositions about something that are felt to be true (Calderhead, 1996). Scholars posit that beliefs are largely cognitive in nature (McLeod, 1992); representing the information, concepts or knowledge that an individual has concerning an object or entity (Havelka, 2003).

Beliefs can determine a person's attitude (Bodur, Brinberg, & Coupey, 2000; Havelka, 2003). Thus, having a certain set of beliefs toward Singapore (e.g., a knowledge that Singapore is a safer place to live compared to other cities or countries), an individual then forms a favorable or unfavorable attitude toward the country (e.g., liking or disliking Singapore), which can ultimately lead to a particular behavior being performed (e.g., staying in Singapore or leaving it). If, as Bodur et al. (2000) and Havelka (2003) suggested, beliefs are foundational to attitudes, then students' beliefs toward Singapore must first be fostered or changed before a positive attitude toward the country can be expected. How, then, is belief change most likely to occur?

Scholars have found that persuasive theories have the potential to change a person's beliefs (Alexander et al., 2002; Gawronski & Bodenhausen, 2006; Murphy, 2001; Sinatra & Kardash, 2004). Persuasion is the process of fostering a shift in judgment about an entity in a certain direction, and is more likely to occur when the individual is given opportunities to engage with reasoned discourse or argument (Sinatra et al., 2012). Although not all persuasive arguments or messages are effective, research has shown that carefully crafted persuasive messages can promote beliefs and attitude change (Hynd, 2003; Sinatra et al., 2012). According to

Chambliss and Garner (1996), a message is considered to be persuasive if it is crafted to counter the current beliefs or knowledge held by a typical reader as well as to present new ones. In other words, belief and attitude changes can occur when: (a) new or unfamiliar persuasive messages are considered, or (b) when additional consideration of already familiar persuasive messages is carried out (Gawronski & Bodenhausen, 2006). In addition, belief change may also be influenced by certain individual dispositions such as their need for cognition. Fig. 1 depicts a possible model of the theoretical framework that frames the current proposed study. In the following paragraphs, we briefly explain these processes.

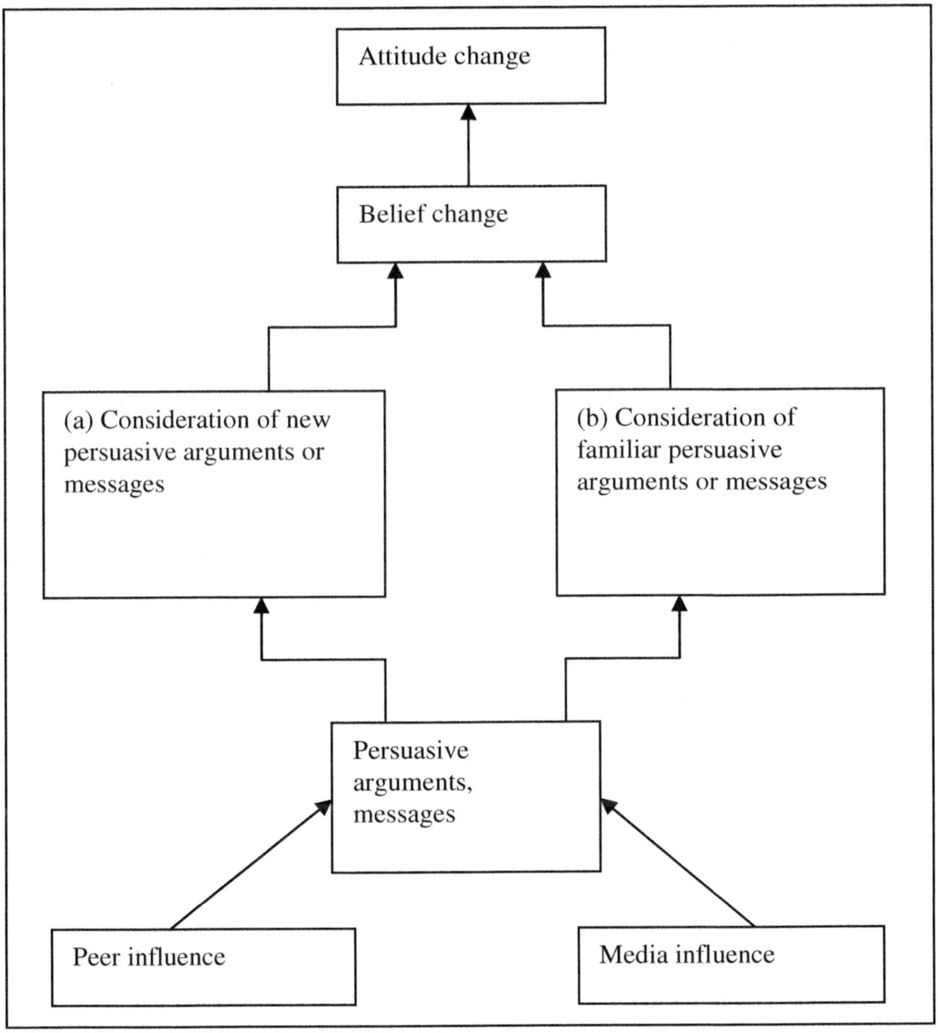

Fig. 1. Processes underlying belief and attitude change

The first case is represented by instances in which individuals are exposed to new or previously unfamiliar persuasive arguments or messages about a particular entity. Sources of persuasive arguments or messages may include peers (e.g., classmates, school mates) and media (e.g., newspapers, Internet, radio). Belief and attitude change can occur when new messages cannot be incorporated into existing ideas (Ertmer, 2005). Gawronski and Bodenhausen (2006) argued that if consideration of the new persuasive messages imply a different evaluation of a given entity, exposure to the new messages is quite likely to lead to belief, and attitude change; on the other hand, if consideration of the new persuasive arguments does *not* imply a different evaluation of a given entity (e.g., no change of view), exposure to the new persuasive messages is *not* likely to lead to any change (Gawronski & Bodenhausen, 2006).

The second case is perhaps best reflected in research on mere thought (Tesser, 1978), or introspection (Wilson, Dunn, Kraft, & Lisle, 1989). Research in these areas has suggested that merely thinking or introspecting about a given entity may lead to belief and attitude change. If mere thought or introspection of already familiar persuasive arguments or messages imply a different evaluation of a given entity (e.g., something that counters the current view held by the individual), additional consideration is quite likely to lead to belief, and subsequently attitude change (Gawronski & Bodenhausen, 2006). However, if additional consideration of already familiar arguments confirm the original belief, no change is likely to occur.

3.2 Use of Asynchronous Online Discussion

From Fig. 1, we may infer that any educational program or project that aims to foster belief and attitude change among students must first require students to reflect, make their preexisting personal beliefs explicit, as well as allow other people to examine, or challenge the adequacy of those beliefs (Kagan, 1992). We suggest that such a program is perhaps best supported by printed materials rather than oral communication. This is because printed materials such as text, images, and video clips are permanent, whereas utterances will disappear once they are spoken.

In this project, we propose the use of an asynchronous online discussion environment. Asynchronous online discussion refers to "the exchange of messages via computer networks where participants need not be online simultaneously" (Cheung & Hew, 2006, p. 2). Every participant in an asynchronous online discussion environment can choose to post and respond to messages at any time or from any geographical location, and can view the messages many times and long after the messages have been posted.

Because the discourse that occurs within the forum is not in real time, students thus have more time to reflect and think about new information before contributing to the discussion (Pena-Shaff & Nicholls, 2004). This is unlike a face-to-face classroom environment where students are constrained by time to respond (e.g., 30 minutes for a typical lesson period in Singapore), and where the face-to-face discussion is usually dominated by a few vocal or outspoken students; hence, leaving the shy students as well as those who wish to have more time to think little or no opportunity to participate in the discussion. In addition, since many of the current asynchronous online discussion forums are text-based, students have little choice but to express themselves in writing. The very process of writing in itself encourages students to reflect and make explicit their beliefs and assumptions — one of the key prerequisites of promoting belief change as suggested by Kagan (1992).

4 Method

The citizenship education project took place at Primary School N, an elementary school in western Singapore. School N was a mixed-gender (boys and girls) school with more than 1,200 pupils. A majority of the pupils in the school were Chinese Singaporean and came from families of middle to high social economic status. Two primary five (equivalent to grade five) classes, each with 30 pupils between the ages of 10 and 11, along with their form teachers took part in the project. Fig. 2 summarizes the overview of the blended learning approach that underpinned the project.

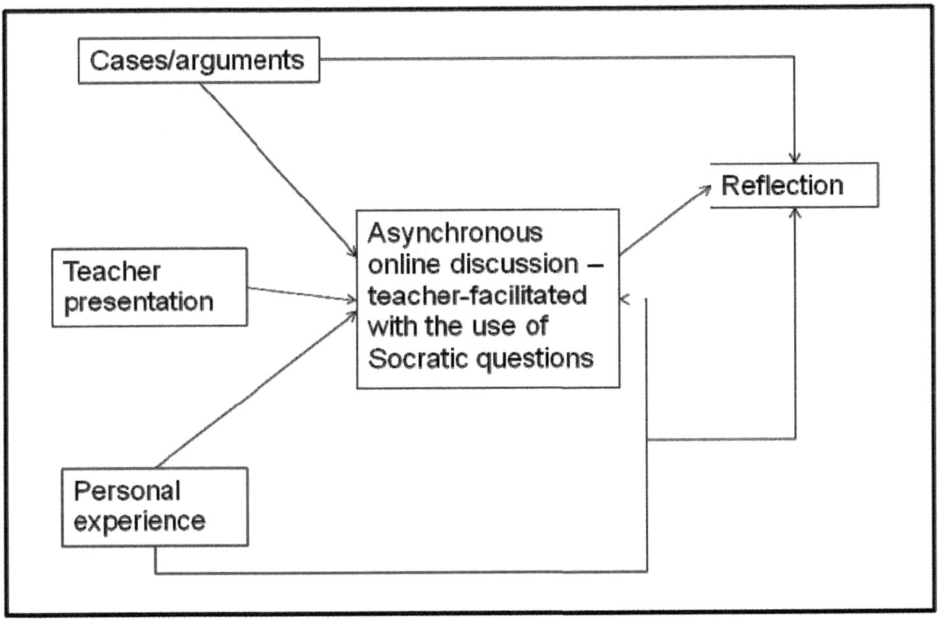

Fig. 2. Blended learning framework

There were three main phases of the project: (a) pre-implementation, (b) actual implementation, and (c) post-implementation.

4.1 Pre-implementation Phase

During the pre-implementation phase, we provided training to the teachers about the use of asynchronous online discussion. Specifically, we introduced teachers to the potential benefits, and challenges of using asynchronous online discussions, as well as ways to engage pupils in the discussions. Teachers were also introduced to the use of Socratic questions. We adopted the use of Socratic questions because of their ability to foster critical thought or introspection in students — one of the key prerequisites of promoting attitude change as suggested by persuasive theories. According to Paul (1990), Socratic questions include: (a) questions of clarification, (b) questions that probe assumptions, (c) questions that probe reasons and evidence, (d) questions about viewpoints, and (e) questions that probe implications and consequences.

After the completion of the teacher training, a training session for the primary five pupils was carried out. Pupils were taught the meaning of discussion. Adopting the work of Bretz (1983) and Henri (1992), we defined discussion as a process of exchanging ideas that involves at least three actions: (a) communication of information, (b) a first response to this information, and (c) a second answer relating to the first. A discussion should not merely involve two actions (person A communicates with person B and a response from person B). Such a process sounds more like a mere question-and-answer activity than a discussion of ideas.

Pupils were also introduced to a set of ground rules and guidelines for the discussion. These include the following: (a) no personal attacks or rude posting, (b) one idea per message posting, and (c) pupils to support opinions with facts or personal experiences. Pupils were introduced to the BlackBoard™ online discussion platform. Essential features of the platform (e.g., creation of discussion threads and messages) were demonstrated. Pupils were also given the opportunity to try out the platform, guided by the teachers and the researchers.

Finally, in the pre-implementation phase, the pupils completed a 10-item *Affective Commitment to Country* questionnaire (Table 1). The *Affective Commitment to Country* questionnaire was earlier pilot tested using a sample of 286 primary six pupils from the same school, i.e., Primary School N. The results of factor analyses such as principal component analysis and confirmatory factor analysis showed evidence of construct validity for the 10-item scale, and an overall Cronbach alpha reliability coefficient of 0.91 (Hew & Cheung, 2011).

Table 1. Affective Commitment to Country questionnaire.

Item	
Q1	I would be happy to spend my whole life in Singapore
Q2	I enjoy discussing Singapore with people from other countries
Q3	I feel as if Singapore's problems are my own
Q4	I am proud to tell others that I live in Singapore
Q5	I feel accepted as a member of society in Singapore
Q6	I feel emotionally attached to Singapore
Q7	I feel a sense of belonging to Singapore
Q8	I love Singapore
Q9	I care about the fate of Singapore
Q10	I am willing to work hard to help Singapore be successful

4.2 Actual Implementation Phase

The actual implementation phase ran for about four months. During this time, we focused on the theme *Appreciating Singapore*. A teacher presented cases or narratives (e.g., real-life stories of people concerning what they appreciated about Singapore, why foreigners should relocate to Singapore) in mass lectures. The teacher also shared what he or she appreciated about Singapore. Pupils, after the teacher presentation, proceeded to participate in an online discussion about the things they appreciated or liked about the country. Pupils were told to comment on one another's online postings. Pupils also visited the *Singapore My Home* website and viewed the competition photographs posted on the web page. They then participated in a separated online discussion thread on what the photographs meant to them personally. In addition, pupils re-visited the *Singapore pledge* and commented on what the pledge actually meant to them in another separate discussion thread. One of the primary five classes participated in the asynchronous online discussion outside of class time (e.g., during their recess, at home), while the other participated within class time. The online discussions were facilitated by the form teachers.

4.3 Post-implementation Phase

At the end of the project, 54 pupils wrote individual reflections on what they had learned from the online discussions, and cases/materials (photographs, narratives of other people). Pupils also wrote whether they had changed their feelings or attitudes toward Singapore and the reason for it. In addition, pupils wrote about the experience of participating in the asynchronous online discussions. Altogether, 53 pupils completed the pre- and post-*Affective Commitment to Country* questionnaire.

5 Results

Table 2 shows the statistical results for the pupils' overall mean pre- and post-questionnaire scores. The results in Table 2 reveal that the pupil's mean scores had indeed improved in terms of their affective commitment to country. The standard deviation had also decreased, indicating that the spread of scores had reduced and that the scores of the pupils varied lesser than before. This suggested that the blended learning approach had narrowed the score differences between pupils.

Table 2. Summary of pupils' mean pre- and post- *Affective Commitment to Country* questionnaire scores

	Pre-		Post-	
Scores	Mean	SD	Mean	SD
Questionnaire	3.23	0.60	3.31	0.57

We also share several insights of the blended learning approach based on the pupils' reflections. Overall, more than 90% of 54 pupils reported positive benefits related to appreciating the country more. For example:

- I feel proud to be a Singaporean.
- I learned that Singapore has a variety of things to enjoy and it is a very peaceful country.
- I feel happy that I am a Singaporean.
- I learned about the Singapore identity and I also learned how to use the discussion forums.
- I felt a great sense of belonging as I learnt that Singapore accepts any religion or race.

A majority of the pupils (80%) reported that they enjoyed the citizenship project morethan the traditional teacher-leddidactic lessons. For example:

- It was very interesting and exciting. I hope we have another project like this.
- I found that this project was very interesting.
- I felt that it was meaningful and I learnt a lot.
- I felt happy but it was too short.
- I feel that we should have more time for the project.
- I feel happy. It is more interesting than normal lessons.

Eighty percent of the pupils reported that they found the use of asynchronous online discussion forums useful and beneficial to them. For example:

- The use of online discussion forums helped me make my beliefs and ideas explicit. It also helped me question or challenge the beliefs or ideas of my classmates.
- It [the asynchronous online discussion] was very useful. We can look at the postings over and over again.
- I feel that it is better to discuss online because it gives people like me who are shy to speak up in class, to voice out our beliefs.
- The online discussion enabled my classmates to question my opinions in order to challenge or improve it. I can think more in-depth.
- I felt that it is convenient because we can participate in the discussion at any place we like.
- I can see [clearly] what other pupils are thinking or feeling.
- I am able to express more about how I feel and it is easier for me to type out some things instead of saying it directly. We can see other classmates' beliefs clearly and express our beliefs freely too.

Some pupils, however, reported negative statements regarding the use of online discussions. For example:

- Though I was able to share my feeling and ideas, not everybody in my class responded to it.
- We can only type.

6 Lessons Learned

We acknowledge that fostering a positive student attitude such as affective commitment to country is not an easy task for educators. Many teachers tend to approach this task through didactic teaching using one-way communication such as lectures aided by PowerPoint slide shows. In our personal communication with teachers, we found that the usefulness of such an approach is questionable. Students tend to "switch off" during these lecture sessions because such teacher lectures sounded preachy. Moreover, many of these didactic sessions focus primarily on factual knowledge such as why one should love or be loyal to one's country. Such presentations tend to address the cognitive domain but fall short on dealing with students' affective domain.

In this citizenship education project, we utilized the use of a blended learning approach that combined the use of Socratic question-mediated asynchronous online peer discussion forum, persuasive cases, reflection, face-to-face classroom discussions, and teacher presentations. We offer the following six major lessons learned.

First, the primary five pupils, on the whole, enjoyed the citizenship education project very much. It was also evident from the pupils' reflections, as well as the increase in mean questionnaire scores that some change of attitude toward the country had occurred. Pupils reported that they learned to appreciate their country more. This suggested that our blended learning approach was able to instill a positive student affective commitment to their country. Of course, we cannot claim actual causal-effect as a result of this blended learning approach due to the absence of a control group. Nevertheless, the positive comments of the pupils were an encouraging sign that at least the blended learning approach was well received.

Second, we found the use of asynchronous online discussion a useful technology to help pupils make explicit their pre-existing beliefs and assumptions about their country. Some of these pre-existing opinions and assumptions about the country may be incorrect. This in turn enabled the pupils to examine, question and challenge these different beliefs, as well as to assimilate new information into their existing belief systems. This is a very important process of fostering attitude change. We believe that if the pupils' pre-existing beliefs had not been explicitly presented as concrete ideas, questioning and examination of these beliefs would not have taken place. However, we realize that some quiet or shy pupils may hesitate to post their views for fear of being attacked or made fun of by their classmates. To overcome this problem, the teacher may consider using anonymity to encourage the pupils to interact and provide critical feedback.

Third, the use of peer online discussion appears to make citizenship education less teacher-centered. Face-to-face classroom discussions often involve teacher-pupil interaction characterized by the Initiate-Respond-Evaluate (IRE) structure. Usually the teacher initiates a question, followed by the pupils answering the question, and the teacher evaluating the response by giving some feedback. In online discussion, however, the IRE structure is usually minimized or eliminated altogether. Interestingly, although the teachers were supposed to facilitate the online discussion, we found that the discussion on the whole was driven mostly by the pupils themselves. Analyses of the discussion posts, for example, revealed that teachers contributed less than 10% of the posts. One possible reason for this is that facilitating an online discussion is very time consuming. Not all teachers could dedicate the time and effort required to do it. At this juncture, it is important to note that this citizenship education posed an extra workload for the two teachers. They were not given any reduction in their regular teaching duties to do the project. Overall, this finding, therefore, infers that it might be best to allow students to take charge or facilitate the discussion on commitment to country themselves because by doing so they would have a greater sense of responsibility and ownership over the direction of the discussion as well as the opinions and arguments generated. In addition, no one pupil dominated the online discussion. This was because everyone could post any idea any time.

Fourth, teachers may wish to consider using asynchronous voice or audio discussion. We realized that not all pupils were proficient in reading or writing. Some preferred to speak rather than type. Hence, the use of asynchronous text discussion may not be very suitable for these pupils. In order to overcome this problem, we suggest that teachers consider using tools such as the Wimba Voice Board which allows pupils to speak a question or comment into a microphone and record it as an audio clip in the online discussion. Moreover, pupils have the option of typing out their comments or questions to be appended to the audio clip. The clips, along with the accompanying text if any, are then posted into a threaded organization of other audio clips (Girasoli & Hannafin, 2008). The use of the Wimba Voice Board could thus potentially meet the needs of both types of pupils — those who prefer speaking to writing and vice versa.

Fifth, there is a need to enforce the ground rules of pupils replying to other individual's postings within 24 hours. One of the main complaints of using asynchronous online discussion was the lack or delay in responses. The delay caused some pupils to feel frustrated especially if their questions went unanswered. So in order to overcome this problem, teachers should establish and enforce the rule of requiring the participants to respond to their peers within 24hours. The choice of a 24-hour rule is not an arbitrary one but based on empirical research (Hewitt & Teplovs, 1999). Hewitt and Teplovs (1999), for example, analyzed over 4,000 online messages from seven graduate level distance education courses and found that responses posted to a thread within 24 hours had the highest chance (0.26 to 0.68) of eliciting additional responses compared to responses posted after a day of inactivity (0.18 to 0.41) and after two days of inactivity (0.12 to 0.31). In other words, responses posted within 24 hours have the highest chance of sustaining the online discussion.

Sixth, we found that pupils participated more (e.g., posted more comments) during asynchronous online discussions in class rather than outside class. Recall that one of the primary five classes participated in the asynchronous online discussion outside class time (e.g., at home), while the other within class time. Although previous research has suggested that participants in an asynchronous online discussion environment can choose to post and respond to messages at any time, we found that this may not necessary apply to the primary school students in our context. One of the main possible reasons for this is that some parents were reluctant to allow their children to access the Internet at home during the day without their supervision for fear that their children might visit undesirable websites. Some pupils were also too busy with tuition in the evenings. Due to these reasons, we suggest that teachers conduct asynchronous online discussions in class, at least for young students such as primary school pupils. In fact, conducting online discussions in class has its own benefits. Students appear to concentrate on the discussion task during online discussions in class as found in this study.

7 Conclusion

In this study, we explored the use of a blended learning approach that combined the use of asynchronous online peer discussion forum, persuasive cases, student reflection, face-to-face classroom discussions, and teacher presentations in an attempt to foster primary school students' affective commitment to country. Overall, we found that pupils enjoyed this blended learning approach very much and there was evidence that a change of attitude toward the country had occurred. We also described six major lessons that we learned from this citizenship education project. In particular, we believe that the use of new persuasive messages and additional consideration of already familiar messages are especially important lessons. These messages have to be authentic and real-life rather than fictional. We believe that these messages, together with the use of online peer discussions which enabled pupils to make explicit their pre-existing beliefs about their country so that these beliefs can be questioned and examined, helped the pupils appreciate their country more.

What are some possible future research directions? First, it is important to note that even with well-designed materials the success of belief change may be affected by certain individual traits or dispositions (Sinatra et al., 2012). According to Stanovich (1999, p. 157), dispositions are "relatively stable psychological mechanisms and strategies that tend to generate characteristics behavioral tendencies and tactics". One of these dispositions is what Cacioppo et al. (1996) referred to as people's tendency to engage in and enjoy effortful cognitive endeavors which could be represented in terms of a single factor called *need for cognition.* Scholars (e.g., Cacioppo & Petty, 1982, 1984; Cacioppo et al., 1986; Cacioppo et al., 1983) have found that individuals low in need for cognition, as well as those high in need for cognition must make sense of their world but they tend to derive meaning, adopt position, or solve problems in different ways. Individuals who are high in need for cognition tend to approach ideas or suggestions open-mindedly, and tend to engage in critical thinking, while those with low degrees of need tend to be close-minded, and less willing to engage in critical thought or discourse (Sinatra et al., 2012). Previous research has suggested that students with a high need for cognition tend to be more accepting of belief change (Sinatra et al., 2003). Future research should therefore examine the relationship between students' need for cognition and their affective commitment to country.

Second, the results of this study cannot be generalized to other schools. The current study was situated within a local mixed gender Chinese school, using a cohort of 11–12–year-old students. Future research should therefore examine other schools such as single gender primary schools, or secondary schools in Singapore and other countries for comparison purposes.

Overall, we believe that we have contributed to the literature on citizenship education. Perhaps the overall strength of this study lies in the design of a blended learning approach which combined the use of Socratic questions, asynchronous online peer discussion forum, persuasive cases, reflection, face-to-face classroom discussions, and teacher presentations. Currently, we are in the process of further testing the effectiveness of this blended learning approach using an experimental research method that utilizes a treatment and control group. Given the importance of citizenship education in today's context, we hope that our blended learning approach will be useful to other researchers and educators who are similarly engaged in efforts to enrich our collective understanding regarding student commitment to their country.

References

Alexander, P.A., Fives, H., Buehl, M.M., Sperl, C.T.: Teaching as persuasion. Teaching and Teacher Education 18, 795–913 (2002)

Banks, J.A.: Citizenship education and diversity. Journal of Teacher Education 52(1), 5–16 (2001)

Barrett, M.: Children's knowledge, beliefs and feelings about nations and national groups. Psychology Press, Hove (2007)

Bodur, H.O., Brinberg, D., Coupey, E.: Belief, affect, and attitude: Alternative models of the determinants of attitude. Journal of Consumer Psychology 9(1), 17–28 (2000)

Bretz, R.: Media for interactive communication. Sage Publications, London (1983)

Cacioppo, J.T., Petty, R.E.: The need for cognition. Journal of Personality and Social Psychology 42, 116–131 (1982)

Cacioppo, J.T., Petty, R.E.: The need for cognition: Relationship to attitudinal processes. In: McGlynn, R.P., Maddux, J.E., Stoltenberg, C.D., Harvey, J.H. (eds.) Social Perception in Clinical and Counseling Psychology, pp. 91–119. Texas Tech University, Lubbock (1984)

Cacioppo, J.T., Petty, R.E., Feinstein, J.A., Jarvis, W.B.: Dispositional differences in cognitive motivation: The life and times of individuals varying in need for cognition. Psychological Bulletin 119(2), 197–253 (1996)

Cacioppo, J.T., Petty, R.E., Kao, C.F., Rodriguez, R.: Central and peripheral routes to persuasion: An individual difference perspective. Journal of Personality and Social Psychology 51, 1032–1043 (1986)

Cacioppo, J.T., Petty, R.E., Morris, K.J.: Effects of need for cognition on message evaluation, recall and persuasion. Journal of Personality and Social Psychology 45, 805–818 (1983)

Calderhead, J.: Teachers: Beliefs and knowledge. In: Berliner, D., Calfee, R. (eds.) Handbook of Educational Psychology, pp. 709–725. Macmillan, New York (1996)

Chambliss, M.J., Garner, R.: Do adults change their minds after reading persuasive text? Written Communication 13(3), 291–313 (1996)

Cheung, W.S., Hew, K.F.: Examining Students' Creative and Critical Thinking and Student to Student Interactions in An Asynchronous Online Discussion Environment: A Singapore Case Study. Asia-Pacific Cybereducation Journal 2(2) (2006), http://www.acecjournal.org/current_issue_current_issue.php (retrieved on June 7, 2007)

Crano, W.D., Prislin, R.: Attitudes and persuasion. Annual Review of Psychology 57(1), 345–374 (2006)

Dziuban, C.D., Hartman, J.L., Moskal, P.D.: Blended learning. Educause Center for Applied Research (ECAR). Research Bulletin 7 (2004), http://net.educause.edu/ir/library/pdf/ERB0407.pdf (retrieved on November 9, 2011)

Eleftherios, K., Theodosios, Z.: Students' beliefs and attitudes about studying and learning mathematics. In: Woo, J.H., Lew, H.C., Park, K.S., Seo, D.Y. (eds.) Proceedings of the 31st Conference of the International Group for the Psychology of Mathematics Education, vol. 3, pp. 97–104. PME, Seoul (2007)

Ertmer, P.A.: Teacher pedagogical beliefs: The final frontier in our quest for technology integration. Educational Technology Research and Development 53(4), 25–39 (2005)

Gawronski, B., Bodenhausen, G.V.: Associative and propositional processes in evaluation: An integrative review of implicit and explicit attitude change. Psychological Bulletin 132(5), 692–731 (2006)

Girasoli, A.J., Hannafin, R.D.: Using asynchronous AV communication tools to increase academic self-efficacy. Computers & Education 51, 1676–1682 (2008)

Han, C.: National education and 'active citizenship': Implications for citizenship and citizenship education in Singapore. Asia Pacific Journal of Education 20(1), 63–72 (2000)

Havelka, D.: Students beliefs and attitudes toward information technology. Information Systems Education Journal 1(40) (2003)

Henri, F.: Computer conferencing and content analysis. In: Kaye, A.R. (ed.) Collaborative Learning through Computer Conferencing: The Najaden Papers, pp. 117–136. Springer, Berlin (1992b)

Hew, K.F., Cheung, W.S.: Examining students' affective commitment toward country: A case study of a Singapore primary school. Asia Pacific Journal of Education 31(1), 19–31 (2011)

Hewitt, J., Teplovs, C.: An analysis of growth patterns in computer conferencing threads. In: Hoadley, C., Roschelle, J. (eds.) Proceedings of the Computer Support for Collaborative Learning (CSCL) 1999 Conference, December 12-15. Stanford University, Palo Alto (1999)

Hynd, C.: Conceptual change in response to persuasive messages. In: Sinatra, G.M., Pintrich, P.R. (eds.) Intentional Conceptual Change, pp. 291–316. Lawrence Erlbaum Associates, Mahwah (2003)

Kagan, D.M.: Implications of research on teacher belief. Educational Psychologist 27(1), 65–90 (1992)

Kerr, D.: Citizenship education: An international comparison. In: Lawton, D., Cairns, J., Gardner, R. (eds.) Education for Citizenship, pp. 200–227. Cromwell Press, Trowbridge (2000)

Kerr, D., Lines, A., Blenkinshop, S., Schagen, I.: England's results from the IEA international citizenship education study: What citizenship and education mean to 14 year olds (Research Report No. 375). Department for Education and Skills, Norwich (2002)

Kerr, D., Cleaver, E., Ireland, E., Blenkinshop, S.: Citizenship education longitudinal study first cross-sectional survey 2001-2002 (Research Report No. 416). Department for Education and Skills, Norwich (2003)

Lee, W.O.: Students' concepts and attitudes toward citizenship: The case of Hong Kong. International Journal of Educational Research 39, 591–607 (2003)

McLeod, D.B.: Research on affect in mathematics education: A reconceptualization. In: Grouws, D.A. (ed.) Handbook of Research on Mathematics Teaching and Learning, pp. 575–596. Macmillan, New York (1992)

Ministry of Education: National Education website (2007), http://www.ne.edu.sg (retrieved on October 26, 2009)

Murphy, P.K.: Teaching as persuasion: A new metaphor for a new decade. Theory into Practice 40(4), 224–227 (2001)

Paul, R.: Critical thinking: What every person needs to survive in a rapidly changing world. Center for Critical Thinking and Moral Critique, Rohnert Park (1990)
Pena-Shaff, J.B., Nicolls, C.: Analyzing student interactions and meaning construction in computer bulletin board discussions. Computer and Education 42, 243–265 (2004)
Sears, A.M., Hughes, A.S.: Citizenship education and current educational reform. Canadian Journal of Education 21(2), 123–142 (1996)
Sim, B.Y.J., Print, M.: Citizenship Education and Social Studies in Singapore: A National Agenda. International Journal of Citizenship and Teacher Education 1(1), 58–72 (2005)
Simpson, R.D., Koballa Jr., T.R., Oliver, J.S., Crawley, F.E.: Research on the affective dimensions of science learning. In: White, D. (ed.) Handbook of Research on Science Teaching and Learning, pp. 211–235. Macmillan, New York (1994)
Sinatra, G.M., Kardash, C.A.: Teacher candidates' epistemological beliefs, dispositions, and views on teaching as persuasion. Contemporary Educational Psychology 29, 483–498 (2004)
Sinatra, G.M., Kardash, C.M., Taasoobshirazi, G., Lombardi, D.: Promoting attitude change and expressed willingness to take action toward climate change in college students. Instructional Science 40, 1–17 (2012)
Sinatra, G.M., Southerland, S.A., McConaughy, F., Demastes, J.: Intentions and beliefs in students' understanding and acceptance of biological evolution. Journal of Research in Science Teaching 40(5), 510–528 (2003)
Stanovich, K.E.: Who is rational? Studies of individual differences in reasoning. LEA, Mahwah (1999)
Tesser, A.: Self-generated attitude change. In: Berkowitz, L. (ed.) Advances in Experimental Social Psychology, vol. 11, pp. 289–338. Academic Press, New York (1978)
Torney-Purta, J., Lehmann, R., Oswald, H., Schulz, W.: Citizenship and education in twenty-eight countries: Civic knowledge and engagement at age fourteen. International Association for the Evaluation of Educational Achievement, Amsterdam (2001)
Wilson, T.D., Dunn, D.S., Kraft, D., Lisle, D.J.: Introspection, attitude change, and attitude-behavior consistency: The disruptive effects of explaining why we feel the way we do. In: Berkowitz, L. (ed.) Advances in Experimental Social Psychology, vol. 22, pp. 287–343. Academic Press, New York (1989)
Wingard, R.G.: Classroom teaching changes in web-enhanced courses: A multi-institutional study. Educause Quarterly 27(1), 26–35 (2004)

Tree-Based Comparison for Plagiarism Detection and Automatic Marking of Programming Assignments

Sin-Chun Ng, Andrew Kwok-Fai Lui, and Lai-Shan Wong

School of Science and Technology, The Open University of Hong Kong, Hong Kong, SAR China
scng@ouhk.edu.hk

Abstract. Programming assignments are usually considered as a major assessment component of a programming course. As the number of students enrolling in programming courses has been always high, it becomes a difficult task to mark a large number of programming assignments effectively in a short period of time. Moreover, plagiarism on program codes has become a serious problem recently. Markers may not be able to locate similar scripts that they have marked before. This paper introduces an online assignment management system which allows programming assignments to be submitted online and marked effectively. The marking of programming assignments involves two processes: plagiarism detection among different submitted source codes and automatic marking of individual assignment which includes program testing on different test cases and checking across the model answer. In this paper, we propose the use of parse tree for checking the similarity between program codes. The method can be employed in plagiarism detection and automatic marking of programming assignments.

Keywords: plagiarism detection, automatic marking, programming assignments.

1 Introduction

Since programming assignments are written using computers, it is very easy and handy for students to copy the program source codes from each other. Plagiarism has been a serious problem recently and it is often found in programming assignments. The most common way is to change the variable names or function names of a program with different names and modify the sequence of the declaration statements of variable or change the location of different modules. After taking these actions a plagiarized program can easily escape the eyes of the markers, and pass off as an original program. It is in fact very difficult and time-consuming for markers to find those plagiarized pairs of programs from a large set of programs. Moreover, students may be allowed to submit their assignments after the original due date, so the marker may have to mark the assignments over a long period of time. They may forget similar scripts that they marked before. Due to the serious problem of plagiarism in programming courses, we aimed to design and implement an assignment management system which includes the submission, plagiarism detection and automatic marking of programming assignments.

K.C. Li et al. (Eds.): ICT 2012, CCIS 302, pp. 165–179, 2012.

Previous program comparison algorithms mainly compare either the syntax or semantics of the programs only. It is not accurate enough for program comparison. Therefore, an efficient and accurate program comparing algorithm should be developed for checking the program similarity. The marking of programming assignments involves two processes, plagiarism detection and effective marking of the assignments. This section first analyses some existing program comparing methods and automatic marking methods in order to develop an accurate and effective program comparing algorithm.

1.1 Program Comparing Methods

Various program-comparing methods have been proposed in the past few decades. They are mainly used for detecting source code plagiarism. Traditional program comparing methods related to detecting plagiarism in program courses are mainly divided into two approaches – metric-based and structural-based.

Metric-based is an earlier approach. This is also called attribute-counting-metric since it compares the frequency of keywords between pairs of programs. Different systems use different metrics. For example, some of the metrics used by the Faidhi-Robinson System (Faidhi & Robinson, 1987) are the number of program statements, repetitive statement percentage, conditional statement percentage, number of modules, module contribution percentage (the number of code lines inside procedures), count of unique identifiers, average spaces percentage per line, average identifier length.

Since metric-based methods compare programs based on the occurrence of keywords, it performs better when the pair of programs is very similar. According to Verco and Wise (1996), metric-based is good for a less experienced group of students because they will not make many changes to the programs, but it is not recommended to use this approach for experienced classes.

A more accurate and reliable approach, structural-based comparison, is then developed. The programs are parsed and transformed to token streams. Table 1 shows an example Java source text and the corresponding tokens (Prechelt, Malpohl and Phlippsen, 2000) and how the token streams are compared. YAP3 (Wise, 1996) and JPlag (Prechelt et al., 2000) are some well-known structural comparison systems, and they use the Greedy String Tiling algorithm (Wise, 1993) for comparing the token strings.

Table 1. Example of Java source text and corresponding tokens

Java Source Code	Generated Tokens
`public class Count{`	BEGINCLASS
`  public static void main(String [] args)`	VARDEF,BEGINMETHOD
`    throws java.io.IOException{`	
`    int count = 0 ;`	VARDEF,ASSIGN
`    while(System.in.read() != -1)`	APPLY,BEGINWHILE
`      count ++;`	ASSIGN,ENDWHILE
`    System.out.println(count+" chars.");`	APPLY
`  }`	ENDMETHOD
`}`	ENDCLASS

Since structural-based only compares the structure of the programs, it is not accurate enough to determine the programs are plagiarized programs. So a new approach using parse tree with comparison of data is introduced for checking plagiarism.

1.2 Program Plagiarism

Program plagiarism refers to the copying of programs and presenting them as one's own without acknowledging the original author. There are many reasons for students to copy programs from each other. The main reasons include a weak student copies and edits a classmate's program because he does not know how to do, or a poorly motivated student copies and edits a classmate's program in order to minimize his job. Common code modification can be classified into two types: lexical change and structural change (Joy & Luck, 1999).

According to Joy and Luck (1999), Lexical change means the change can be performed without the knowledge of the language. An example of the changes includes

- Modifying the comments, such as adding, deleting and using other words in the comments.
- Modifying the format, such as adding or deleting spaces.
- Modifying the identifier names.

On the other hand, structural change requires knowledge of the language. The changes depend on the language. An example of the changes includes

- Replacing loops, such as replacing while loop with for loop and vice-versa.
- Replacing if statements with case statements and vice-versa.
- Changing the order of the statements without affecting the output of the program.
- Changing the operand without affecting the output of the program. E.g. x>y is replaced by y<=x, true is replaced by not false.
- Changing in-line code into procedure calls and vice-versa.

A powerful program plagiarism system should be able to detect plagiarized programs after students make lexical and structural changes on their programs.

1.3 Automatic Marking

Automatic marking system for programs usually uses test harness for checking programs. It uses the black box technique because it is a quick and easy method. The system does not need to look into the program code or the structures. First, the programs are executed to see if they are error free. Tutors should provide test cases for checking. The number of test cases should depend on the type of assignments because some assignments need more test cases. The test cases should include cases of normal expected output and special cases, such as boundary cases. Mark scaling is also considered. Usually, the mark is evenly distributed to the test cases. Some marking systems for programming courses have been developed, JavaMarker (Ahmadzadeh, Namvar, & Soltani, 2011), CourseMarker (Higgins, Hegazy, Symeonidis, & Tsintsifas, 2003), and ASSYST (Jackson & Usher, 1997).

However, students may know the outputs from the assignment question and they may hard code the outputs in their program. The student's program can then give the correct output without using the required technique. For example, the assignment requires printing 1 to 10 using a for-loop, but the student can hard code printing 1 to 10 line by line. This cannot be detected if the test harness approach is used. So another approach is to check the similarity between the program and the model answer.

1.4 Comparison on Existing Systems

Table 2 is a comparison of some available systems in the market, an online submission system BOSS (Joy, Griffiths, & Boyatt, 2005), a software plagiarism detecting system JPlag (Prechelt, Malpohl, & Phlippsen, 2000), an Eclipse plug-in marking system JavaMarker (Ahmadzadeh et al., 2011).

Table 2. Comparisons on BOSS, JPlag and JavaMarker

	BOSS	**JPlag**	**JavaMarker**
Online submission system	Y	N	N
Plagiarism Detection	Y	Y	N
Checks on	Text	Source Code	Source Code
Automatic Marking	N	N	Y
Plagiarism Detection Algorithm	Sherlock (on text and comments)	Structural-based approach + Greedy String Tiling	N/A
Automatic Marking Algorithm	N/A	N/A	Test Harness

Currently, the existing systems mainly support online submission, plagiarism detection or automatic marker for programming courses. There are not many "one-stop service" systems including all these features in the market at the moment. A system with these features is needed in order to reduce the workload of the markers.

2 System Architecture

An online assignment management system is developed to evaluate the comparator as a plagiarism detection tool and an automatic marking tool. Fig. 1 shows the system architecture. Students can submit their assignments through the online system and instructors can upload the model answers. All the files submitted are sent to the database. In plagiarism detection, only program files of the same question from an assignment are compared since inter-question comparison is unnecessary. A pair of files is loaded from the database for each comparison. A table of similarity rate is shown for each question. In automatic marking, each program is compared with all the model answers of that question (since a question may have different program solutions) and the highest score is taken. The markers should be able to adjust and confirm the final mark of each question.

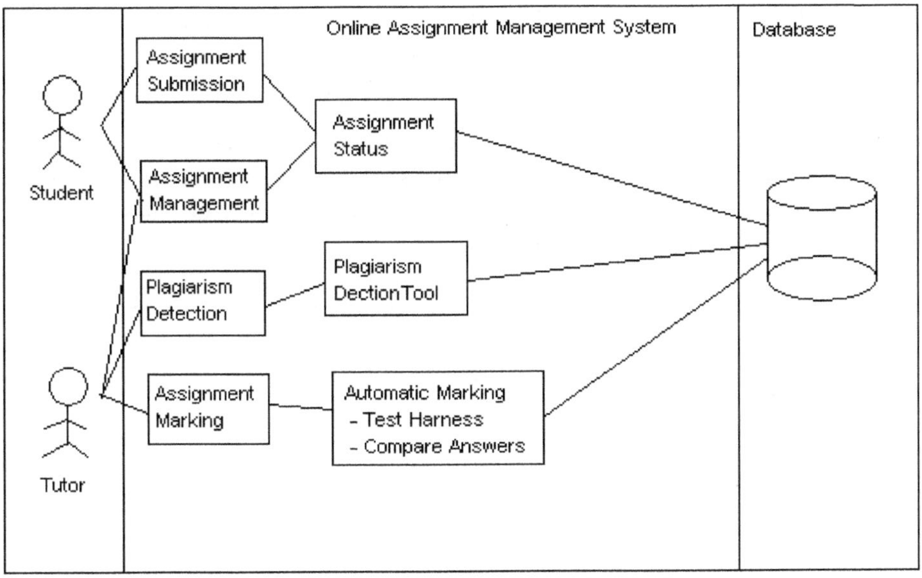

Fig. 1. System architecture

3 Methodology

3.1 Overview

Different types of program comparing algorithms have been analyzed. To develop our own online assignment management system, the tree comparing approach is chosen because it can compare both the content and the structure of the programs. Each program is transformed into a parse tree with nodes and tokens. Then, a program comparator is developed. It compares the trees in pairs and produces a similarity score for each pair.

After the comparator is developed, it is applied as a plagiarism detection tool. A threshold rate is defined. If the similarity rate of a pair of programs is higher than the threshold rate, the pair is considered as plagiarized programs.

The comparator can also be applied as an automatic marking tool. The more similar they are, the higher the score of the program.

3.2 Parse Tree

First, each program is transformed into a parse tree. The comments, spaces and line breaks are ignored since they do not affect the program result. Each tree node contains a node part and a token part. The node part is used to compare the structure of the program, while the token part is used to compare the content of the program. Fig. 2 shows an example of a simple parse tree. “Class” is the node and “HelloWorld” is the token, the rest tree nodes share the same format. Sub-trees of the same type of node are compared in order to compare the program structure. For each node, the token part is also compared in order to compare the program content. This approach, which considers both program structure and program content, should be more accurate as compared to former approaches since metric-based approach compares mainly program content and structural-based approach compares mainly program structure.

Source code:

```
public class HelloWorld {
    public static void main(String [] args) {
        System.out.println(1);
        System.out.println(2);
    }
    public String getA() {
        return a;
    }
}
```

The corresponding parse tree:

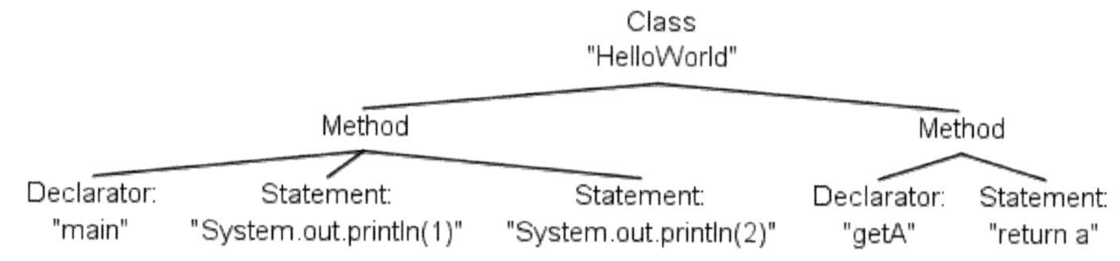

Fig. 2. Example of a simple parse tree

A powerful program comparator should be able to detect similar programs even after lexical change and structural change are made. Table 3 shows some common types of changes and the solution when using tree-based approach.

The parser should be language dependent, different programming language should use a different parser. JJTree in JavaCC (Kodaganallur, 2004) is chosen as the parser for parsing Java programs in this paper.

Table 3. Common types of changes and the solution in tree-based approach

Change	Solution
Modify comments and format	Ignore comments and extra spaces while parsing.
Modify identifier names	The ratio of node and token is adjusted so node is more important than token, hence the detected rate will be high even all the names are changed.
Changing the order of statements	The comparison is in tree based, so statements of different order are still in the same level.

3.3 Program Comparator

Programs are compared in pairs. Since the parse tree approach has been chosen, the pair of programs is parsed into trees by the parser first, one tree for each. The trees generated are complicated so they are broken down into sub-trees. Each sub-tree represents a sub-part of the program where sub-parts are categorized as a package, import, class or interface, constructor, field, method, expression and statement. Fig. 3 shows an example of the hierarchy of a parse tree. Different sub-trees are compared with sub-trees of the same structure type from the other parse tree, so it can detect similarity even with different order. For example, a method is compared with other methods from the other program. In each comparison, a similarity score between the two sub-trees is produced. The final similarity score of the pair of programs is the sum of scores for all sub-trees.

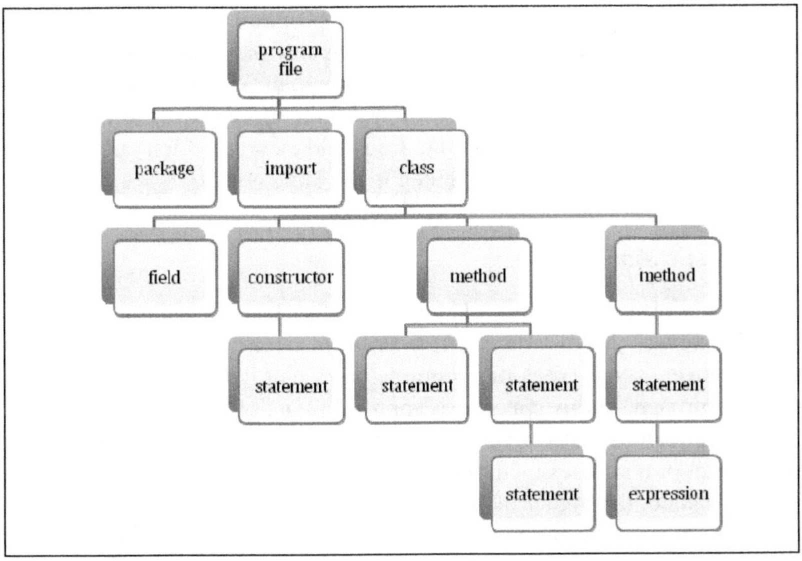

Fig. 3. An example of the hierarchy of a parse tree

The comparator uses depth-first approach to compare the two sub-trees. It compares the nodes and the tokens in the two sub-trees and the similarity score returned will be 0 if both nodes and tokens are not same, 9 if both nodes are the same, 10 if both nodes and tokens are same. The ratio of return value of the node and token can be adjusted to reflect the importance of variable names. The sub-tree will match to the sub-tree of the other program with the highest score. Once a sub-tree is matched, it cannot be matched with other sub-trees.

Lastly, the similarity rate of the pair of programs is calculated by

Similarity = (sum of similarity score of all sub-trees / maximum similarity score) ×100%

where the maximum similarity score is calculated by

maximum similarity score = 10 × number of sub-trees in the program

3.4 Plagiarism Detection

The program comparator is then implemented in an online assignment management system that can detect plagiarism. Student programs are sent to the system before checking plagiarism. For a set of n programs, there will be n×(n-1)/2 comparisons. After checking, a table of similarity scores for each program pair is shown. The higher the similarity score, the higher the possibility that plagiarism occurs. Smaller programs will have a higher similarity rate as the base is smaller, so the comparator is not aimed at detecting plagiarism on programs that are too small (less than 10 lines of code). Plagiarism detection should be used for larger programs, for example programs with more than 50 lines of code. The size of the program should affect the chance of being similar, so a threshold rate should be defined. If the similarity score of a pair of programs is higher than the threshold rate, the pair is considered as plagiarized programs. A table of the similarity rate of each pair of programs in the set is shown. Those similarity rates higher than the threshold score, which are considered as suspected plagiarized pairs, are highlighted in the table.

3.5 Automatic Marking

For automatic marking, existing systems usually uses test harness to check the programs. However, this is not accurate enough since students can hard code the outputs. Moreover, some types of programs, such as GUI, cannot be detected using test harness approach. In this paper, two approaches are employed.

The first approach is test harness. The system runs the programs and compares the input and output of test cases including normal expected output and special cases. The more cases matched, the higher the score of the program.

Other than the test harness approach, the comparator is added to check the similarity between the submitted program and the model answers. The more similar they are, the higher the score of the program. However, a question may have different program solutions. The instructor can provide more than one model answer for a programming question. A program is compared with all the model answers and the highest score is taken into account. This is suitable when different program structures will be used to solve the problem.

4 Results

4.1 Parse Tree

Programs are successfully parsed into desired trees using JJTree (Kodaganallur, 2004). Fig. 4 shows an example of converting a simple Java program into a tree structure with nodes and tokens. Space indentation represents the depth of the node. Each line shows a node and token as quoted text.

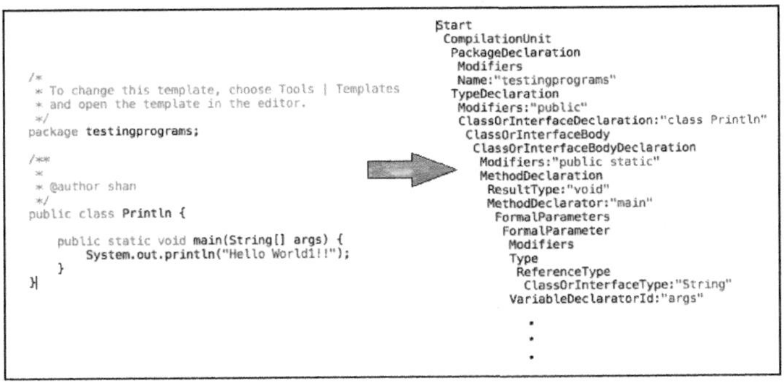

Fig. 4. Example of converting a Java program into a tree structure with nodes and tokens

4.2 Program Comparator

Since the parse tree is complicated, it takes some time to parse it into trees. Some simple programs shown in Table 4 are being compared for different program-comparing algorithms. The comparison results are shown in Table 5.

Table 4. Simple testing programs

File	Description
HelloWorld.java	Contains a main function which assigns “HelloWorld” to a string “a” and prints a.
HelloWorld2.java	Contains a main function which assigns “HelloWorld” to a string “b” and prints b.
IfElse.java	Contains a main function with a simple if-else statement
IfElseCopy.java	A copy of IfElse.java
WhileLoop.java	Contains a main function with a simple while loop and the program function is same as ForLoop.java
ForLoop.java	Contains a main function with a simple for loop and the program function is same as WhileLoop.java

The results for tree-based algorithms are more reasonable. The first pair has different variable names, so the rate should be high (97%). It is not 100% as the two programs are not exactly the same. The third pair has totally different structure and content, so the rate should be low. The fourth pair has similar content but still different in structure, so the rate should be high but not as high as 100%. From the result, it confirms that the use of tree-based approach as a comparator is a feasible method. It gives a realistic and accurate comparison result.

Table 5. Comparison of our proposed tree-based method and other methods

Compared files	Description	Tree-based	Metric-based	Structural-based	JPlag
HelloWorld.java **HelloWorld2.java**	Programs with same content but different variable	Score: 97, Maximum: 100 Rate: 97%	Score: 65, Maximum: 65 Rate: 100%	Score: 14, Maximum: 14 Rate: 100%	Rate: 100%
IfElse.java **IfElseCopy.java**	Programs with same structure and content	Score: 140, Maximum: 140 Rate: 100%	Score: 98, Maximum: 98 Rate: 100%	Score: 18, Maximum: 18 Rate: 100%	Rate: 100%
HelloWorld.java **IfElse.java**	Programs with different structure and content	Score: 68, Maximum: 140 Rate: 49%	Score: 65, Maximum: 98 Rate: 66%	Score: 12, Maximum: 16 Rate: 75%	Rate: 10%
WhileLoop.java **ForLoop.java**	Programs with different structure but similar content	Score: 119, Maximum: 140 Rate: 85%	Score: 212, Maximum: 212 Rate: 100%	Score: 16, Maximum: 20 Rate: 80%	Rate: 10%

4.3 Plagiarism Detection

The comparator is implemented as a plagiarism detection tool. A few set of programs is tested and compared with JPlag's (Prechelt, Malpohl & Phlippsen, 2000) result.

Set 1: this set contains 6 simple Java program files. Each program contains a main method with one or two simple statements including print, if-else, for-loop, while-loop. The results are listed in Table 6.

The result is different from that of JPlag. JPlag shows only one pair in range 90% to 100%, which is an exact copy pair. The other files fall into the low range of rate may be because programs are too small so it does not consider them as plagiarism.

Set 2: this is a larger set that contains 121 Java program files. The programs are larger and more complicated as compared to Set 1. The results are listed in Table 7.

Table 6. Comparison results of our proposed tree-based and Jplag

Our Tree-based approach		JPlag	
Similar Rate	**Pair Number**	**Similar Rate**	**Pair Number**
0% to 9%	0	0% to 9%	14
10% to 19%	0	10% to 19%	0
20% to 29%	8	20% to 29%	0
30% to 39%	5	30% to 39%	0
40% to 49%	0	40% to 49%	0
50% to 59%	0	50% to 59%	0
60% to 69%	1	60% to 69%	0
70% to 79%	0	70% to 79%	0
80% to 89%	0	80% to 89%	0
90% to 100%	1	90% to 100%	1

The results look similar for obvious plagiarized pairs. The distribution is different for non-obvious plagiarized pairs. This may be due to the use of different comparing approaches. However, this is insignificant since the lower ranges are usually not considered in plagiarism detection.

Table 7. Comparison results of our proposed tree-based and JPlag

Our Tree-based approach		**JPlag**	
Similar Rate	**Pair Number**	**Similar Rate**	**Pair Number**
0% to 9%	589	0% to 9%	109
10% to 19%	446	10% to 19%	1478
20% to 29%	333	20% to 29%	0
30% to 39%	108	30% to 39%	0
40% to 49%	2	40% to 49%	1
50% to 59%	0	50% to 59%	0
60% to 69%	0	60% to 69%	0
70% to 79%	0	70% to 79%	0
80% to 89%	1	80% to 89%	0
90% to 100%	5778	90% to 100%	5672

4.4 Automatic Marking

The automatic marking process will involve two phases: program testing according to test harness and similarity check between the program and the model answers. Instructors are required to input test cases and model answers for each question.

The same tree-based comparator (as discussed in the above section) will be applied as an automatic marking tool for checking the similarity of the student's program with respect to the model answers. Since both the contents and the structures of the programs will be checked, the suggested score will provide an indicative and a reliable mark for the marker to further adjust.

4.5 Online Assignment Management System

Our system consists of three main functions:

1. It is an online system (Fig. 5) that provides an easy and comfortable interface for students, instructors and markers to submit and manage programming assignments.
2. The markers can check plagiarism for programming assignments. Students' program files are checked according to each question, a table showing similarity of each pair is shown for each question. Fig. 6 shows an example of checking plagiarism. Each box shows the similarity rate between the corresponding row and column. Boxes of files not successfully parsed (i.e. rate equals -1, usually because the programs have syntax errors) or students who did not submit are darkened, and boxes of similarity rate higher than a threshold (the current threshold is 85%) are highlighted in the table. The similarity rates are linked to view the pair of the two files. The text highlighted in red is the similar part of the two files. Fig. 7 shows two files that have low similarity.
3. The system provides automatic marking (Fig. 8) on test harness and comparison with the suggested model answer. It also provides an interface (Fig. 9) for the

markers to input the final mark, as the automated marking should be used for reference. The left hand side will show the program code and the right hand side will show the result of the test cases.

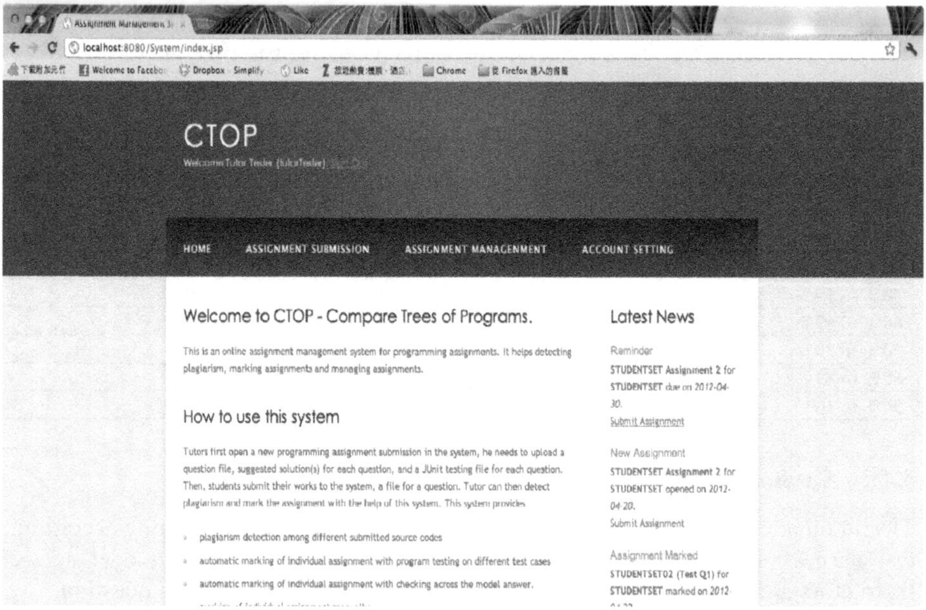

Fig. 5. The Online Assignment Management System

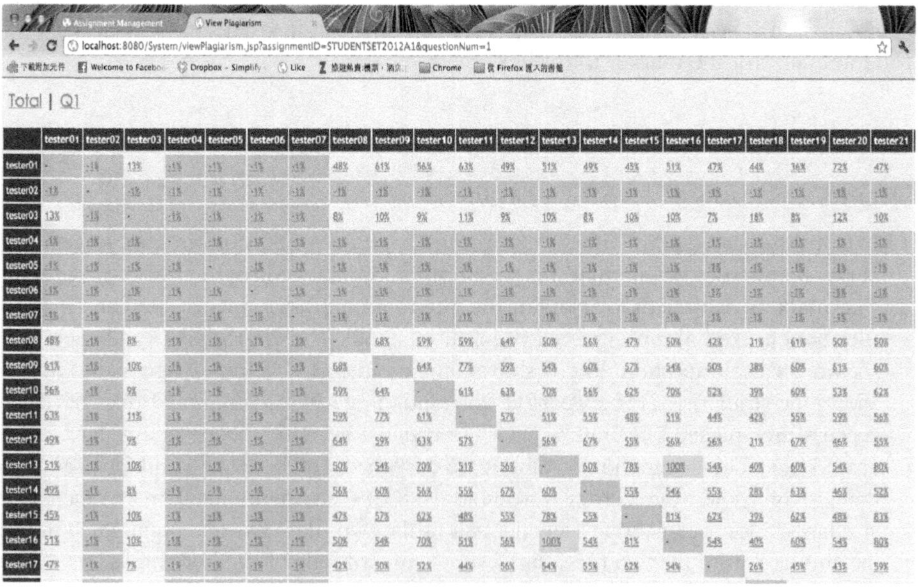

Fig. 6. Example of checking plagiarism

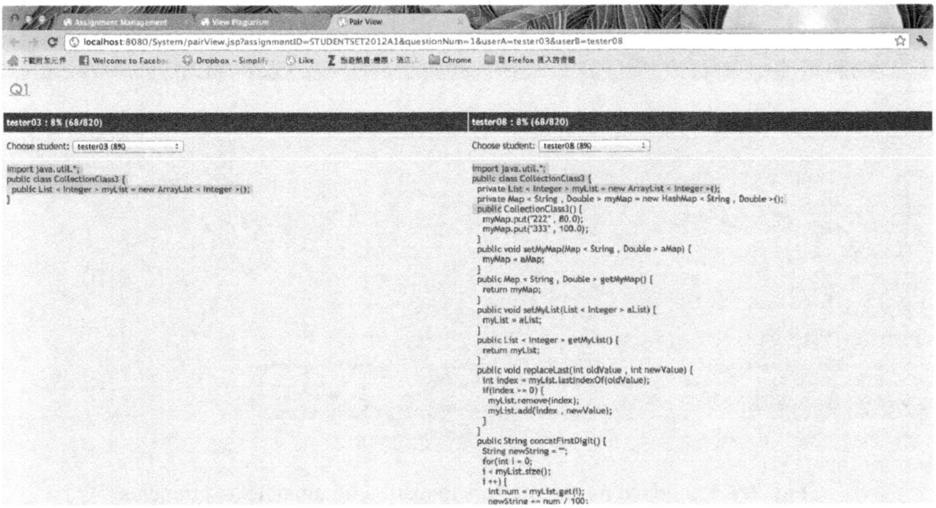

Fig. 7. A view on two files that have low similarity

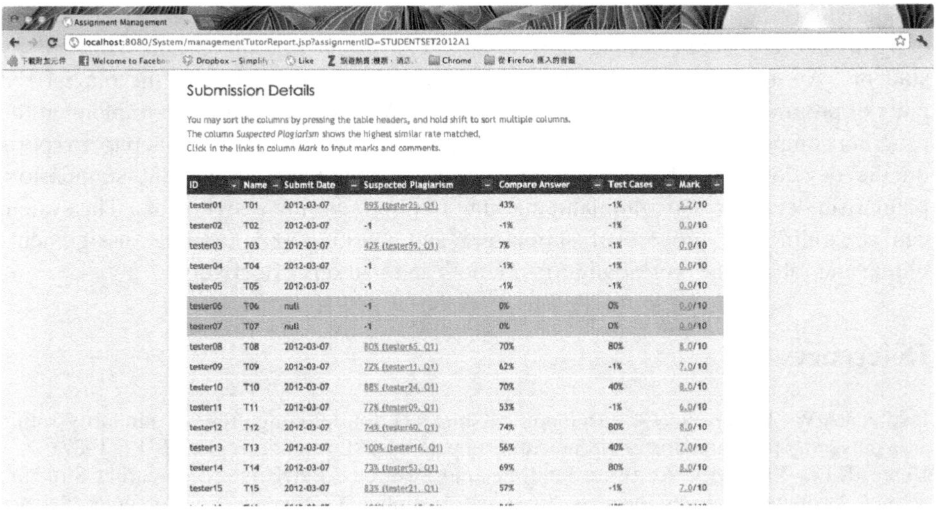

Fig. 8. A view after automatic marking

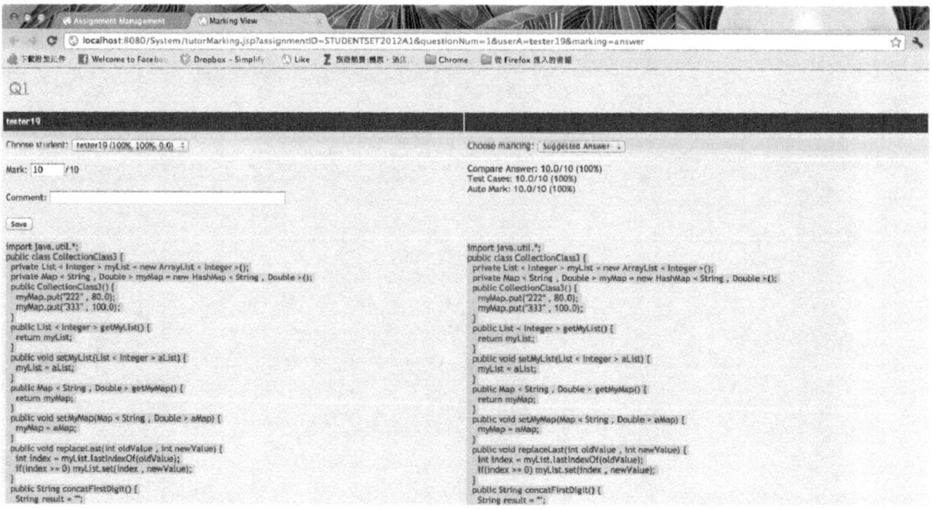

Fig. 9. An interface for the markers to mark programming assignments

5 Conclusions

Plagiarism is currently a serious problem in academic institutions. Programming assignments, especially computer programs, can easily be copied and modified by students. An accurate and flexible system can help markers identify the plagiarized pairs of program among a large set of programs. A parse tree is used to implement the program comparator for checking the similarity between programs. This paper reports on the development of an integrated online system with assignment submission, plagiarism detection and automatic marking of programming assignments. The system can streamline the process of submitting and marking programming assignments online and relieve the workload of instructors and markers effectively.

References

Faidhi, J.A.W., Robinson, S.K.: An empirical approach for detecting program similarity within a university programming environment. Computers and Education 11(1), 11–19 (1987)

Verco, K.L., Wise, M.J.: Software for Detecting Suspected Plagiarism: Comparing Structure and Attribute-Counting Systems. In: First Australian Conference on Computer Science Education, ACSE 1996, Australia (1996)

Prechelt, L., Malpohl, G., Phlippsen, M.: JPlag: Finding plagiarisms among a set of programs. Fakultät für Informatik Technical Report 2000-1. Universität Kalrsruhe, Germany (2000)

Wise, M.J.: YAP3: improved detection of similarities in computer program and other texts. In: Proceedings of the Twenty-Seventh SIGCSE Technical Symposium on Computer Science Education, SIGCSE 1996, Philadelphia, USA (1996)

Wise, M. J.: String similarity via greedy string tiling and running Karp-Rabin matching. Department of Computer Science, University of Sydney (1993), `ftp://ftp.cs.su.oz.au/michaelw/doc/RKRGST.ps` (retrieved)

Joy, M., Luck, M.: Plagiarism in Programming Assignments. IEEE Transactions of Education 42(2), 129–133 (1999)

Ahmadzadeh, M., Namvar, S., Soltani, M.: JavaMarker: A Marking System for Java Programs. International Journal of Computer Applications 20(2), 15–20 (2011)

Higgins, C., Hegazy, T., Symeonidis, P., Tsintsifas, A.: The CourseMarker CBA system: Improvements over Ceilidh. Education and Information Technologies 8(3), 287–304 (2003)

Jackson, D., Usher, M.: Grading student programs using ASSYST. In: Proceedings of the Twenty-Eighth SIGCSE Technical Symposium on Computer Science Education, SIGCSE 1997, San Jose, USA (1997)

Joy, M., Griffiths, N., Boyatt, R.: The BOSS online submission and assessment system. ACM Journal on Educational Resources in Computing 5(3), 1–28 (2005)

Kodaganallur, V.: Incorporating language processing into Java applications: A JavaCC tutorial. IEEE Computer Society 21(3), 70–77 (2004)

Research on the Learner Guide Mechanism in the Virtual Experiment Platform of Physics Based on the Theory of User-Centered Design

Yuanyuan Hu, Zuyuan Wang, Yu Lu, and Ruiheng Sun

Department of Physics, Tongji University, China
19irishu@tongji.edu.cn

Abstract. This paper applies the theory of user-centered design to the learner guide mechanism in facilitating the development of the virtual experiment platform. In order to form an appropriate guide mechanism, it incorporates the findings from the learner activity models and learner-centered principles into an improved learners' mental model. According to the guide mechanism, three detailed guiding suggestions have been put forward to make the learning atmosphere more friendly and efficient.

Keywords: guide mechanism, virtual experiment, user-centered design, learner model.

1 Introduction

Various researchers are attempting to build their own psychological models of user experiences during the network process. User-centered ideas have revolutionized Web research to the extent that feelings in the process of human–computer interaction should be also taken into account. Nowadays, the techniques, algorithms and functions are probably the most often discussed in the research on the virtual experiment platforms. However, the virtual experiment, as a marriage of Web and education, also needs the guidance of research on users' activities or experience. Since learners are the main user groups, doing research on learner–computer interactions is necessary and beneficial to the development of our virtual experiment platform.

1.1 The Virtual Experiment Platform for Physics

Virtual labs have been developed for reforming the teaching and learning conditions for the provision of distance education and technical support. Learners can enter the virtual laboratory apparatus at any time to carry on various experiments (Li, Zhou, Li, Chen, & Peng, 2002). In America, there are many good and famous virtual labs such as Carolina State University's LAAP (Learn Anytime Anywhere Physics), and the laboratory of organic chemistry of the University of Illinois at Chicago. There are also

K.C. Li et al. (Eds.): ICT 2012, CCIS 302, pp. 180–189, 2012.

many excellent domestic ones. For example, the VCM Simulating Lab for middle school students, the Web Virtual Labs of Beijing University of Posts and Telecommunications, the Virtual Experiment Education Platform for Multi-Subjects and so on (Hu, Wu, & Wang, 2012).

The Virtual Experiment Platform for Physics and Automatic Control is a multi-function platform of labs for students manipulating instruments and observing virtual phenomena in physics and control areas. It was developed by a team at Tongji University, which consists of teachers and students from different departments including: Computer Science, Physics and Automatic Control. Our platform embraces six physics experiments and five automatic ones. Fig. 1 shows a scene of the single pendulum experiment. It has eight menu options: “Experiment Principles”, “Related Knowledge”, “Experiment Instruments”, “Research Scheme”, “Operate the Experiment”,“Conclusions and Rethink”, “Reports”, and “Manuals”.

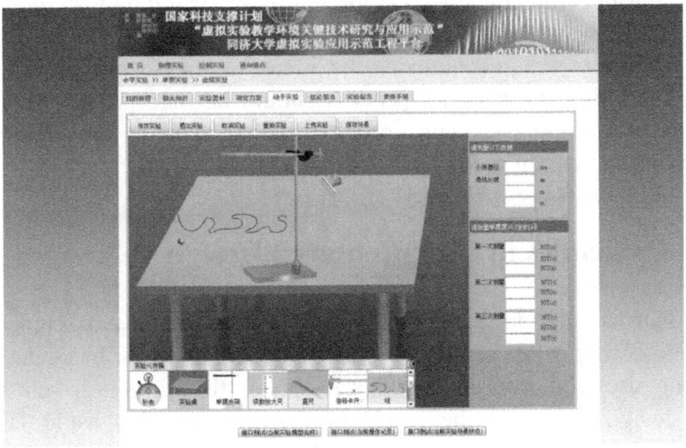

Fig. 1. A screenshot of the single pendulum experiment

1.2 The Learners’ Mental Model

The learners’ mental model (Cooper & Reinmann, 2003) derived from our previous paper based on Norman’s User Mental Model. The learners’ mental model is composed by cognition, motivation, destination and expectation. They guide the learners’ activities and experience. We had conducted a survey on learners’ experience during the process of the mentioned virtual platform among senior high school students. According to the learners’ mental model, we designed 10 questions in our distributed questionnaires. This survey exposed many drawbacks of the platform including excessive words usage, unreasonable manual arrangement, lack of approachability, and the absence of audio files. It also gives overall suggestions for improving the design such as “survey before design”, “more graphics and videos”, “a suitable user”, “implant the manuals” and so on. However, the details are still ambiguous. The learner guide mechanism is essential to the design detail in virtual experiment platforms.

1.3 The Learner Guide Mechanism

The learner guide mechanism derived from the concept of the User Guide since the learners are the main part of the user groups in virtual labs. This mechanism clarifies a detailed process during the interactions between learners and virtual experiment platforms. Researching on the learner guide mechanism could help develop our Web product. What's more, the theory of user-centered is the core concept of the user guide.

User guide concepts or ideas used to appear as a book-like guide document or a manual for software applications. Recently, a whole new concept in interactive design areas has emerged. Just like the meaning of the word "guide", the user guide is a process design that is aimed to direct the users to be familiar with the digital products as soon as possible. It also demands this experience should be friendly and interesting. Thus, we suggest that the manual should be implanted into the pages as invisible signals to help users when they need them, but making sure they are not too evident as well.

In order to build this mechanism, the ideas of user-centered and the learners' activity model during the network process should be incorporated into the learners' mental model. According to an appropriate guide mechanism, the detailed revision for our platform could be exhibited.

2 The Principles in User-Centered Design

Donald A. Norman, as an academic in the field of cognitive science, design and usability engineering, proposes three concept models and four basic design principles in advocating user-centered design. Norman uses the term user-centered design to describe a design based on the needs of the user, leaving aside what he deems secondary issues like aesthetics (Norman, 2002).

2.1 Three Concept Models

The three concept models in the process of the interactions between user and products are design model, user's model and system image:

- The design model describes the design minds of the designers or the original goals that they mean to unfold.
- The user's model or user's mental model means, their intuitive opinions on the operating methods when they face the product.
- The system image states the actual contents that the products passed on to users.

Since these models build bonds between designers, users and products, they play important roles in the design processes. Fig. 2 embodies the relationships of these three models.

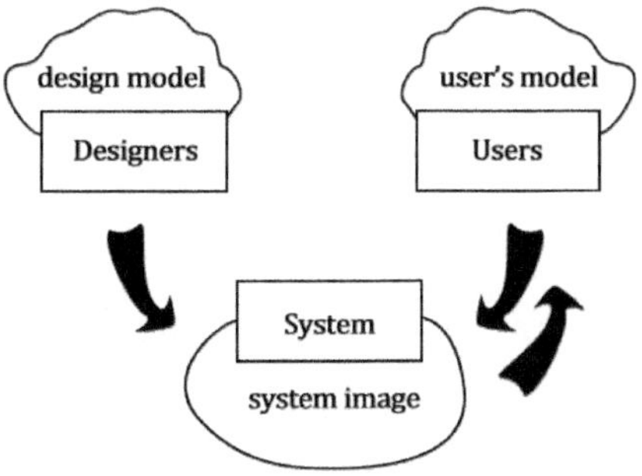

Fig. 2. The relationships of design model, user's model and representing model

2.2 Seven Principles

Norman also exalts seven important principles in interactive design: applying the knowledge in representing systems, simplifying the structure of tasks, making things visible, getting the mapping available, exploiting the powers of constraint, explaining affordances, and standardizing.

The principle of visible and mapping available are frequently mentioned in Norman's descriptions. Making things visible embodies that every controller should match a specific goal. What's more, the guidance should be easily understood. Getting the mapping available is so called "response compatibility" in the domain of ergonomics. It means designers should create a product that users feel familiar with at first sight in the way of physical analogies and cultural customs. It figures in the principle of feedback. This principle claims that systems need to provide information in time when a user finishes an action or wants to know the following effects.

These models and principles are not only the core concept of user-centered design, but also the necessary elements to form the learner guide mechanism. Combining these ideas with the learner's activity model can build a better learners' mental model.

3 A Supplement to the Learners' Mental Model

Since the learner guide mechanism needs the direction of the learners' mental model, an improved model has been put forward by consolidating "the activity model during the network learning process" and "the learner-centered psychological principles".

3.1 The Activity Model during the Network Learning Process

The structure of the learner model (Du, Zheng, Li, & Yuan, 2005) has been separated into two parts: personality model of learner and behavior model. As shown in Fig. 3, the public and private information, and the no-intelligence factor are two main elements. However, it is obvious that this model paid more attention to the personality studying style, but ignored the activities model towards the efficiency of learning.

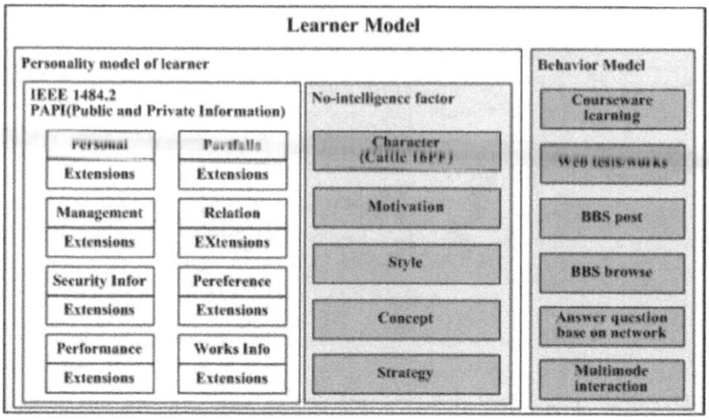

Fig. 3. The structure of learner model: Personality model & behavior model

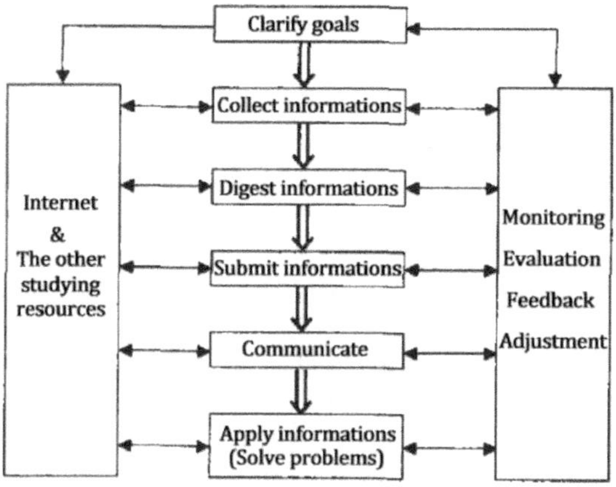

Fig. 4. The multidimensional network learning model

The multidimensional network learning model (Pen & Yang, 2006) has been proposed based on the structure of the learner model. This model not only elaborates on information activities in time order, but also the relationships between the learners and online resources, involving monitoring, evaluation, feedback and adjustments. As every element could interact with another, it forms a cyclical system to connect each part. Compared with Du's structure of the learner model, learners in this model become more active and could also impact the network resources. The learners are not passive receivers any more. It gives a lot of enlightenment for our leaner mental model.

3.2 The Learner-Centered Psychological Principles

Lepper and Malone (Lepper & Malone, 1987) surveyed learners' motivation in many different kinds of educational games. They considered that the four factors which encourage learners' motivation were challenge, curiosity, control, and imagination. Inspiring learners' curiosity could maintain the interactions between learners and the system. And the BECTA (British Educational and Communications Technology Agency) put forward that the factors which enlighten the learners' motivation were internal and quick feedback, challenging and achievable goals, and uncertain final results. "The learner-centered psychological principles" (Alexander & Murphy, 1998) states briefly that mild anxiety could also focus learners' attention on the special studying content. Thus, the encouragement mechanism, the learning atmosphere with mild anxiety, curiosity, quick feedback, uncertain results are considerable elements in the learner guide mechanism.

3.3 An Improved Learners' Mental Model

Combining the structure of the learner model and multidimensional network learning model, an improved learners' mental model has been built as Fig. 5 shows.

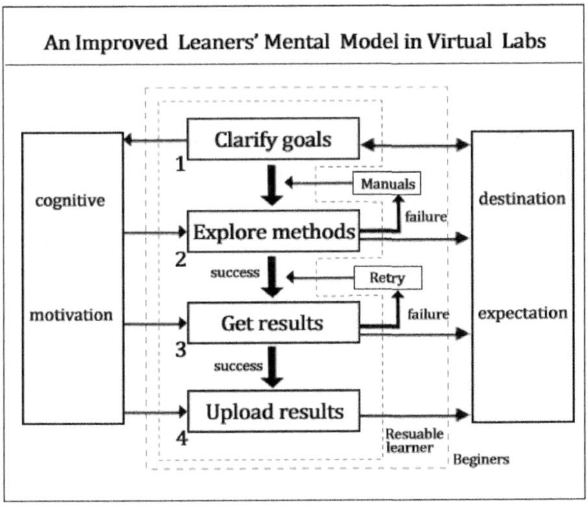

Fig. 5. An improved learners' mental model in virtual labs

- This model involves four main steps in the virtual experimenting process: "clarify goals", "explore methods", "get results" and "upload results".
- The four psychological elements (cognitive, motivation, destination and expectation) that used to be the main components of the former mental model have become the important factors that have impacts on the whole process; however, the arrows' directions are not all the same.
- In the step 2, if a learner couldn't find the right approach, he or she would turn to the "manuals" for help (means "failure" in Fig. 5).
- In the same way, when a learner wants to find some other results, he or she might have a retry before uploading the final results.

- That is to say, in steps 2 and 3, they might have another choice rather than just carrying on to the next step directly.
- This model includes two kinds of learners: beginners and reusable ones. Thus, dashed boxes have been used in the figure to distinguish the two different groups.

4 The Learner Guide Mechanism and Design Scheme

According to the principles in the user-centered and the improved learners' mental model in virtual labs, the guided mechanism for learners in virtual experiences could be established. The mechanism embraces three parts: invisible guide, beginner's guide and encouraging guide. Within this chapter, our guide mechanism would be clarified not only in a theoretical form, but also in some detail.

4.1 Invisible Guide

The scene of the virtual lab itself could be the best guide tool, since the learners could independently explore the methods to manipulate the experiments without external assistance. It also could be known as the invisible guide. The right colors and shapes could create an advantageous atmosphere for learners to immerse themselves in the scene. The distinctive color contrasts make the themes outstanding and the appropriate shapes make the controllers (the buttons, links, etc.) more understandable.

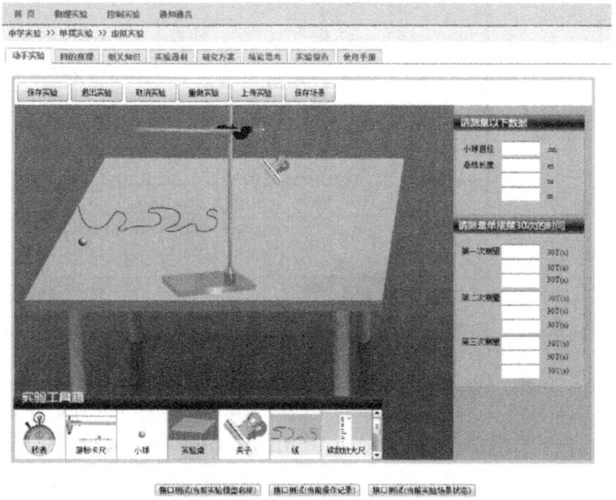

Fig. 6. The design scheme of visual guide in experiment scene

Fig. 6 shows that the "Operate the experiment" has been put in the first place in order to ditch the word illustration that used to clarify the goals and theories. The scene folding in a direct way gives the learner an interesting start. What's more, the outstanding color guidance makes the tool box and data recording space more easily recognized, so that this function would be hardly ignored in the experiment process.

4.2 Beginners Guide

On account of the two groups of learners having different situation recognition levels, beginners and the reusable learners should be worked with separately. Although the scene itself is the best guidance, it also demands a quick way to understand the labs. Beginners need to take a comprehensive view of the overall situation since they have never met this kind of virtual product before. The overall tour is a good problem-solving method. However, a choice should be given out first in order that the reusable learners could actively avoid this assistance.

Fig. 7 clarifies the beginner dialog box. It is obvious that there are two options (yes and no). If beginners choose "yes", they can start a function named overall tour to begin immersion in the experiment. However, if they choose "no", they can skip this part and start the experiment directly. Thus, Fig. 8 shows a detailed guide of the overall tour. It is clear that learners could understand how to carry on with this platform without additional word manuals.

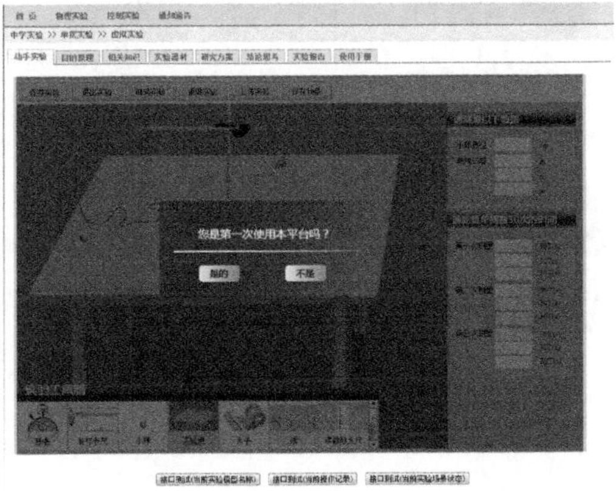

Fig. 7. The design scheme of the beginners' dialog box in the experiment scene

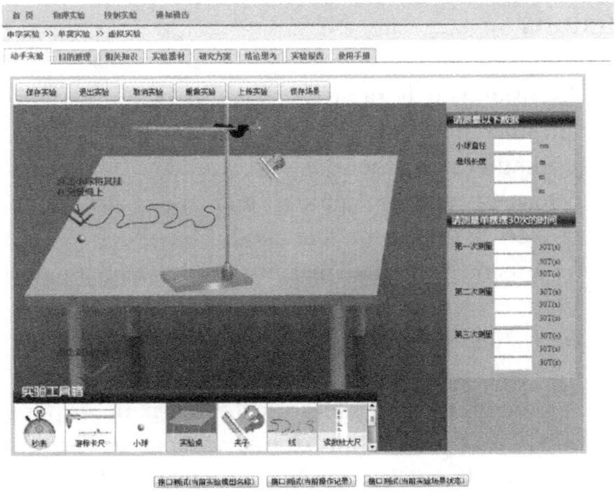

Fig. 8. The design scheme of the overall tour in the experiment scene

4.3 Encouraging Guide

The encouraging guide could provide an attractive factor to inspire the learners' motivation as well. The mild anxiety and encouraging method should be introduced into the process of the virtual experiment. Thus, a timer could enter the labs, and the scoring system should be transformed from negative to positive. Different uses of time should be awarded for different scores. Fig. 9 illustrates the application of the timer and scoring systems. These measures could help learners focus on the experiment process.

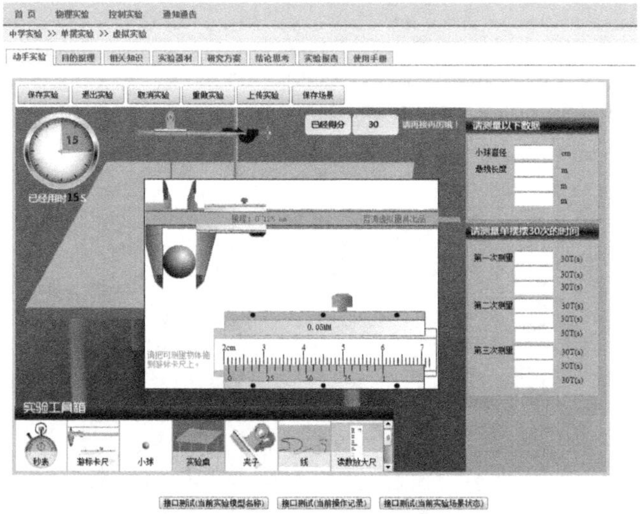

Fig. 9. The design scheme of encouraging guide in the experiment scene

5 Conclusions

From the above discussion, it is obvious that this paper has introduced the theory of user-centered design into the virtual experiment platform. That is to say, the research on the learner-computer interactions is guided by user-centered ideas. By incorporating the learner activity model and the learner-centered psychological principles, an improved learners' mental model has been proposed to construct our learners guide mechanism. It is clear that our guide mechanism involves three parts: invisible guide, beginners guide and encouraging guide. What's more, it is not only put forward in a theoretical level, but also applied to the improvements of our virtual platforms.

It is important to recognize, stressing on the learners' experiences in the learner-computer interactions could revolutionize educational software or websites. In order to create a friendly and efficient learning atmosphere, the ideas of learner-centered have been interpenetrated into the design processes. However, there are still some questions which need to be addressed by future research:

- How should the virtual experiments be represented (including the instruments, phenomena and layouts of laboratories and so on)?
- How to create a virtual experiment with not only one approach or how to design more than one logical manipulating method?
- How to design resource sharing schemes for multiple learners online at the same time?

Addressing these questions could help us build a much greater virtual learning atmosphere. As the developments of technology means to serve our lives, the users' feelings and demands are the most important goals for Web products. Thus, learner-centered ideas should be endowed in every design segment of virtual experiments.

Acknowledgement. This Paper is Supported by the Key Project in the National Science and Technology Pillar Program of China Under Grant No.2008BAH29B00.

References

Alexander, P.A., Murphy, P.K.: The research base for APA's learner-centered psychological principles. In: Lambert, N., McCombs, B.L. (eds.) How Students Learn: Reforming Schools through Learner-Centered Education. American Psychological Association, Washington, DC (1998)

Cooper, A., Reinmann, R.: About Face 2.0 The essentials of interaction design. Wiley Publishing, Inc., US (2003)

Du, J., Zheng, Q., Li, H., Yuan, W.: The Research of Mining Association Rules Between Personality and Behavior of Learner Under Web-Based Learning Environment. In: Lau, R., Li, Q., Cheung, R., Liu, W. (eds.) ICWL 2005. LNCS, vol. 3583, pp. 406–417. Springer, Heidelberg (2005)

Hu, Y., Wu, T., Wang, Z.: Research on the Web Interface of Virtual Experiment Platform Based on the Theory of User Experience. Paper presented at the Automatic Control and Artificial Intelligence, Xiamen, China (2012)

Lepper, M.R., Malone, T.W.: Intrinsic motivation and instructional effectiveness in computer-based education. Aptitude, Learning, and Instruction 3, 255–286 (1987)

Li, R., Zhou, Z., Li, F., Chen, Y., Peng, H.: Network Architecture of Virtual Lab. Acta Simulata Systematica Sinica 3, 91–94 (2002)

Norman, D.A.: The design of everyday things. Basic Books, New York (2002)

Pen, W., Yang, Z.: Research on the Network Learning Activity and Model. China Educational Technology 10 (2006)

Overcoming Copyright Hurdles in the Development of Learning Materials in the Digital Era

K.S. Yuen, Linda Chow, Simon K.S. Cheung, K.C. Li, and Eva Y.M. Tsang

The Open University of Hong Kong, Hong Kong, SAR China
{ksyuen,lchow,kscheung,kcli,etsang}@ouhk.edu.hk

Abstract. Developing teaching or course materials poses many challenges, and copyright is one of them. This paper provides teachers and developers of learning materials with an overview of what they should know about copyright, and provides suggestions on ways to overcome copyright hurdles. Of importance is an understanding of the clauses on fair use and fair dealing under copyright law, as these legally permit reproduction of copyrighted material for certain purposes and circumstances without the need to apply for permission.

This paper also notes a changing copyright landscape and a growing culture of resource-sharing among the educational community. Teachers or developers of learning materials can now consider another option — accessing *free* digital learning materials which can be used, adapted and shared, without any copyright fees. The final part of the paper explores the use of some types of free online materials: works produced under the Creative Commons licence and public domain materials.

Keywords: copyright, Creative Commons licence, open educational resources, public domain.

1 Introduction

When developing teaching and learning materials to distribute to students, we often uncover copyrighted materials we would like to include in our course(s). The paper discusses how, based on our experience at the Open University of Hong Kong, one can sometimes overcome copyright restrictions and effectively use such resources in teaching and developing teaching materials. Whilst the suggestions for overcoming copyright hurdles are useful, nowadays—in the digital era—more changes are evident in the copyright landscape. Teachers or developers of learning materials have another option that they can consider—accessing *free* digital learning materials to use, adapt, share, and reuse—at no copyright cost. The latter part of the paper explores how we can use, open educational resources and public domain materials in our development of teaching and learning materials.

2 Copyright

What is copyright? Copyright is a right granted by law to the author or originator of certain literary, artistic, and musical productions whereby he or she controls the use of

K.C. Li et al. (Eds.): ICT 2012, CCIS 302, pp. 190–200, 2012.

the product for a limited period of time. Permission from the copyright owner is needed for reproduction and distribution of most copyrighted materials, otherwise you may be infringing copyright and put your institution and yourself at legal risk.

3 Developing Learning Materials

If you are given the task of writing a set of instructional materials, no matter whether for self instruction or as teaching materials for use in the classroom, you may first think of writing them from scratch by yourself. This is a common approach, but it is also the most time consuming.

As a subject expert, you probably already have a set of notes you lecture from. You may have been given (or you have developed) a framework for the course, and the task in front of you now is to write the teaching content based on the materials you already have. The following provides some issues relating to copyright that you need to consider when you start writing materials for your course.

4 Writing Your Own Course 'Based On' Existing Learning Materials

In the digital era of developing course materials, you will likely come across useful and relevant materials online developed by others which you would like to use, i.e. copy, paste, edit the source, and probably also post to the Web. Laws on copyright that were created long before the emergence of the Internet make it hard to legally perform such actions that we take for granted on the network. The default setting of copyright laws requires all of these actions to have explicit permission, granted in advance by the right owner, whether you are an artist, teacher, scientist, librarian, policymaker, or just a regular user (Creative Commons, n.d.).

Instead of copying directly the copyrighted materials, you can always write your materials based on the *ideas* of existing copyrighted materials. If the ideas and concepts in the materials are quite unique you probably have to cite the source of such, as a matter of courtesy and to avoid plagiarism. However, using others' ideas in your work does not require permission, as ideas or concepts are not copyrightable – only the specific expressions of them are. So, for example, making a summary of an existing business case for students' reference does not infringe copyright.

5 Copying a Small Amount of Other People's Work

There are instances when you wish to copy just a small amount of materials, such as an extract of 250 words, a single chart, a table, or a diagram, for inclusion in your course. You may wish to copy an excerpt of a business case or an article from a journal, or you may like to include a small amount of digitized multimedia materials in your online study unit that you will provide to your students. With proper acknowledgment of such usage, this can probably be considered as 'fair dealing' or 'fair use', and does not constitute copyright infringement.

What is fair use, and what is fair dealing? It is the use of copyright materials that is considered fair and reasonable, and does not infringe copyright. The fair use approach is adopted by the US and other countries, and whether a usage is considered fair and reasonable depends on the following factors — purpose and character of your use (commercial, educational), the nature of the copyrighted work, what amount and proportion of the whole work was taken from the work, and the effect of the use upon the potential market for or value of the copyrighted work (Committee on the Judiciary, 2001). Judging your own situation against the factors just mentioned (for example, you are teaching in a public school; the materials, which you are copying are from a journal, are academically inclined, and not for profit; the amount you copy is small – like 250 words; and you believe your act will not stop students buying the journal), you will decide for yourself whether you have satisfied the fair use principles, and you can use the materials fairly.

In fair dealing, a number of specific circumstances are defined by law that allows the use of copyrighted materials without the copyright holder's agreement. These include: private copying for personal use, research and study, review and critique, news reporting, and the giving of professional advice (i.e. legal advice). Again, you should check if your usage falls into one of the specifically permitted categories.

Section 45 of Hong Kong's Copyright Ordinance allows photocopying of literary, dramatic, musical and artistic works *to a reasonable extent* by or on behalf of educational establishments for instructional purposes where no relevant licensing schemes are available.

In 2007, Hong Kong's Copyright Ordinance was further amended to include a 'fair dealing' exemption clause (Section 41A) which aimed to help teachers and students make use of reasonable portions of copyright works in a *fair* manner for teaching and learning in a specified course of study. Teachers can judge for themselves whether their use of any amounts and kinds of copyrighted materials is allowed against some factors similar to the fair use factors mentioned above.

So if you wish to use a limited amount of copyrighted materials without permission from the copyright owner, you have to check the copyright law in your country to see if you can do it. Does your country offer fair dealing, or fair use, or both, with regards to copyright materials? In the case of fair dealing, check to see what the specific instances are that the law allows. Is there any consensus on the reasonable extent that can be used without infringing copyright? It is not that difficult to find out, and knowing the law in detail is important as this will have implications on how you develop your teaching materials for distribution.

6 Providing Links to Materials on the Web

As mentioned earlier, you are not permitted to reproduce substantial amount of materials from the Web, as everything on the Web is copyrightable, unless otherwise stated by the owner. In addition, you are not allowed to download materials on the Web and reproduce them on your own course website. But there is one way you can 'make available' (actually this is just leading students to) substantial amounts of other people's materials to students, e.g. the whole article, or whole chapter of a book, or the whole book, and yet you do not have to pay a copyright fee. This is when you only provide a hyperlink (URL) to your students, which will lead students to the website containing the materials. However, you must be careful about deep linking, i.e. linking to a deeper webpage (not the homepage) within a website, which may make it appear that the webpage is part of your own site. The downside of using hyperlinks is, of course, that the site may not be working or the article is withdrawn. Then your students will be at a loss when access to the materials is denied.

7 Using Copyrighted Material: By Permission of the Copyright Owner

If substantial amounts of third party copyrighted materials are used in a course you develop you will need to obtain permission from the copyright owner for reproduction and distribution, and a fee is often charged. Seeking permission to use copyright materials from copyright owners is often a tedious task. The copyright right owner is often difficult to identify and locate, and when this is done the response to the request is often slow. Some commercial bodies impose horrendous copyright fees. Prof J Turow of the University of Pennsylvania reported that he had to pay around US$17,000 in fees and royalties for a total of three minutes of video clips used in a multimedia CD for his medical students. *Harvard Business Review* charges OUHK US$2.80 per copy for a case (US$1.00 for translation rights). Cases developed by local universities in Hong Kong are similarly priced (HK$20 per case). Local newspapers usually charge a flat fee (typically HK$400 to HK$1200 for each article) irrespective of the number of copies reproduced. Open and distance learning institutions are more prepared to pay such fees, but conventional universities and schools usually have not made such budgetary provisions.

8 Using Copyrighted Material: Through a Copyright Collective Administration

There is an alternative for applying permission to copy directly from the copyright owners and that is via through licensing societies which are available in many countries (including Hong Kong). Licensing societies act on behalf of copyright owners and grant licenses at a fee to third parties to copy materials; the copyrights of which are owned by their members. Users may save time in their copyright applications as they report and pay the licensing society rather than having to locate and apply directly to the copyright owners.

Hong Kong, for photocopying of text materials, has the Hong Kong Reprographic Rights Licensing Society (HKRRLS) and Hong Kong Copyright Licensing Association (HKCLA). The former covers textbooks and journals and the latter focuses on newspapers. Similar associations exist for music and songs, and movies and videos. HKRRLS now offers licenses for photocopies and scanned copies of print materials. Unfortunately, no licensing body yet exists to license online rights for digitized materials. Many publishers are still reluctant to provide licenses to allow others to copy digitized materials (journal articles and textbook chapters) online.

HKRRLS offers tertiary institution a fixed charge per page per copy of printed copyright materials (presently at HK$0.50), and for primary and secondary schools a fixed annual charge per school (see http://www.hkrrls.org).

9 Copyrighted Material with CC Licenses

Do we have to pay copyright fees for every item of copyrighted materials? Not necessarily: there are some people who like to make contents they produce freely available to others. A resource-sharing culture is spreading amongst the educational community and this culture of sharing resources and practices will help facilitate change and innovation in education (OER Commons, n.d).

The offer of free usage is facilitated when authors place a copyright permission declaration on their works. Today, they can do it easily through the use of standardized legal tools such as Creative Commons (CC) licences instead of having to pay a lawyer to draft the copyright permission requirement.

Creative Commons (CC) was established (a) to aid universal access to creative works offered by those who wish to make their work freely available, and (b) to provide a free, public, and standardized infrastructure (licenses) which common people can adopt easily (Creative Commons, n.d). Creative Commons licenses are easy-to-understand copyright licenses that allow creators of content to inform others which rights they reserve and which rights they waive for the benefit of other users. CC licenses were designed specifically to work with the Web, so that content with such licenses is easy to search for, discover and use. With Creative Commons licenses labelled on copyrighted materials by the right owner, users of such materials do not have to negotiate individually over specific rights for their usage.

There are six CC licenses, specifying whether or not you mind your work being modified, being used in a commercial context, and whether you want to insist that others keep the same license in any derivative works. All licenses require that users provide attribution to the original creator and licensor (Creative Commons, n.d.).

There are now many content creators who use Creative Commons licenses, and we see more and more websites offer content with such licenses on the Internet. Flickr incorporates it into its framework allowing users to select whether to publish their images under any of the licenses. Wikipedia publishes its content under a Creative Commons Attribution-ShareAlike license; Al Jazeera launched a selection of its videos in a Creative Commons Repository; Whitehouse.gov releases data under Creative Commons Attribution license; and OpenLearn of The Open University in the UK makes educational resources freely available on the Internet under a CC license. Some videos in YouTube have a Creative Commons Attribution licence which allows re-use.

10 Open Education Resources (OER)

A major contribution to the Creative Commons contents comes from the Open CourseWare Movement. In 2002, the Massachusetts Institute of Technology (MIT) started an initiative called MIT OpenCourseWare (MIT OCW, 2007), the ultimate goal of which is to put all of the educational materials from its undergraduate- and graduate-level courses online, and to make them freely available to all people in the world. Such materials are offered under a CC Attribution-NonCommercial-ShareAlike license. MIT OCW is part of MIT's mission to advance education and discovery through knowledge open to everyone. While a few of these courses are limited to chronological reading lists and discussion topics for a course, the majority provide homework problems and examinations (often with solutions) and lecture notes. Some courses also include interactive Web demonstrations in Java or Matlab, complete textbooks written by MIT professors, and streaming video lectures. The project started in October 2002 with 32 courses, and at present, over 2000 MIT courses are available online. In 2005, MIT, along with other leading universities around the world, formed the Open CourseWare Consortium (OCW Consortium, 2007), which 'seeks to extend the reach and impact of open course materials, foster new open course materials and develop sustainable models for open course material publication'. The initiative has encouraged a number of institutions worldwide to make their course materials available as open educational resources under CC licenses. The OCW Consortium is now a collaboration of more than 100 higher education institutions and associated organizations from over 20 countries.

A term synonymous to open courseware is open educational resources (OER). Like the MIT OpenCourseWare project, we also see similar OER movements. The OER movement which aims to provide high quality teaching and learning resources to teachers and learners everywhere for free is growing rapidly supported by foundations and supporters around the world (Matkin, 2010). OER resources include content, software tools, licenses and best practices and usually include a Creative Commons license.

Generally OER are made available in digital format for easy sharing and adaptation (NY Times, 2010). OER programmes and projects range from entirely user-generated content such as Wikipedia and institution-led open courseware, to digital repositories of learning objects and textbooks. Some OER websites are given in Appendix 1.

11 Open Textbooks

Open textbooks are one particular type of open educational resources. They are high-quality textbooks allowing online access under an open license that allows users to read or download them freely. With the open license, teachers may tailor the text to fit their course better by removing unneeded chapters or adding new material. Some examples of open textbooks projects are given in Appendix 2.

As a form of OER, open textbooks are completely digitized textbooks that are accessible online at no cost, and also available in affordable-to-purchase printed copies. The open content can be revised, reused, often remixed and customized under a Creative Commons license that permits the authors to retain ownership of their content, yet establish the rights under which the content may be used by others. In short, open textbooks can be distinguished by the following aspects:

- They are freely available for use and adaptation by anyone using the OER site.
- They invariably consist of digital material. Content can be delivered in many formats, including web, audio, pdf, e-reader, and print versions.
- They are coherent in content and are aligned with particular curricular guidelines and standards, and can be customized to meet individual needs.
- Their copyright is governed by a Creative Commons license which clearly states a list of permissions by the author.

Generally, the minimum baseline rights allow users to, at least:

- Use the textbook without compensating the author;
- Copy the textbook, with appropriate credit to the author;
- Distribute the textbook non-commercially; and
- Shift the textbook into another format (such as digital or print).

Making use of Creative Common licenses, authors may further grant users the rights to:

- Add, remove or alter content in the textbook, often on the condition that derivative works must have the same license;
- Copy and distribute the textbook without giving credit to the author; and
- Use the textbook commercially.

The advantage of open textbooks compared to general OER is that the former are more aligned to a course and may form a major part of its content, while the latter are often scattered resources. If you can identify an open textbook for use in your course, you can write your course 'wrapping around' the book, and in such a case a lot less effort will be required in developing it. If the open textbook does not restrict derivatives, you can even modify the book to suit your course's needs.

12 Public Domain Resources

Public domain resources are works that is not protected by copyright and which can be freely used by everyone. They include:

- generic information like facts, numbers, ideas, titles, blank forms, and the like,
- works granted or donated to the public domain,
- works by the government, and
- works whose copyright has expired.

The copyright for literary, dramatic, musical or artistic works has a limited duration. In Hong Kong the copyright generally ends 50 years after the death of the author. Works of Shakespeare, many songs of the 19th century and earlier now fall under public domain.

One local example of government works is the HKSAR Government's Bilingual Legal Information System (BLIS), which houses the laws of Hong Kong, and is public domain material.

13 Other Free Materials

There are also some free digital resources that are free for use and distribution but there may be some restrictions. You should always check the terms of use carefully as free use may be restricted for use in certain countries.

The Apple Store, for example, has many eBooks available from Project Gutenberg which are available for free download (see Appendix 2). Some of those materials provide a declaration of permission to use, together with a requirement for acknowledgement.

Another useful resource is the World Development Indicators which provides global development data from the World Bank collection. Users are permitted to copy, distribute, adapt, display or include the data in other products for commercial and noncommercial purposes at no cost subject to certain limitations.

There are also sites which offered many peer-reviewed scientific and scholarly journals published online.

Besides materials, there are also open source software solutions such as Moodle or Mahara which educators can use to create their own online learning platforms. Users can redistribute and/or modify it under the terms of the license.

14 Conclusion

This paper provides content writers with the general copyright requirements, related copyright laws, and suggests a number of ways to overcome copyright hurdles when they develop teaching and learning materials. It also provides a discussion of digitally *free* resources which are free to use, though some may have specific restrictions. All these can be valuable resources for educators and at no cost!!

References

Creative Commons. (n.d.). About. About-Creative Commons, http://creativecommons.org/about (retrieved April 18, 2012)

Hong Kong Copyright Ordinance. Section 45. Reprographic copying made by educational establishments or pupils of passages from published works (2007), http://www.legislation.gov.hk/blis_ind.nsf/e1bf50c09a33d3dc482564840019d2f4/3484dc1af84653c148257338001769a0?OpenDocument (retrieved April 18, 2012)

Hong Kong Copyright Ordinance. Section 41A. Fair dealing for purposes of giving or receiving instruction (2007), http://www.legislation.gov.hk/blis_ind.nsf/CURALLENGDOC/7B90EA57827AED8C4825730F003496E0?OpenDocument (retrieved April 18, 2012)

Massachusetts Institute of Technology. In Free Online Course Materials MIT Open CourseWare (2012), http://ocw.mit.edu/index.html (retrieved April 18, 2012)

Matkin, G.W.: The open educational resources movement: current status and prospects (2010), http://unex.uci.edu/pdfs/dean/matkin_apru_paper.pdf (retrieved April 18, 2012)

NY Times. For exposure, universities put courses on the web. New York Times (November 1, 2010), http://www.nytimes.com/2010/11/01/world/europe/01iht-educLede01.html?pagewanted=all (retrieved April 18, 2012)
OER Commons. (n.d.), http://www.oercommons.org/ (retrieved April 18, 2012)
Committee on the Judiciary. Technology, education and copyright harmonization act of 2001 (Senate report 107–31) (2001), http://thomas.loc.gov/cgi-bin/cpquery/z?cp107:sr031 (retrieved March 19, 2012)
The World Bank. World Development Indicators (2012), http://data.worldbank.org/data-catalog/world-development-indicators (retrieved April 18, 2012)

Appendix 1: Some OER Websites

- OER Commons
  http://www.oercommons.org
- WikiEducator
  http://wikieducator.org
- Open High School of Utah
  http://www.openhighschool.org
- Khan Academy
  http://www.khanacademy.org
- Open CourseWare Consortium
  http://www.ocwconsortium.org
- OUHK Free Courseware
  http://openlearn.ouhk.hk/free-coursewares
- OpenLearn, UK Open University
  http://openlearn.open.ac.uk
- Virtual University for Small States of the Commonwealth
  http://www.vussc.info/for-learners
- African Virtual University
  http://oer.avu.org
- Curriki
  http://www.curriki.org
- SOL*R - BC Commons
  http://solr.bccampus.ca
- Science Commons
  http://sciencecommons.org/

Appendix 2: Examples of Open Textbooks and OER Projects

- College Open Textbooks, http://www.collegeopentextbooks.org

  The College Open Textbooks aims at driving awareness and advocacy for open textbooks and training teachers to adopt open resources, conducting peer review of open textbooks, and growing online professional networks which support authors who open their resources. The project has a website containing a few hundred tertiary-level open textbooks.

- Connexions, http://cnx.org

  Connexions is a dynamic system consisting of an educational content repository and a content management system optimized for the delivery of educational materials. It has more than 19,000 learning objects or modules in mathematics, science, history, English, psychology, sociology, etc. in its repository which have been accessed by over 2 million people per month. Schools can also order low cost hard copy sets of the materials (textbooks).

- California Free Digital Textbooks Initiative, http://www.clrn.org/fdti; http://instructionaltech.rusd.k12.ca.us/digital_textbooks.htm

  In May 2009, California planned for a state-approved list of standards-aligned, open-source digital textbooks for high schools. The initiative reviews existing free digital textbooks and invites content developers to submit textbooks for review against California's academic content standards. Currently it has textbooks on 47 subjects, each of which covers several grades.

- CK-12 FlexBooks, http://flexbooks-wiki.ck12.org

  CK-12 Foundation is a non-profit organization with a mission to reduce the cost of textbook materials for the K-12 market both in the US and worldwide. Using an open-content, web-based collaborative model called the 'FlexBook', CK-12 intends to create re-mixable texts packed in 30-plus open textbooks for high schools.

- Open Access Textbooks, http://www.openaccesstextbooks.org

  The Open Access Textbooks Project is a two-year initiative to create a sustainable model for the discovery, production, and dissemination of open textbooks. Funded by a grant from the Fund for the Improvement of Postsecondary Education (FIPSE), this project builds on lessons learned in open textbook efforts across the United States and seeks to create a collaborative community to further sustainable implementation of open textbooks.

- Flat World Knowledge, http://www.flatworldknowledge.com

  Flat World Knowledge (FWK) claims to be the world's largest publisher of free and open college textbooks. Its books are written are professionally developed and supported by supplementary materials, audio, video and interactive features. It is completely free online but there is a low cost charge for print, e-books for the iPad, Kindle, Nook and other e-readers and downloadable PDFs.

- Project Gutenberg, http://www.gutenberg.org/

  The project offers over 33,000 free e-books to download on PC, iPad, Kindle, Nook, Sony Reader, iPhone, iPod Touch, Android or other mobile or cell phones. No fee or registration is required. All of its e-books are quality assured, and previously published by *bona fide* publishers. The project has digitized and diligently proof-read them with the help of thousands of volunteers.

Open Access Textbooks: Opportunities and Challenges

Simon K.S. Cheung, K.S. Yuen, K.C. Li, Eva Y.M. Tsang, and Alex Wong

The Open University of Hong Kong, Hong Kong
{kscheung,ksyuen,kcli,etsang,jwwong}@ouhk.edu.hk

Abstract. Different from traditional textbooks, open access textbooks are by nature open education resources that are free to use and can be delivered in electronic or printed form. Not only that the development of open access textbooks is cost-effective, the continuous revisions and updates can be made efficiently. Open access textbooks also allow easy adaptation to cater for the students' learning differences. However, for the successful adoption of open access textbooks, a number of challenges need to be overcome, such as on soliciting contributors of textbook contents, assuring the quality of textbooks, and establishing a culture of sharing education resources. This paper investigates these opportunities and challenges, and proposes a solution for the implementation and sustainable development of open access textbooks in Hong Kong. Some overseas successful projects are referenced and discussed. It is believed that open access textbooks would effectively resolve the pressing issues of high price and frequent revisions of textbooks, while offering many pedagogical advantages.

Keywords: open access textbook, open education resource, textbook development, e-learning.

1 Introduction

Traditional printed textbooks have a long history and good track record of serving as a core component in the process of teaching and learning. There are however a number of problems. The contents of printed textbooks are relatively static, and costly to update, and become even more expensive when bundled with multimedia elements. By nature, these textbooks are not flexible enough to cater for the students' learning differences as they cannot be customised for different learning objectives and contexts. The traditional publishing industry would finds it increasingly difficult to keep pace with the rapid curricular development without significant increase in production costs, and consequent charges to students and parents. In recent years, the escalation in textbook prices become widespread public concerns, and at the same time there are also growing demands for active and flexible learning that traditional printed textbooks may not be able to meet.

With the advent of information and communication technologies and the prevalence of digital cultures together with the latest copyright practices, educators and researchers have been exploring the use of education resources that are openly shared and distributed over the Internet, or Open Education Resources (OER). OER is formally defined as the "digitized materials offered freely and openly for educators,

K.C. Li et al. (Eds.): ICT 2012, CCIS 302, pp. 201–210, 2012.

students and self-learners to use and re-use for teaching, learning and research" (Organization for Economic Cooperation and Development [OECD], 2007, p. 2). In North America, vast amount of OER for higher education have been developed. The innovations are now diffusing to the primary and secondary education levels (Kamenetz, 2010; Guttenplan, 2010; Curriki, 2011),. These motivate us to explore the possibilities of developing textbooks as OER.

As a form of OER, open access textbooks are basically digitized textbooks that can be accessible online at no costs, and also available in affordable-to-purchase printed copies (EDUCAUSE, 2011). The textbook contents can be revised, reused, often remixed and customized under a Creative Commons license that permits the authors to retain ownership of their contents, yet establish the rights under which the content may be used by others (Creative Commons, 2002). Open access textbooks offer many definite advantages. Fot one thing, they are inexpensive to students, teachers and parents. Rapid revision and timely updates of textbook contents can be made efficiently. As well, they allow easy adaptation and modifications to cater for the students' learning differences. Open access textbooks can be easily accessed online. They can be readily available for use in multi-media, whether in printed form or other digital forms (Leung, 2012).

The successful adoption of open access textbooks depends on at least three factors. First, there should be sufficient enthusiastic contributors who are willing to produce the textbook contents as authors, editors and reviewers. Second, the quality of the open textbooks should be well assured so that teachers and students have the confidence to use them. This requires a system for continuous quality assurance and control. Third, a culture of sharing education resources should be well established. In Hong Kong, such a culture is still lacking, partly because a common platform to enable sharing of education resources among teachers has not yet existed. It may take long time to build up the culture.

The paper will start with an elaboration on open access textbooks: the concept, opportunities and challenges will be discussed. In the later part of a solution to implement and to sustain an open access textbook system will be proposed.

2 Open Access Textbooks

Originating from open learning, distance learning and e-learning, open education resources (OER) have evolved as a promising means of teaching and learning. According to OECD, OER is defined as the "digitised materials offered freely and openly for educators, students and self-learners to use and re-use for teaching, learning and research" (OECD, 2007, p. 2). OER range from the user-generated contents and software tools such as Wikipedia (Wikipedia, 2012) and institution-led open courseware (The Open University of Hong Kong [OUHK], 2012; The Open University, United Kingdom [OUUK], 2012; Massachusetts Institute of Technology, United State [MIT], 2012; African Virtual University [AVU], 2012; Commonwealth of Learning [COL], 2012; Open High School of Utah [OHSU], 2012; Open Courseware Consortium [OCW], 2012), to digital repositories of learning objects, learning materials and textbooks (Community College Open Textbooks Collaborative [CCOTC], 2012; Connexions [CXN], 2012; California Learning Resource

Network[CLRN], 2012; CK-12 FlexBook, 2012; Florida Distance Learning Consortium, 2012; Flat World Knowledge, 2012; Khan Academy, 2012; Gutenberg, 2012; Wikibooks, 2012).

With the advent of information and communication technologies, OER are made available online and in digital format for easy sharing and adaptation (Wikipedia, 2012). Under various types of open licenses, the author of OER grants users the freedom to use, reuse, revise, remix and redistribute the resources. In other words, with proper attribution, users can share OER with others, revise, translate or improve them and, in turn, share these new versions with others. Users can also make printed copies of the resources as they wish. There is no need to pay any copyright fees for using the resources.

Open access textbooks are a specific type of OER which can be used as official textbooks for classroom-based teaching and learning in universities, institutions and schools. They are by nature digitized textbooks that can be accessible online and downloadable for offline usage, as well as in printed copies. As OER, the contents of open access textbooks can be freely used, reused, revised, remixed and customized. In essence, open access textbooks can be characterized in the following aspects:

- They are freely available for use and adaption.
- They invariably consist of digital materials. The contents can be delivered in many formats, including web, audio, e-reader and printed versions.
- They are coherent in contents and are aligned to particular curricular guidelines and standards, and can be customized to meet individual needs.
- Their copyrights are governed by the Creative Commons or similar license which clearly states a list of permissions by the authors.

In principle, the baseline rights allow users to use the textbooks without compensating the authors, copy the textbooks with appropriate credit to the authors, distribute the textbooks non-commercially, and shift the textbooks into another format. Through Creative Common licenses, authors can further grant users the rights to add, remove or revise the textbook contents, often on the condition that derivative works must have the same licenses. Users may be granted the rights to copy and distribute the textbooks without given credit to the authors and/or use the textbooks commercially (EDUCAUSE, 2011).

In North America, vast amount of OER for higher education have been developed. The innovations are now diffusing to textbooks for primary and secondary schools. Some successful textbook projects are quoted as follows.

- College Open Textbooks (2012) aims at driving awareness and advocacy for open access textbooks, training teachers to adopt open resources, conducting peer review, and growing online professional networks which support authors to share the resources. The project has a website containing hundreds of tertiary-level open access textbooks. It also developed a detailed guide for adopting open access textbooks and creating associated teaching and learning materials.
- Connexions (2012) is a dynamic system consisting of an educational content repository of educational materials and textbooks. More than 19,000 learning objects or modules in mathematics, science, history, English, psychology and sociology are available in the repository which is accessed by over 2 million

people of all ages per month. Materials and textbooks can be easily downloadable to almost any mobile device for use anywhere and anytime. Institutions and schools can also order low cost hard copy sets of the materials and textbooks.

- In 2009, California planned for a state-approved list of standards-aligned and open-source digital textbooks for high schools. This initiative, called California Free Digital Textbooks Initiative (2012), reviews the existing free digital textbooks which could be used in California's classrooms. It has stipulated 16 free digital textbooks for high school mathematics and science classes, alleged to have met at least 90% of the California's academic standards. At present, it offers open access textbooks on 47 subjects, each of which covers several grades.
- CK-12 FlexBook (2012) is a non-project organization with a mission to reduce the cost of textbooks for K-12 market both in the United States and worldwide. Using an open-content and web-based collaborative model, CK-12 intends to create re-mixable texts packed in 30+ open textbooks for high schools.
- The Open Access Textbooks project (2012) is a two-year initiative to create a sustainable model for the discovery, production and dissemination of open access textbooks. Funded by a grant from the Fund for the Improvement of Post-Secondary Education, this project builds on lessons learned in open access textbook efforts across the United States and seeks to create a collaborative community to further sustain the implementation of open access textbooks.
- Flat World Knowledge (2012) claims to be the world's largest publisher of free and open college textbooks. Its books are written by leading experts and are peer-reviewed, edited and highly developed. They are supported by test banks, Powerpoint notes, instructor manuals, print desk copies, and knowledgeable service representatives. Its whole stock is completely free online. The texts come with integrated audio, video, interactive features, and powerful search capabilities.
- Khan Academy (2012) is a not-for-project organization with a goal of changing education for better by providing free educational resources to anyone. At present, it has over 2,400 videos as well as thousands of exercises covering K-12 mathematics and science subjects such as biology, chemistry and physics, and reaching into the humanities with playlists on finance and history.
- Project Gutenberg (2012) offers over 33,000 free e-books to download on PC, iPad, Kindle, Note, Sony Reader, iPhone, iPod Touch, Android or other mobile or cell phones. No fees are required. All of its e-books are quality assured, and previously published by bona fide publishers. The project has digitized and diligently proof-read them with the help of thousands of volunteers.

Open access textbooks offer many advantages. First, they are free. Even when hardcopies are ordered, students need to pay only the basic printing costs. Second, rapid revisions and timely updates of the textbook contents can be made efficiently. Teachers and students need not wait long for the revised textbooks, as the revisions and updates can be made online for instant accesses. Third, open access textbooks allow easy adaptation and modification to cater for the students' learning difference. Teachers may select and customize the textbooks to fit specific teaching and learning needs of individual groups. Fourth, they can be easily accessed online that supports active and flexible learning. Fifth, as open access textbooks are in digital forms, they are readily available for use with multi-media elements. Students' learning experience can be enriched.

On the other hand, a number of challenges have to be tackled for the successful adoption of open access textbooks. As the authoring of open access textbooks are on voluntary basis, there requires a substantial group of enthusiastic contributors who are willing to produce the textbook contents, including the authoring, revision and review of the contents. Open access textbooks are by nature OER that allow revision, remix and redistribution. Hence, the quality of textbooks, especially after each revision, should be well assured. This requires a system for continuous quality assurance and control. Another challenge is to establish a sharing culture in the community, where teachers and students are willing to share their resources with others. Though difficult to achieve, this is especially important as the sharing of resources is the core concepts of OER.

3 Implementation of Open Access Textbooks

In this section, we propose a solution for the implementation of open access textbooks. It essentially has four components. The first component is a platform for hosting the open textbooks. The second component is the textbook contents. The third component is a system for assuring the quality of textbooks. The fourth component is the support for continuous cultural building and capacity building.

3.1 Open Access Textbook Platform

The open access textbook platform serves many functions. First, it provides a repository for hosting the textbook contents and resources. Teachers can select appropriate textbook contents and resources, and customize them to meet specific teaching and learning needs. Second, it supports a two-way interactive and iterative process, whereby teachers can download, revise, remix and upload contents. The built-in architecture would anticipate and accommodate on-going growth of contents driven by the bottom-up involvement of an ever expanding body of users, stakeholders and volunteers.

Moreover, the platform allows users to download and print out the selected and customized textbook contents. It also allows users to send online requests to printing houses for mass printing of the textbooks. Besides, electronic versions of the selected customized textbooks are available to support online learning and mobile learning. The platform also provides a function for schools and teachers to generate an individual school site to house the selected and customized textbooks and resources.

3.2 Open Access Textbook Contents

The repository of textbook contents include both newly developed open access textbooks and those open access textbooks and OER which are already available elsewhere for possible adaptation by teachers and students. For the development of new open access textbooks, the following strategies can be applied.

- *Aggregating and selecting from the Web relevant and usable resource materials.* This saves users tremendous time and efforts on sifting through the massive information online and removes uncertainty of the relevance to their teaching and learning.
- *Borrowing and adopting open resources for reuse, revision and redistribution by Creative Commons Licenses.* Many of these open resources are specifically developed and comprehensive for teaching and learning, albeit for different curricular and national standards. They can be translated, easily modified and adapted as a fast-track and economical way of content development.
- *Enlisting the support of practitioners to cooperate and collectively develop the contents and resources for both individual and common needs.* A substantial number of schools and institutions should have already engaged in creating teaching resources in-house. Mutual cooperation would provide some extra incentives, and reduce the workload of single-handed development by individuals who are scattered among various educational organizations.
- *Deploying and recruiting professionals and experts to create original content where necessary.* Like the traditional textbook development process, textbooks can be developed by a team of recruited professionals and experts.

3.2 Quality Assurance System

Open access textbooks are free learning resources available to anyone. To alleviate the worries and scepticism over the quality of free learning resources, a quality assurance system should be set up and overseen by a team of subject experts, editors and education technologists to monitor the textbook development process, assess the quality of textbooks, and review each item admitted to the system. These professionals take the role of co-authors as well as gate-keepers for the quality of the textbooks. The textbook contents would be continually reviewed, updated, improved and enriched with reference to the ratings and feedback gathered online and offline. Apart from internal quality procedures, the following recourses should be in place:

- *Peer review.* Where appropriate, the developed contents are forwarded to individual peers or groups from professional organizations, by voluntary or paid service.
- *Government review panels.* In case of open access textbooks for primary and secondary education, the final products would be submitted for assessment by Government's review panels of school textbooks.
- *Open review and rating.* There should provide an opportunity for teachers, educators and other users to review and rate the open access textbooks in an open way. Such transparency helps identify shortcomings, ensure the effectiveness of the particular resources and in turn further bolster the quality.
- *Systematic evaluation and research.* There are institutions and schools which have the necessary expertise to carry out systematic studies and timely research to evaluate the outcomes and assess the level of satisfaction.

3.3 Continuous Culture and Capacity Building

Coherent groups of potential contributors and beneficiary schools and organizations, which subscribe to the spirits and principles of OER, should be established to share expertise, input manpower, coordinate efforts, and spread the knowledge in support of the continuous development of open access textbooks and resources at societal level. At the individual level, those interested and qualified authors, editors, teachers from primary and secondary schools, and professors from tertiary institutions could join the developers and contributors of open access textbooks at different levels.

Training should be provided to teachers and professors, mainly on the teaching practices with the use of open access textbooks and other learning resources. The training can help them master the skills to produce these open access textbooks and learning resources. It can nurture their abilities to search, filter and select appropriate and legitimate learning resources on the Internet as well as to write, edit and digitize materials for textbook contents. It can also explain what is good instructional design, how quality is upheld and what tools and techniques should be used.

In addition, there should be a public platform providing services primarily to teachers and students, and any other users with the enthusiasm to collaboratively contribute to the textbook contents, whether by way of authoring, editing, enriching, commenting, amending or remixing. The expanding community and capacity thus generated would ensure a clear understanding of quality standards and requirements, and provide ample energy, relevant experiences and favourable conditions for the continuous improvement of the programme and achievement of successful outcomes.

4 Sustainable Development of Open Access Textbooks

As mentioned earlier, the successful adoption of open access textbooks depends on at least three factors, namely, contributors of textbook contents, high quality of textbooks, and the culture of sharing education resources. Strategic measures should be in place in order to sustain its long-term development. This section discusses these measures in the steering, governance, community, culture and capacity building, and the on-going development and maintenance of open access textbooks.

- *To garner public support of open access textbooks.* A group of supporters is required. Institutional supports should be solicited. Public seminars should be arranged in order to raise public awareness and to promote the use of open access textbooks. It is believed that substantial savings and flexibility to adjust to students' learning needs, arising from open access textbooks, is a strong motivation for users' participation as well as a vehicle to obtain public support.
- *To form a group of volunteers.* There is much anecdotal evidence showing that it is possible for volunteerism alone to drive a massive project, such as Wikipedia, and Linux. It is believed that the vision of social equity and the motivation of knowledge sharing as well as the benefits of widened dissemination would be sufficiently strong drivers to enlist volunteers to participate as authors, editors and reviewers to offer some services for non-monetary rewards and recognition.

- *To solicit philanthropic and community support.* Some local and overseas foundations, charitable bodies or commercial organizations have pledged their support to sustain OER projects, such as Bill Gate Foundation and Hewlett Foundation. Some open and free online services, such as Wikipedia, manage to survive and flourish with mass donations from individuals. In the long term, it is necessary to solicit philanthropic and community support for open access textbook development.
- *To provide training for teachers.* Training workshops would be provided to teachers and practitioners, mainly on the use of open access textbooks, the associated teaching materials and other OER. These aim to nurture teachers' abilities to select appropriate and legitimate open access textbooks and other learning resources, and write, edit, revise, remix and digitize the contents. Instructional design and quality assurance practices would be covered.
- *To launch a forum for practitioners of open textbooks.* Online forums for teachers and practitioners of open textbooks would be organized. It serves to provide a 7x24 platform for teachers and practitioners to share views, express opinions and discuss issues on open access textbooks and OER.
- *To sustain the open access textbook platform.* On-going maintenance of the platform, including technical system administration, account administration, and regular system updates, for the platform is essential to ensure its proper and smooth running. On-going technical and user support, such as hotline and helpdesk, is also required for answering technical queries from end-users.
- *To maintain the quality of open access textbooks.* On-going maintenance of the developed textbooks, including annual evaluation, review and revision, is also required in order to assure the quality of textbooks. As multiple versions of an open access textbook are allowed, versioning need to be properly controlled. Reviews would be done both by experts, users and peer review groups.
- *To review the scope and identify the need for new open access textbooks.* From time to time, reviews would be carried out on the scope of available textbooks, and the need of new textbooks should be identified. On-going enhancement of the developed open access textbooks is equally important. This includes major revision, and addition of OER associated with the open access textbooks.

5 Conclusion

With the rapid development and wide acceptance of OER, we found the opportunities of using open access textbooks to replace, or at least to complement, the traditional printed textbooks for good reasons. Apart from resolving the pressing issues of high price and frequent revisions of textbook, which has been perplexing the students and educators for years, there are pedagogical advantages such as on catering for the students' learning differences, promoting flexible and active learning, and enriching the students' learning experience with multimedia elements. In North America, there are many successful projects that prove the effectiveness of OER for teaching and learning. It is therefore a corollary that the same concepts can also be applied to school textbooks.

As a revolutionary change in practices, the successful adoption of open access textbooks has a number of anticipated challenges, such as soliciting the contributors of textbook contents, assuring the quality of textbooks, and establishing a culture of sharing education resources. Continuous public support and user participation are crucial in order to sustain the long-term development of open access textbooks. In this paper, we elaborate the concepts of open access textbooks, discuss the opportunities and challenges, and propose a solution for the implementation together with some strategic measures for the sustainable development. Overseas successful projects are referenced and discussed.

We are pleased to see that the sharing of resources on the Internet is becoming a common practice. Wikipedia, iTuneU, Curriki and Open Courseware are some good examples of sharing information resources and learning resources. Linux, Moodle and open source codes are other good example of sharing software resources. Todays, the development of many intellectual properties have shifted to a paradigm of collective and cooperative development with the open access and shared resources. It is undeniable the advent of information and communication technologies have changed the traditional practices in different walks of life. Teaching and learning practices would not be the exception, and we optimistically believe that open access textbooks would be the order of the day soon.

References

African Virtual University, Kenya. (n.d.), `http://oeravu.org` (retrieved March 31, 2012)

California Learning Resource Network. CLRN: Website of California Digital Textbooks Initiative (2012), `http://www.clrn.org/fdti` (retrieved March 31, 2012)

Organisation for Economic Cooperation and Development, OECD: Giving Knowledge for Free: The Emergence of Open Education Resources (2007)

CK-12 FlexBook. (n.d.), `http://flexbooks-wiki.ck12.org` (retrieved March 31, 2012)

Creative Commons. (n.d.), `http://creativecommons.org` (retrieved March 31, 2012)

Commonwealth of Learning. COL: Website of Virtual University for Small States of the Commonwealth (2012), `http://www.vussc.info` (retrieved March 31, 2012)

Community College Open Textbooks Collaborative. (n.d.), `http://www.collegeopentextbooks.org` (retrieved March 31, 2012)

Connexions. (n.d.), `http://www.cnx.org` (retrieved March 31, 2012)

Curriki. (n.d.), `http://www.curriki.org` (retrieved March 31, 2012) EDUCAUSE. Open Textbook Publishing. Educause Learning Initiative (March 2011), `http://www.educause.edu/eli` (retrieved March 31, 2012)

Flat World Knowledge. (n.d.), `http://www.flatworldknowledge.com` (retrieved March 31, 2012)

Florida Distance Learning Consortium. FDLC: Open Access Textbooks: Website of Open Access Textbooks (2012), `http://www.openaccesstextbooks.org` (retrieved)

Guttenplan, D.D.: For Exposure, Universities put Courses on the Web. New York Times (November 1, 2010), `http://www.nytimes.com/2010/11/01/world/europe/01iht-educLede01.html?pagewanted=all` (retrieved March 31, 2012)

Gutenberg. (n.d.), `http://www.gutenberg.org` (retrieved March 31, 2012)

Khan Academy. (n.d.), `http://www.khanacademy.org` (retrieved March 31, 2012)

Kamenetz, A.: Eliminate Print Textbooks, Go Digital. New York Times (July 25, 2010), http://www.nytimes.com/roomfordebate/2010/7/25/the-real-cost-of-college-textbooks/eliminate-print-textbooks-go-digital?scp=1&sq=%22Eliminate%20Print%20Textbooks%22&st=Search (retrieved)

Leung, C.M.: Open Textbooks are a Solution to Publishers' Costly, Bundled Schoolbooks. South China Morning Post (February 11, 2012)

Massachusetts Institute of Technology, United States. MIT: Website of MIT Open Courseware, http://ocw.mit.edu/index.html (retrieved March 31, 2012)

Open High School of Utah. (n.d.), http://www.openhighschool.org (retrieved March 31, 2012)

Open Courseware Consortium. (n.d.), http://www.ocwconsortium.org (retrieved March 31, 2012)

The Open University, United Kingdom. OUUK: Website of Open Learn (2012), http://openlearn.open.ac.uk (retrieved March 31, 2012)

Wikibooks. (n.d.), http://en.wikibooks.org (retrieved March 31, 2012)

Wikipedia. (n.d.), http://www.wikipedia.org (retrieved March 31, 2012) The Open University of Hong Kong. OUHK: Website of OUHK Free Courseware (2012), http://openlearn.ouhk.hk/free-coursewares (retrieved March 31, 2012)

Wikipedia. Open Educational Resources, Wikipedia (2012), http://en.wikipedia.org/wiki/Open_educational_resources (retrieved March 31, 2012)

*e*Volution from Conventional Textbooks to Open Textbooks: A Way Out for Hong Kong

K.C. Li, K.S. Yuen, Simon K.S. Cheung, and Eva Y.M. Tsang

The Open University of Hong Kong, Hong Kong SAR, China
kcli@ouhk.edu.hk

Abstract. This paper attempts to first briefly review the difficulties concerning textbooks that Hong Kong faces. Summarising issues into five problems — high and increasing prices, inflexibility in revision, weight, bundling with teachers' materials, and costly marketing means, it outlines measures the government has been taking to tackle them and concludes that there has been little success in solving the problems. By explaining that Hong Kong is not the only place confronted with this worldwide bugbear, it highlights that, to be free from the constraints of conventional textbooks, we may capitalise on information and communication technology to take us to a new paradigm and that open textbooks are a promising solution to the aforementioned burdens and constraints.

Keywords: conventional textbook, open textbook, *e*learning, mobile learning, student engagement.

1 Introduction

In Hong Kong, conventional textbooks pose persistent problems which confront stakeholders in the education field: government officers, teachers, students and parents. Despite great efforts and various measures to tackle the taxing problem, there has been little improvement. (Education Bureau, 2009, p. 6)

This paper attempts to summarize the problems in Hong Kong, outlining major problems of textbooks in the territories. It also highlights that the problem has been a common one, worrying not only Hong Kong.

Putting relevant issues in the perspective of the global trend to capitalize on information and communication technology (ICT) and to evolve into electronic textual media, this paper explicates the advantages and disadvantages of *e*books. Then it puts forward an immensely promising solution — open textbooks. Besides explaining the nature of open textbooks, it elucidates how open textbooks may remove problems and constraints of conventional textbooks and make disadvantages of *e*books irrelevant, before drawing a conclusion.

2 Conventional Textbooks: Taxing Problems to the Authority and Parents

In Hong Kong, among various problems that the government has been tackling, the problems of conventional textbooks have been among the most taxing and has drawn

K.C. Li et al. (Eds.): ICT 2012, CCIS 302, pp. 211–225, 2012.

much public concern (Education Bureau, 2010; Legislative Council Secretariat, 2011c). Related problems can be summarised into the following five:

2.1 High and Increasing Prices

According to the annual textbook price surveys conducted by the Consumer Council between 2000 and 2009, the average prices of textbooks have kept rising above the Composite Consumer Price Index (CCPI) over the past years, at a rate from around 2% in 2004 to over 7% in 2008, with a sharp drop to around 1.5% in 2009. In 2006, textbook prices on average increased by 4.2% and 5.2% respectively for the primary and secondary school sectors, which far exceeded the average rise of 1.5% in CCPI in the preceding 12-month period. The respective increases rose to 5.4% and 3.0% in 2007, and 5.9% and 6.0% in 2008, compared with only 2.0% rise in CCPI in 2007 and 4.3% in 2008. (Consumer Council, 2010a)

In 2010, the average expenses for secondary and primary form textbooks increased by 6.9% and 0.2 % respectively when compared to the average textbook expenditure in 2009. (Consumer Council, 2010b) Then in 2011, the average expenditure of primary school textbook increased 4.1% as compared with that of the previous year. There was a slight increase of 1.6% to 2.0% in the average textbook expenditure for junior secondary grades and the average textbook expenditure, however, has decreased by 3.5% with reference to that of last year. This was mainly due to a substantial drop of nearly 40% in the average expenditure of Form 6 (Senior Secondary 3) students, thus resulting in the substantial reduction in the average textbook expenditure for secondary schools. (Consumer Council, 2011)

2.2 Inflexibility in Revision or Updating

In the last few decades, there were often complaints that publishers revised textbooks too often, making it difficult for textbooks to be reused and pushing parents to purchase new textbooks, rather than used ones. The general public commonly believe that publishers use textbook revisions as a means to increase prices and to prevent students from using second-hand books. In view of these, the government set up a "three-year rule of no revision" in 2003 (Education Bureau, Textbook Committee, 2008) Under the textbook review mechanism, all textbooks that have been reviewed by the Education Bureau and are recommended to be put on the "Recommended Textbook List" are not eligible for revision within three years. Publishers may improve a textbook no less than three years after its publication. In 2009, this three-year directive became a five-year rule (Education Bureau, 2009, p. 64), though textbook publishers may provide schools with printed pamphlets on necessary revisions of textbook revisions free of charge.

This, however, poses problems relating to the suitability of each textbook. It is essential that textbook contents are up-to-date, match the school curriculum well and reflect the latest status of the world or real life. Textbook revisions are vital and indispensable. According to a survey conducted in 2009, the Consumer Council compared the new and old editions of nine volumes of secondary textbooks, including three on Chinese History, four on Chinese Language and two on Mathematics. It also invited experts in the education field to give comments on the necessity of the revisions and justifications for changes to the contents, chapter sequence and design of the textbooks. The survey found that the sampled textbook revisions were either necessary or quite necessary. (Consumer Council, 2009)

2.3 Weight

School textbooks are intended for classroom learning and study, rather than being carried around in backpack as an excessive load on students' shoulders. However, according to a survey conducted by the Professional Teachers' Union on schoolbag weights, the schoolbags of primary school children weighed 11 pounds on average, and for secondary school children, the average schoolbag weight was about 14 pounds. That is, the weight of the schoolbags of more than 90% of the primary school children and 80% of the secondary school students covered in this survey exceeded the recommended standard of the then government — 10% of the student's own weight. (Hong Kong Professional Teachers' Union, 1998)

As a precautionary measure, the Department of Health has recommended that school children should avoid carrying school bags which exceed 15% of their body weight for long periods of time. This means, for example, a child of 30 kg should carry a bag of not more than 4.5 kg. (Consumer Council, 2007). However, improvement has been slow and parents are concerned that children's school bags are often overweight and much of this is caused by the weight of textbooks.

2.4 Bundling Students' Textbooks with Teaching Materials for Teachers

While students, or their parents, pay for textbooks they use, school teachers are normally given complimentary copies of the textbooks they have chosen for their classes. In addition to textbooks, they are usually given supplementary teaching materials, which include the teacher's edition of the textbooks with answers, wall charts, worksheets, CD-ROMs with additional teaching materials, data files for project study, presentation files for use in lessons, assessment tasks, and assessment item banks. In addition, there may be supporting websites for teachers' access only to provide them with further materials to complete their teaching duties. It is believed that the cost of these items is one of the key factors which cause the prices of textbooks to become unreasonably high. Since schools have different needs on teaching materials, such free provision of uniform sets of teaching materials by publishers, without doubt, result in wastage of various degrees. (Education Bureau, 2009, p. 33) The cost of such additional materials inevitably raises the textbook prices (Ibid, p. 58).

2.5 Marketing Strategy

To introduce textbooks to teachers and encourage them to adopt them for their classes, publishers often run promotional functions (such as talks to introduce their textbooks and useful pedagogical methods related to their textbooks) in expensive hotels, and offer teachers small gifts and large items (such as computing equipment), besides providing them with complimentary copies of the textbooks. (Apple Daily, 2008; Legislative Council Secretariat, 2011b, para. 97 and 99) Publishers may sometimes even offer cash grants to schools for the purchase of equipment or teaching aids to be used jointly with particular textbooks or series of textbooks, and may provide funding for school functions, sponsorships for school publications as advertisements, speech day floral baskets, or scholarships. The government has already called a halt to these and sent official guidelines to schools making clear that these are not acceptable. (Education Bureau, 2010, para.13)

3 Approach Adopted by the Government / Education Bureau

The Government has been holding fast to their adoption of the free market principle. It does not publish textbooks. Textbooks are published freely and are priced by publishers with considerations of their market and development costs. In textbook supply, the role of the Education Bureau (EDB) has been no more than monitoring the quality of textbook content and reviewing the textbooks submitted by the publishers. After the review, the textbooks having an acceptable quality are included in EDB's "Recommended Textbook List". Teachers choose the textbooks from the list for their classes and parents pay for the books.

In response to public concern about textbooks, the EDB set up in 2008 the Working Group on Textbooks and e-Learning Resources Development (the Working Group), which was chaired by the Under Secretary for Education, and included parents, school teachers and principals, textbook publishers, representatives from the information technology sector, the Consumer Council and legislators. The group conducted in-depth analyses of the textbook problems, held regular meetings, organised seminars, focus discussions, open seminars, student forums, administered school questionnaire and collected views of parents on the web, looked into study of overseas experience and measures as well as visited schools. Besides, they also consulted professional bodies and community groups, including the Curriculum Development Council, Panel on Education of the Legislative Council, school councils, Consumer Council and university academics before making recommendations to the government. (Education Bureau, 2009, p. 33 & 58)

Based on the working group's recommendations, the government has introduced and implemented relevant measures to resolve the textbooks issues. For instance, according to the Working Group's recommendation, the government made it clear to publishers that the teaching materials provided to the teachers and gifts to schools should not be included in the cost of textbooks which is ultimately borne by parents, with a view to reducing the price of textbooks.

4 Results Thus Far

Despite accusing fingers being pointed at them, publishers argue that the problems are not with them. Regarding the high textbook prices in Hong Kong, they maintain that operational costs such as salary and rental in Hong Kong are among the highest in the world, but its student population size is among the lowest worldwide which means that the number of students to share out the production cost is small. For example, the student population in Guangdong can be as large as about one million per level, while that of Hong Kong is only around 40,000 per level. They also reason that the frequent changes in the curriculum have also contributed to the high prices. (Legislative Council Secretariat, 2011b, para. 103). These major contributing factors (salary, rental, student population and textbook content) are to a large extent out of the control of the publishers or the government.

Over the years, EDB has adopted various measures to assist in lowering the textbook prices. However, despite the reduction in production costs as a result of the economic downturn in the last decade, textbook prices have kept rising.. (Education Bureau, 2009, para. 1.5 and 1.6)

Regarding weight, EDB issued Guidelines for Printing of Textbooks for the publisher's reference. Among others, it recommended that paper used for printing textbooks should be of light weight, thin, resistant and matt finished and the textbooks to be separated into a few thin volumes or printed in separate modules to reduce the weight of textbooks (Education Bureau , 2007)

The government has recently made it a policy to debundle textbooks from materials supplied to schools. (Secretary for Education, 2011a) Yet, despite the government's strong push for debundling which was scheduled to take place in 2010, the implementation had to be put on hold for one year on the request of publishers to allow them more time to resolve copyright issues. The Secretary for Education then announced that if the textbook publishers still refused to debundle teaching materials for pricing after one year, the EDB would tender out the publication of textbooks and teaching materials to introduce more competition into the market. Nevertheless, the situation has not improved much. In 2011, debundling was implemented in only a small number of textbooks. For the few textbooks that had been debundled, the prices remained unchanged or were nominally lower. (Ming Pao, 2011a)

To stop malpractice related to marketing strategy of textbooks, EDB set up rules that schools are not allowed to accept from publishers complimentary teacher's books and teaching materials. In addition, they are not allowed to accept any donations or any form of benefits from textbook publishers or textbook retailers. (Secretary for Education, 2011b)

However, in practice, it is impractical for schools not to accept complimentary books and teaching materials. First, publishers normally distribute such materials before they have decided on the price of textbooks. Second, for decades, schools have enjoyed the provision of the materials for free. They are not prepared to pay for the materials by squeezing money from their existing school budgets in other areas. The government soon realised that they cannot at least at the initial stage stop schools from accepting such materials. For the school year 2011/12, EDB had to allow schools to use materials supplied by publishers in the guise that they are on loan to the schools, rather than given as gifts. (Secretary for Education, 2011a)

Notwithstanding the government's efforts, the problems with traditional textbooks have been dragging on for years without any substantial improvement and the public feel disappointed with the government (Mingpao, 2011b).

5 Textbook Problems – A General Phenomenon

Textbooks cause headache not only in Hong Kong, it appears to be a common phenomenon around the world and is not a recent problem (Curwen, 1979; Academic Senate for California Community Colleges, 1997; Carbaugh & Ghosh, 2005). Among the textbook problems, the most pressing is the price. In the United States, for example, prices have skyrocketed for decades (United States Government Accountability Office, 2005; Koch, 2006, September; Reininger, 2010; Harvey, 2011). There is also common discontent with frequent revision of textbooks, for instance, as Kim and Jung (2010, p. 249) report about South Korea.

Similar to the situation in Hong Kong, governments have taken measures to tackle the problems and experienced much resistance. For example in the United States, there is intense dissatisfaction not only with high prices set by and practices of publishers (Carbaugh & Ghosh, 2005) but also teachers' discontent with interference of the bureaucracy. For instance, in their study, Silver, Stevens, Clow and Howard (2011) point out problems in the implementation of government measures. Business law professors showed strong resistance to university, legislative, and publisher actions that infringe on their options in selecting textbooks and how long they would have to use a specific textbook before replacing it with a newer edition. They were not in favour of the university policy to require adoption of low cost textbooks and keep textbooks for all classes for at least three years. Lewis (2009) complains that the federal government micromanages colleges and universities and causes more trouble, rather than solves the problem of textbooks.

6 From Conventional Textbooks to the eWorld

For centuries, textbooks have been a foundation for standardized teaching. It shows how courses are taught in schools around the world and is the culmination of publishing subject and teaching expertise derived from studies on learning effectiveness, testing, and technological opportunities. (Abram, 2011) While textbooks' place in education has seldom been challenged, the trend to shift away from the conventional form of textbooks is gaining strong momentum.

6.1 Constraint of Conventional Textbooks

The call for any change originates in dissatisfaction and constraints with conventional textbooks. The five problems listed in section 2 of this paper are among the major ones. Reininger (2010) also highlights constraints of the conventional textbooks. Besides the points that textbooks are expensive and may become out of date easily which concur with subsections 2.1 and 2.2 above, he further points out three constraints. First, the breadth and depth of a textbook seldom fits well with the curriculum for which it serves. Second, in order that textbooks can be sold to the widest audience, they are often "watered down" to be politically correct to avoid offending any group. Third, they are "dumbed down" to allow less skilled readers to understand the material, so that textbooks are comprehended by the majority of students and their markets maximised. Table 1 provides a summary of the major constraints.

Table 1. Constraints of conventional textbooks

Problem areas	Constraints
Prices	High and increasing
Content updating	Too frequently needed
Weight	Too heavy for children and causing inconvenience
Bundled sale with teaching aids	Students/parents who purchase the textbook also pay for teachers' aids or tools for instruction
Marketing strategy	Expensive means to promote textbook sales by offering teachers various kinds of benefits
Breadth and depth	Seldom fits well with the curriculum
Contents on sensitive topics	Watered down
Contents for intelligent students	Dumbed down

6.2 The Move towards ICT

Conventional textbooks, however, are not the only kind of effective learning materials. With its advancement, ICT has been widely applied in education. To minimize problems caused by constraints of conventional textbooks, *e*learning or the use of electronic learning materials such as *e*books has become an obvious way ahead. In Hong Kong, when the government set up the Working Group to look into the textbook problems, it assumed that *e*learning is a solution and thus the group was entitled "the Working Group on Textbooks and e-Learning Resources Development".

In Hong Kong, the Government has implemented three strategies of ICT in Education since 1998 and has invested about $8 billion, aiming to shift school education from a textbook-based and teacher-centred mode to a more interactive learner-centred mode. Integration of *e*learning into learning and teaching has since then been gradually introduced, though schools have varied in their pace of development. In support of the development of *e*learning resources in schools, EDB provided schools with a one-off grant in the 2010–2011 school year, amounting to some $30,000 to $70,000 per school, for the purchase of teaching materials as might be required over a three-year period. (Legislative Council Secretariat, 2011c, para 11).

At the same time, many parts of the world are attempting to capitalise on ICT applications in books. For example, the education ministry of Singapore has been exploring the use of digital textbooks in their schools (Kwang, 2011,). The production and sale of *e*book reader devices other than personal computers, such as Amazon Kindle, Barnes and Noble Nook, Sony Reader, PDAs and cell phones, have been rising especially in recent years (Foasberg, 2011; Herther, 2011). Libraries in many parts of the world are increasing the yearly budgets on *e*books (Chong, Lim, & Ling, 2009).

The advantages of making digitised books and its promise can be summarised into five key points. First, electronic books are portable and can be carried around and used anywhere with a notebook computer or reader device. This makes learning ubiquitous. Second, a large quantity of texts together with graphics or pictures that a small device can store brings convenience and saves storage space and greatly reduces the weight to carry around. Third, it provides additional functions that printed books cannot without additional devices. The wide variety of functions include text-to- speech, instant dictionary, note taking, text or index search, adjustable text/picture sizes, sharing of parts of texts with friends, internet browsing as well as communications through social media. Fourth, electronic books can respond to input from the reader by, for example, changing the level of details to show and checking answers to questions in exercises. Fifth, like software updating through the internet, contents of *e*books can be updated conveniently by connecting to the publisher or the source.

Despite these advantages and the growth of the digitised book market, there are considerable reservations and the market growth has not been as fast as what many *e*book sellers and reader device manufacturers might have wished. (Foasberg, 2011; Herther, 2008). Studies (e.g. Gregory, 2008; McCullough, 2005) have indicated that students prefer conventional textbooks to digitized textbooks. Reservations also arise from dissatisfaction with the design of *e*books (Chong, Lim, & Ling, 2009) and general reluctance to carry multiple devices with them (Herther, 2011).

The limitations of *e*books, including *e*textbooks in general, can be summarized in six points. First, the use of *e*books inevitably relies on compatible hardware devices, as well as suitable software installed in them. The high upfront cost of reader apparatus prevents *e*books from being widely used. For the same reason, unless schools and the government provide sufficient support for every student to have a reader device, *e*textbooks can hardly be utilized for general education. Second, to different extents, devices are yet limited by the size, resolution and colour support of their screen, and the fragile nature of their hardware. Third, also to various extents, the available software for reading is limited by the interactivity it allows and their reading capacity is limited by its compatibility with the *e*book content. This is also related to the design of the software in association with the device in which it is used. Ease of use such as convenient navigation within a book and across books decides how acceptable the reading tool can be. Fourth, *e*books from publishers and institutions come in highly diverse formats (e.g. DJVU, FBreader, PDF, XPS and Plucker) and global standardization still appears remote. Fifth, *e*books are not library friendly, using them requires much accommodation in format integration, as Gibbons (2001) pointed out long ago and the situation has not improved much. Sixth, the general habit of reading books and using textbooks have yet to change though it is evident that in many places, those who are technologically savvy and able to access reader devices available are switching their reading behaviours. To a substantial extent, students and teachers are not yet ready for a paradigm shift away from paper-form textbooks (McCullough, 2005; Gregory, 2008).

The above advantages and disadvantages of *e*books are summarized in Table 2. It should be noted that the effects of the disadvantages are diminishing with the advancement of ICT. As Lewis (2008) shows that while pointing out the preference for *e*books depends on a variety of demographic factors such as age and sex, we can anticipate that this preference is not static and is gradually changing with the adoption of ICT in daily life and education.

Table 2. Advantages and disadvantages of *e*books

Positive features	**Advantages of *e*books**
Portable	Ubiquitous learning
Large storage	Light weight and space saving
Versatile additional functions	Enhanced reading effectiveness
Responsive to reader input	Interactiveness
Content renewable via internet	Convenience to update contents timely
Limitations	**Disadvantages of *e*books**
High cost of reader devices	Use limited to those who can afford or those who are supplied with devices
Technological limitations of devices	Dissatisfaction among users
Compatibility and design limitations of software	Limitations to use
Diverse format of *e*books	Limitations to use
Much accommodation required for format integration	Library unfriendly
Stock habit of using books in paper form	Reluctance to switch to electronic reading

For students to benefit from the advantages of *e*textbooks, besides overcoming the disadvantages, there should be clear evidence that constraints of the conventional textbooks can be removed with the use of the electronic medium so that there is a good cause for them and their school to switch to *e*textbooks. However, of the constraints listed in Table 1, only the problem of content updating can be improved as new *e*book contents can be timely updated and distributed electronically quickly to only those who have bought the previous edition without going through the arduous processes such as typesetting, printing, selling and hardcopy distributing. The other problems can hardly be solved by simply evolving to *e*books. The high price of reader devices may escalate the financial burden of the amenable groups. The weight of reader devices may not cut down the overall school-bag weights even when conventional textbooks are replaced. With publishers' role in the textbook market, the rest of the constraints cannot be removed either.

7 Open Textbooks: A Promising Solution

To really solve the problems of textbooks, following the conventional supply chain model and simply transforming the textual carrier from paper to electronic devices does not appear feasible. This calls strongly for a new paradigm of textbook supply and open textbooks to fit in well with the current impasse.

7.1 Characteristics

Open textbooks are a kind of open educational resources (OER) and have emerged out of the OER movement, which seeks to offer free learning materials for learning and teaching as well as research (UNESCO, 2006, June). The learning materials are in general made available for 4R's — **r**euse, **r**evise, **r**emix and/or **r**edistribution (Wiley, n.d.) — through open licenses such as Creative Commons to regulate the copyrights involved. In brief, open textbooks are textbooks that are made freely available with nonrestrictive licenses (ISKME, 2008; Petrides, Jimes, Middleton-Detzner, Walling, & Weiss, 2011). The distribution and redistribution of open textbooks have been rendered feasible through ICT applications. Open textbooks are digitized materials for learning and teaching and made available through the internet. Contents of open textbooks are licensed to allow anyone to download, customize, read or print without expressed permission from the author (Harley, 2009, p. 3).

7.2 Strengths

As books available in electronic formats, open textbooks enjoy the advantages of *e*books. Besides these advantages, open textbooks enjoy a distinctive combination of four major strengths. First, these textbooks are distributed and obtained through open licenses. This usually involves no costs. Students and their teachers may simply access their desired texts via the internet free-of-charge, no matter whether the textbook is written or compiled by their teacher. Students and their parents therefore typically pay nothing or very little for online access and use of open textbooks. They therefore serve well the potential solution to high textbook costs (Baker & Hood, 2011). Second, for those who need a paper version or a book in a specific digitized format, a range of formats are available at affordable costs. The cost is normally a small fraction of the expense of a traditionally published text. In addition, the business model and market structure motivate publishers to develop their business by offering a wider range of products at fair prices (Allen, 2010). Third, students as well as their teachers and parents may freely print the whole or part of them, or have them printed, as hardcopies for use. This means that the need for students and teachers to adjust to a new form of textbook is minimized. Fourth, since no single textbook fits a curriculum well for all student groups, under open licenses, a teacher may freely select parts from different open textbooks and compile his or her textbook or adapt substantially an existing one for his or her class. This, being impossible with conventional textbooks, is fully permissible and encouraged with open textbooks.

Table 3. Distinctive advantages of open textbooks (in addition to advantages of *e*books)

Positive features	Advantages of open textbooks
Open license	Free-of-charge download and use
Other forms available on demand	Different modes of use catered to
Conventional paper version possible	No need for reader devices or any dramatic change in conventional ways of using textbooks
Remixing and revision allowed	Content tailoring for effective school/class/group-based learning

These distinctive strengths obviate the constraints as listed in Table 1. Open textbooks dramatically cut down the cost of textbooks, allow immediate updating or revision by the author or teacher as frequently as desired, reduce weights to carry by permitting selective or partial printing of a book, free textbook sellers from bundling and carrying out expensive marketing practices. The need to water or dumb down contents for catering to a broad market no longer exists either.

In addition, the availability of paper-form open textbooks makes the limitations detailed in Table 2 irrelevant. Using open textbooks does not require any upfront purchases of reader devices for individual students. Technological limitations of *e*book devices may cause little difficulties to the use of open textbooks. There is no need to adjust to the change from conventional textbooks.

All these suggest that open textbooks are a promising solution to the problems of conventional textbooks. Hong Kong appears to be an ideal place for implementing this solution. Hong Kong has a high internet penetration rate (68.7% as of December 31, 2011) (Internet World Stats, 2012), and schools have necessary ICT infrastructure and the Government has already launched the Internet Learning Support Programme to help low-income families to acquire affordable computers and Internet access services (GovHK, 2012). In addition, the government has been investing substantially on ICT applications to learning and teaching. For example, in 2010, $140 million was proposed for the promotion of e-learning in the school sector (Legislative Council Secretariat , 2011a, pp. 4–5).

8 Conclusion

This paper has analyzed the predicament concerning textbooks in Hong Kong, summarizing five key problems, namely high prices, inflexibility in revision, heavy, bundling with teachers' materials, and expensive marketing strategies. It has examined the role of the local government and briefly evaluated the results of the government's efforts, highlighting that textbook problems that confront the territory are universal and common around the world.

Considering the textbook problems from a general development perspective, rather than that of a local problem, this paper has studied the move towards using electronic media through ICT. It has summarized the constraints which cause dissatisfaction with textbooks. The advantages and disadvantages of *e*books have then been expounded, pointing out that *e*books hardly solve most of the textbook problems.

Offering a solution, this paper has put forward the idea of open textbooks. Having explained the nature and characteristics of open textbooks, it has elucidated the distinctive strengths of such textbooks as a kind of OER. With these and the general advantages of *e*books, it has highlighted that open textbooks may free readers from the constraints of conventional textbooks and disadvantages of general *e*books.

Open textbook projects have been implemented and utilised in many parts of the world and successful stories abound, for example, the Rice University's Connexions and the Community College Open Textbook Project (Baker, Thierstein, Fletcher,

Kaur, & Emmons, 2009; Petrides, et al. 2011), as well as Flat World Knowledge (Shelstad, 2011).

The immensely promising outlook hardly implies that the adoption of open textbooks has been and will be plain sailing. On the contrary, resistance has been common place. For instance, teachers could be reluctant and unprepared for change in terms of their skills to use the open textbook and their knowledge to appreciate the versatility and advantages of this new tool for learning (Petrides, et al., 2011). As Lewis (2008) predicts, the resistance from publishers and some textbook authors will be strong. Three major publishers have sued a new open textbook company, Boundless Learning, in a federal court of the United States (DeSantis, 2012).

Lessons others have learned (e.g. Baker, et al., 2009) from their open textbook projects should be worthy of attention. The open textbook trend, though new, is gaining massive evolutionary momentum. Given the promising prospect of alleviating the textbook problems, Hong Kong should join the open textbook movement and succeed through the lessons we imbibe from how things are happening in other parts of the world.

References

Abram, S.: Whither the Textbook? Opportunity Knocks. LOUD, 20–22 (November/December 2011), http://www.internetatschools.com/ (retrieved March 20, 2012)

Academic Senate for California Community Colleges. Textbook Pricing Policies and Student Access (Research Report No. 143) (1997) Education Resources Information Center website, http://www.eric.ed.gov/PDFS/ED414962.pdf (retrieved March 5, 2012)

Allen, N.: A cover to cover solution: How open textbooks are the path to textbook affordability. (The Student PIRGs CSD5956).(2010) Student PIRGs (Public Interest Research Groups) website, http://www.studentpirgs.org/sites/student/files/reports/A-Cover-To-Cover-Solution_3.pdf (retrieved March 20, 2012)

Apple Daily. Publishers make donations to schools and raise Textbook prices (書商向學界捐款向學生加價). Apple Daily (April 22, 2008), http://hk.apple.nextmedia.com/template/apple/art_main.php?_id=20080422&sec_id=4104&subsec_id=11867&art_id=11018229 (retrieved January 12, 2012)

Baker, J., Hood, J.: 7 Things you should know about Open Textbook Publishing (2011), http://net.educause.edu/ir/library/pdf/ELI7070.pdf (retrieved March 23, 2012)

Baker, J., Thierstein, J., Fletcher, K., Kaur, M., Emmons, J.: Open Textbook Proof-of-Concept via Connexions. International Review of Research in Open and Distance Learning 10(5) (2009), http://www.irrodl.org/index.php/irrodl/article/view/633/1390 (retrieved March 21, 2012)

Chong, P.F., Lim, Y.P., Ling, S.W.: On the design preferences for ebooks. IETE Technical Review 26(3), 213–222 (2009)

Carbaugh, G., Ghosh, K.: Are college textbooks priced fairly? Challenge 48(5), 95–112 (2005)

Consumer Council. A timely reminder to relieve the burden of heavy school bags on children and teenagers. [Press release] (August 15, 2007), http://www.consumer.org.hk/website/ws_en/news/_releases/p37005.html (retrieved March 15, 2012)

Consumer Council. Annual survey gives the green light to all revised textbooks sampled [Press release] (November 16, 2009), http://www.consumer.org.hk/website/ws_en/news/press_releases/p39705.html (retrieved March 15, 2012)

Consumer Council. Comments from Consumer Council on Prices of school Textbooks and e-Learning Resources (消費者委員會就教科書價格及電子學習資源的發展呈交立法會教育事務委員會的意見), (Legislative Council Paper No. CB(2)868/09-10(03)) (February 2, 2010a), http://www.legco.gov.hk/yr09-10/chinese/panels/ed/papers/ed0208cb2-868-3-c.pdf (retrieved March 15, 2012)
Consumer Council. Average Textbook Expenditure on the Rise [Press release] (September 15, 2010b), http://www.consumer.org.hk/website/ws_en/news/press_releases/p40701.html (retrieved March 15, 2012)
Consumer Council. Heavy Burden on Primary Student Parents In Textbook Expenditure [Press release] (September 15, 2011), http://www.consumer.org.hk/website/ws_en/news/press_releases/p41905.html (retrieved March 15, 2012)
Curwen, P.J.: The price commission report on books – a short critique. The Journal of Industrial Economics 27(3), 295–299 (1979)
DeSantis, N.: 3 Major Publishers Sue Open-Education Textbook Start-Up. The Chronicle of Higher Education (April 5, 2012), http://chronicle.com/blogs/wiredcampus/3-major-publishers-sue-open-education-textbook-start-up/35994?sid=pm&utm_source=pm&utm_medium=en (retrieved April 6, 2012)
Education Bureau. Guidelines for Printing of Textbooks (2007), http://www.edb.gov.hk/index.aspx?nodeID=2844&langno=1 (retrieved February 3, 2012)
Education Bureau. Working Group on Textbooks and e-learning Resources Development Main Report. Education Bureau (October 2009), http://www.edb.gov.hk/FileManager/EN/Content_689/wg%20final%20report.pdf (retrieved March 12, 2012)
Education Bureau. Information Note of Legislative Council (Legislative Council Paper No. CB(2)1249/10–11(01)) (2010), http://www.legco.gov.hk/yr10-11/english/panels/ed/papers/ed0214cb2-1249-1-e.pdf (retrieved March 10, 2012)
Education Bureau. Textbook Committee, A Parental guide to Textbook Matters. HK: Education Bureau, HKSAR Government (2008)
Foasberg, N.M.: Adoption of e-book readers among college students: a survey. Information Technology and Libraries 30(3), 108–128 (2011)
Gibbons, S.: Ebooks: some concerns and surprises. Libraries and the Academy 1(1), 71–75 (2000)
GovHK. Internet Learning Support Programme (2012), http://www.gov.hk/en/theme/ilearnathome/news/ (retrieved March 25, 2012)
Gregory, C.L.: But I want a real book: an investigation of undergraduates' usage and attitudes towards electronic books. Reference and User Services Quarterly 47(3), 266–273 (2008)
Harvey, D.: Analytical Chemistry 2.0 – an open-access digital textbook. Analytical and Bioanalytical Chemistry 399, 149–152 (2011)
Herther, N.K.: The ebook reader is not the future of ebooks. Searcher 16(8), 26–29, 33–40 (2008)
Herther, N.K.: The sizzling ebook marketplace. Searcher 19(3), 14–18, 42–43, 46–47 (2011)
Hong Kong Professional Teachers' Union. Result of Survey on the Weight of Schoolbags: Teachers Consider Schoolbags Too Heavy. (書包重量調查結果反映教師感同身受認爲過重). PTU NEWS (1998), http://www.hkptu.org/ptu/director/pubdep/optunews/373/3737.html (retrieved March 1, 2012)
Institute for the Study of Knowledge Management in Education. What are open textbooks? Connexions Module (2008), http://cnx.org/content/m15226/latest/ (retrieved March 14, 2012)

Internet World Stats. Asia Marketing Research, Internet Usage, Population Statistics and Facebook Information (2012), http://www.internetworldstats.com/asia.html (retrieved March 31, 2012)

Kim, J.H.Y., Jung, H.Y.: South Korean Digital Textbook Project. Computers in the Schools 27, 247–265 (2010)

Koch, J.V.: An Economic analysis of Textbook Pricing and Textbook Markets (September 2006), http://www.eric.ed.gov/PDFS/ED497025.pdf (retrieved March 5, 2012)

Kwang, K.: Singapore sees digital textbooks in future. ZDNet Asia (July 11, 2011), http://www.zdnetasia.com/singapore-sees-digital-textbooks-in-future-62301144.html (retrieved February 14, 2012)

Legislative Council Secretariat. Minutes of Meeting of the Panel on Education of the Legislative Council held on 11 May 2009 (Legislative Council Paper No. CB(2) 2127/08-09) (2009), http://www.legco.gov.hk/yr08-09/english/panels/ed/minutes/ed20090511.pdf (retrieved March 12, 2012)

Legislative Council Secretariat. Background brief prepared by the Legislative Council Secretariat for the meeting on 11 April 2011: Debundling of textbooks and teaching and learning resources for pricing (Legislative Council Paper No. CB(2)1444/10-11(06)) (April 7, 2011a), http://www.legco.gov.hk/yr10-11/english/panels/ed/papers/ed0411cb2-1444-6-e.pdf (retrieved March 12, 2012)

Legislative Council Secretariat. Minutes of Meeting of the Panel on Education of the Legislative Council held on 11 April 2011 (Legislative Council Paper No. CB(2)1984/10–11) (June 10, 2011b), http://www.legco.gov.hk/yr10-11/english/panels/ed/minutes/ed20110411.pdf (retrieved March 12, 2012)

Legislative Council Secretariat. Updated background brief prepared by the Legislative Council Secretariat for the meeting on 21 June 2011: Debundling of textbooks and teaching and learning resources for pricing (Legislative Council Paper No. CB(2)2083/10-11(02)) (June 17, 2011c), http://www.legco.gov.hk/yr10-11/english/panels/ed/papers/ed0621cb2-2083-2-e.pdf (retrieved March 12, 2012)

Lewis, D.W.: How to Make Good Affordable Textbooks (2009), https://scholarworks.iupui.edu/bitstream/handle/1805/1881/How%20to%20Make%20Good%20Affordable%20Textbooks.pdf?sequence=11 (retrieved March 5, 2012)

Lewis, S.: E-Book Discovery and Use Behaviour is Complex. Evidence Based Library and Information Practice 3(2), 38–41 (2008)

Matkin, G.W.: Open Learning: What Do Open Textbooks Tell Us about the Revolution in Education? (Research & Occasional Paper Series: CSHE.1.09) (2009) Center for Studies in Higher Education website, http://cshe.berkeley.edu/publications/docs/ROPs-Matkin-OpenLearning-03-31-09.pdf (retrieved March 31, 2012)

McCullough, E.: E-books and E-content: A Panel Discussion at Charleston. Against the Grain 17(1), 50–52 (2005)

Mingpao: Textbook Debundling. Editorial. Mingpao (June 1, 2011a), http://edu.sina.com.hk/news/42/4/1/89402/1.html (retrieved February 3, 2012)

Mingpao: Textbook Debundling. Editorial. Mingpao (December 16, 2011b), http://edu.sina.com.hk/news/42/4/1/104167/1.html (retrieved February 4, 2012)

Petrides, L., Jimes, C., Middleton-Detzner, C., Walling, J., Weiss, S.: Open textbook adoption and use: Implications for teachers and learners. Open Learning 26(1), 39–49 (2011)

Reininger, J.: My Text: An alternative to the traditional textbook. Computers in Human Behavior 26, 119–121 (2010)

Secretary for Education. The Implementation of the Policy of Debundling Textbooks and Teaching/Learning Materials for Pricing: Special Measures (Education Bureau Circular Memorandum No. 95/2011) (2011a), http://www.edb.gov.hk/UtilityManager/circular/upload/EDBCM/EDBCM11095E.pdf (retrieved March 12, 2012)

Secretary for Education. The Implementation of the Policy of Debundling Textbooks and Teaching/Learning Materials for Pricing, and Notes on Selection of Textbooks and Learning Materials for Use in Schools (Education Bureau Circular Memorandum No. 67/2011) (2011b), http://www.edb.gov.hk/UtilityManager/circular/upload/EDBCM/EDBCM11067E.pdf (retrieved March 12, 2012)

Shelstad, J.: How Flat World Knowledge is Transforming College Textbook Publishing. Publishing Research Quarterly 27(3), 254–258 (2011)

Silver, L.S., Stevens, R.E., Clow, K.E., Howard, R.W.: Business law professors' perspectives of the cost of college textbooks. Mustang Journal of Law and Legal Studies 2, 18–30 (2011)

UNESCO, Open educational resources: Deliberations of a community of interest. ICDE SCOP. Lillehammer, Norway (June 2006)

United States Government Accountability Office. College textbooks: Enhanced offerings appear to drive recent price increases (GAO Report No. GAO-05-806) (2005), http://www.gao.gov/htext/d05806.html (retrieved March 12, 2012)

Wiley, D.: (n.d.) Defining the "Open" in Open Content. Open Content website, http://opencontent.org/definition/ (retrieved March 13, 2012)

Author Index

GPSR Compliance

The European Union's (EU) General Product Safety Regulation (GPSR) is a set of rules that requires consumer products to be safe and our obligations to ensure this.

If you have any concerns about our products, you can contact us on ProductSafety@springernature.com

In case Publisher is established outside the EU, the EU authorized representative is:

Springer Nature Customer Service Center GmbH
Europaplatz 3
69115 Heidelberg, Germany

Batch number: 10844619

Printed by Printforce, the Netherlands